Jim Glanville

Dec 1989

D1010675

Nature's Gambit

Nature's Gambit

Child Prodigies and

the Development

of Human Potential

DAVID HENRY FELDMAN

WITH LYNN T. GOLDSMITH

Basic Books, Inc., Publishers   *New York*

Library of Congress Cataloging-in-Publication Data

Feldman, David Henry.
  Nature's gambit.

  Bibliographic Notes: p. 251
  Includes index.
  1. Gifted children—Case studies. 2. Genius—Case
studies. 3. Child development—Case studies. 4. Gifted
children—Family relationships—Case studies. 5. Gifted
children—United States—Case studies. I. Goldsmith,
Lynn, T., 1950–   . II. Title.
BF723.G5F43 1986   155.4'55   85–73880
ISBN 0–465–04861–7

For Grandpa Howie and the girls

CONTENTS

PREFACE

I WAS STANDING on the deck of his house in Geneva looking out at the lake and the mountains when my friend Howard Gruber said: "So you have written a book about evolution once again." I had been describing this book to him, explaining that it was a report of my work with prodigies but also a speculation about how the prodigy phenomenon may shed light on other issues such as the expression of potential and the importance of a long-term perspective on the development of abilities. When Gruber had written six years ago that an earlier book of mine was about evolution he had taken me somewhat by surprise, since I thought I had written about developmental psychology and education. Not that I was totally unaware of thinking about evolutionary matters in relation to my topic, but Gruber's characterization of the book as being fundamentally about evolution was more than I had anticipated. When I reflected on what he had said, though, there was a certain plausibility in his statement. When he said it again, about this book, I should not have been as surprised as I was. Either Gruber's own extended study of Darwin had left him so obsessed with evolution that he interpreted everything through that lens, or he had once again recognized a deeper theme in my work and was bringing it to my attention.

As before, it is not that I was unaware that issues concerning evolution were a significant aspect of the prodigy work. Evolutionary themes have always played a prominent role in my thinking. Although I have no formal training in disciplines like biology or ethology, it has been apparent to me for many years that psychologists must consider evolutionary issues if they are to create a complete picture of human behavior. This has been true ever since my student days. When I entered graduate school in developmental psychology several professors asked me about my interests. I replied, with the naiveté and arrogance that only a first-year student can muster, that the only thing that really interested me was understanding how thought could evolve from primitive to advanced reasoning, both for individuals and for the species as a whole. It is a testimony to the patience and wisdom of my teachers that they allowed me these preoccupations within the confines of developmental psychology, gently weaning me away from topics too general to be addressed in my discipline. I guess that in spite of my real identification with investigating the psychology of

development, I still find irresistible this long-standing tendency to speculate about the broader meaning of what I study.

For better or for worse, then, this is a book about prodigies, about
development, and about evolution. Prodigies provide more than enough
justification for research solely on the basis of their remarkable capabilities
and fascinating lives. Yet for me the prodigy phenomenon has also provided a challenge to long-accepted ways of thinking about ability and
about change. It has caused me to stand back and consider anew certain
conceptions of ability and development that have been generally accepted,
but that could not account for the anomalous, puzzling, extraordinary
behavior of the prodigy. Prodigies had either been ignored entirely in the
psychological literature or interpreted as freaks of nature—exceptions or
anomalies to be described but not explained. I took the phenomenon as the
impetus for proposing a broader developmental framework to encompass
the extraordinary ability of the prodigy as well as the more modest talents
that most of the rest of us display. I wanted to construct a way of looking
at human thinking and development that specifically considered the
prodigy phenomenon, and recognized it as a lawful example of development rather than as an anomaly. The phenomenon of the prodigy thus
became for me a challenge to existing theories of development, to current
ideas about education and child rearing, and indeed a challenge to how we
think about intelligence itself. It was my effort to integrate the prodigy
phenomenon into conceptions of intellectual development that led me to
take the broader stance that Gruber interpreted as evolutionary. Having
assumed this stance, I have come to see the prodigy as uniquely capable
of illuminating certain secrets of the developmental process.

The prodigy provides this illumination, I think, at two levels—that of
the individual and that of the culture. First, the prodigy offers the opportunity to examine how development proceeds in the rarefied situation in
which extraordinary ability in a particular domain develops exceedingly
quickly. Although the prodigy's gifts are awesome and extremely uncommon, I believe that the *processes* by which they grow and flower are nonetheless similar to the ones by which all intellectual development proceeds.
Thus, understanding something about the development of prodigious ability will tell us something fundamental about the development of ability
in general.

Second, I believe that the prodigy stands both as exemplar and beacon,
demonstrating the power of optimal early expression of potential and
pointing to the fact that, through judicious use of that potential, humanity
is capable of influencing its own future development. Here is where the
evolutionary theme is most in evidence. The prodigy is the embodiment

of a remarkable confluence of biological and cultural potential; the extraordinary and precocious achievement within a particular domain that is the prodigy's hallmark points to the possibility for future large-scale changes in the organization of knowledge. Such changes, it seems to me, cannot be explained solely in terms of variation and selection at the biological level. An explanation constructed at a different level of analysis—one that emphasizes cultural modes of transmission of knowledge and behavior—is needed to begin to account for these sorts of transformations and their effects.

I am not alone in proposing that humans are subject to cultural as well as biological evolution; biologists and geneticists have turned their attention to developing quantitative models of the processes of cultural transmission. By emphasizing cultural evolution, I do not intend to suggest that a nonbiological process supersedes classical Darwinian evolution, effectively separating humanity from the rest of the living world. Yet, because so much of what we do and know comes to us through cultural routes, I believe that there is a dimension to human evolution that is different from evolution in cats or pansies. I want to draw attention to the importance of the ways in which people select, transform, extend, and transmit qualities in environments we have shaped ourselves, some of which irrevocably change the human landscape, perhaps even exerting biological selection pressures in turn.

Prodigies clearly point to the existence of such tendencies for cultural transmission and transformation. They represent a remarkable coincidence of biological proclivity and cultural readiness and response. The power of their talent is awesome; yet it should also be a reminder that proclivities are realized as talent only through the arrangement of conditions that identify, engage, sustain, and fuel its development. Ultimately, I hope that prodigies will be fully appreciated both for what they can contribute to the enrichment of cultural life and for their unique expression of certain processes of human development and evolution.

The prodigy is an individual child with the gift of an extraordinary talent. But I think that the prodigy is also much more. The very existence of the prodigy is itself a gift of immense importance, for the phenomenon offers insights into the workings of the human mind. The prodigy teaches us about the expression and development of potential and about something deeper as well—something about how humanity has gotten where it is, why it has gotten there, and perhaps how we might better choreograph our uniquely human dance.

Winchester, Massachusetts
April, 1986

ACKNOWLEDGMENTS

ALTHOUGH this book bears the name of a single author, like the prodigy phenomenon itself it is in reality the result of contributions from a number of different people. It is my pleasure to acknowledge them here and to thank them for their generous support and help.

My deepest thanks go to the six boys who were the subjects of my inquiry, and to their families and teachers. Their dedication to the development of extreme talent, their insights into the process, and their generosity in sharing their time and lives with me has been extraordinary. They have become friends as well as subjects in my study of the prodigiousness that they know firsthand.

I have been fortunate to have been supported in this work by grants from The Spencer Foundation during H. Thomas James's tenure as president, and also by John Sawyer of the Andrew Mellon Foundation. Grants from these foundations were catalytic to my research effort. A number of colleagues and friends have also provided intangible support by engaging in lively discussion, offering examples, advice, and criticism, and sharing their own points of view in ways that have enriched my conceptualization of early prodigious achievement and enhanced its presentation here. I would particularly like to acknowledge the contributions of Jeanne Bamberger, Art and Betty Bardige, Susan Carey, John and Ethel Collins, Mihalyi Csikszentmihalyi, Sylvia Feinburg, Howard Gruber, Pat Gunkel, Frank and Mathilda Holzman, George Kane, Bernard Koser, Rima Laibow, Scott McVay, Dean and Janice Randall, Seymour Sarason, Bob and Pat Sears, Shlomo Sharan, Morris Shepard, Varda Shoham-Salomon, Amy and Everett Shorey, Samuel Snyder, Julian Stanley, Sidney Strauss, Yoram Yarose, and David Zissenwine. Howard Gardner, my close colleague and collaborator, generously read an early draft of the book and, as always, offered many helpful comments and suggestions.

The early phases of this study also benefited greatly from the able assistance of staff and students, particularly Gary Bean, Richard Bensusan, Ellen Reuter, and Constance Stolow. More recently, Ann Benjamin, Martha Morelock, and Janet Stork have helped move the manuscript along. Rose Chicocarello prepared much of the manuscript, with assistance from Louise Clancy and Tillie Nelder. They wrestled simultaneously with my rough drafts and the mysteries of word processing, managing this double challenge with cheerfulness and equanimity.

I would also like to thank Arthur Schwartz, my literary agent, and Jo Ann Miller, my editor at Basic Books, for their support, advice, and encouragement through the various stages of preparation of this book. Sheila Friedling competently ushered the manuscript into production, despite frequent last-minute alterations.

Finally, although her name appears on the title page with mine, it does not begin to do justice to the contributions of my wife and collaborator, Lynn Goldsmith. In more ways than I can express she has sustained this effort. Were it not for Lynn, this book would not have seen the light of day. When I think of what we might have done with all the days and nights spent on *Nature's Gambit*, well, that is another book.

PART I

Prodigies and

Development

Unless otherwise stated in the text,
children, parents, siblings, teachers,
and schools are identified herein by pseudonym.

1

Out of the Usual Course of Nature

THIS BOOK is about six unusual children. It is about a child who read music before he was four, two children who played winning chess before they entered school, another who studied abstract algebra in grade school, a youngster who produced typed scripts of original stories and plays before his fifth birthday, and a child who read, wrote, began learning foreign languages, and composed short musical pieces before he was out of diapers.

I set out to find a group of such children in 1975. I wanted them as subjects for a straightforward psychological experiment I had designed to refute a rather esoteric point in cognitive developmental psychology. I knew even at the time, although perhaps not consciously, that my interest in prodigies exceeded the obscure academic issue motivating me to seek out a group of prodigies. When I began this study I was not a stranger to children with exceptional abilities. I have studied creativity for more than twenty years, and although prodigious achievements and creative ones are not directly related, there is nonetheless at least an intuitive connection between the two. Thus it came as no surprise when I found myself drawn to those complexities of the phenomenon of early prodigious achievement that transformed my small, controlled investigation into a broader, much more open-ended effort to observe, interview, and understand the children in my study.

The prodigy phenomenon is seductive. There is something uncanny about children who display talents that are only supposed to be the province of gifted and highly trained adults. When feats that are rare even among adults are performed by a mere child—composing a symphony, for example, or beating a chess master in a match—they seem to violate the natural order of things. I wanted to find out more about how these things can be explained and understood.

The prodigy phenomenon is not new. There have probably always been child prodigies. It is likely that some children have displayed extreme talent for as long as people have recognized that there are variations in ability. But the reception and treatment of prodigies have varied widely over the centuries. Historically the prodigy was part of a prophetic tradition signaling impending change. The term "prodigy" originally connoted a much broader set of phenomena than it does today, referring to any sort of sign or portent: "a monstrosity; something out of the usual course of nature, like a comet or a meteor."[1] Such deviations from daily, predictable events were seen as indications of impending change in the world. Occasionally such signs were welcomed as the promise of a better future (such as the appearance of the religious prodigy Jesus as the awaited herald of the Messianic Age). More often than not they were seen as signaling an irreparable rent in the fabric and functioning of society. For example, Claudius alludes to such "prodigious" portents of his reign's end at the close of Robert Graves's historical novel, *Claudius the God*:

> My eyes are weary and my hand shakes so much that I can hardly form the letters. Strange portents have been seen of late. . . . Phoenix, comet and centaur, a swarm of bees among the standards of the Guards Camp, a pig farrowed with claws like a hawk, and my father's monument struck by lightning! Prodigies enough, soothsayers?[2]

While the connotations of the prodigy phenomenon have narrowed and changed over the years, one aspect seems to have remained intact. Child prodigies are still perceived as unexplained and somehow unnatural occurrences, and they have been greeted over the generations with an ambivalent mix of emotions that accompany the expectation of change: fear and wariness, mystery and myth, skepticism and contempt, awe and wonder. Prodigies would often tour the countryside as freakish sideshow attractions, drawing crowds both curious and cautious about their unusual talents. Hans Eberstark, himself a mental calculator, has described the alienation of children with unusual talent in this way:

> We are an odd lot, often at odds with the society we were born into. We are out of context. Few, if any . . . were socially adapted conformists. Some were slandered and ridiculed.[3]

Prodigies from past eras were frequently isolated from normal activities and friendships, their talents exploited by friends and family for financial purposes. The obituary notice of Jacques Inaudi (1867–1950) captures some of the flavor of this itinerant life.

> M. Inaudi was a Piedmontese by birth and came to France as a shepherd boy. His extraordinary faculty for mental arithmetic soon attracted notice, and in 1892 he was presented to the French Academy of Sciences, which gave official recognition to his phenomenal performances. After that M. Inaudi travelled all over Europe and America demonstrating his mental powers. His most sensational performance was a match with three calculating machines set to work out three different arithmetical problems simultaneously. M. Inaudi always gave the answers before any of the three machines stopped ticking. Although the walls of his house were covered with testimonials from crowned heads, after court performances, M. Inaudi died in relative poverty. He had been living a retired life since 1934, but he continued to amuse his neighbors with his powers until the end of his life.[4]

Demonstrating abilities both awesome and incomprehensible, the prodigy has been greeted with uneasiness partly because the phenomenon threatens to upset what appears to be the order of things.[5] One of life's most basic tasks is to construct a set of expectations that allows for the perception of stability, continuity, and predictability of experience: the prodigy is often an unwelcome intrusion into such a construction. By performing feats that should be impossible in ones so young, prodigies at the very least violate expectations about personal ability. It simply does not seem right or fitting for a seven-year-old to play a virtuoso violin concerto or a nine-year-old to solve complex algebraic equations. It is virtually impossible to reconcile our assumptions about the developing abilities of children with reports like the one from a family in my study that their child spoke two and three word sentences at three months of age and began reporting his dreams to them at six months, calling them "television in my head." In general, most of us would prefer to avoid confrontations with such incomprehensible achievement. We would just as soon dismiss or devalue the prodigy's accomplishments as accept evidence of such extraordinary talent. Perhaps this is how child prodigies originally became associated with unwelcome change: they make us recognize that the world is not as neat and orderly as we might like.

From our twentieth-century perspective it is difficult to accept the antique notion that the prodigy presaged actual changes in the natural or social order. Perhaps, as in the conditioned response, prodigies were associated with major changes often enough historically to become psychologically linked with them: a prodigy appears and the world changes; surely the prodigy must have had something to do with the change. More than likely there have always been prodigies, through usual and unusual times alike, but perhaps they were only perceived as significant during more active, turbulent periods. Perhaps this pattern holds for our own age as well. After more than half a century of neglect within the scholarly community, prodigies have once again become the object of curiosity, interest, and attention; is it coincidental that the second half of the twentieth century is characterized by extraordinarily rapid technological and social change?

Yet this recent attention has damned the prodigy by faint praise. Within our own time the phenomenon has been whitewashed and sanitized, deftly separated from its original meaning and power to portend change. The prodigy has been assimilated into the peculiarly American notion of the "intellectually gifted," or high-IQ, child. Current explanation for early prodigious achievement is that the prodigy focuses extremely high levels of general intellectual capability on a specific field, such as mathematics or art or music. This explanation assimilates prodigies' talents to the psychometrician's notion of high general intelligence. From this perspective prodigies are considered unusual because high-IQ individuals are relatively rare: less than 1 percent of the population has an IQ of 145 or more. The psychometric viewpoint assumes that intelligence is by and large a unitary quality, so that a high IQ indicates more intelligence and a low IQ less of the same kinds of abilities. Thus the prodigy's abilities are considered to be no different—only more extreme—than those of all other children.

Therefore, on those rare occasions when scholars have specifically considered the phenomenon of the prodigy, they have found such children to be similar in kind to the thousands of children nationwide who are labeled "gifted." This assimilation to an IQ-based framework of ability has homogenized the notion of the prodigy. The extraordinary and specific talent that is the prodigy's hallmark has been ignored in the effort to demystify the phenomenon by fitting it into established beliefs.

For example, there have been efforts to account for chess skill in terms of strong ability to recognize patterns of pieces and to remember a "dictionary" of standard moves.[6] While these skills do seem to distinguish chess novices from seasoned players, they don't go very far toward explaining how one of my subjects at age nine played twelve simultaneous chess matches against strong adult players, winning seven games, drawing one, and losing only four! And even when one encounters examples of extraordinary retentive abilities, it is hard to see how they help explain the overall talent: the other chess prodigy I studied could easily and accurately recall both his and his opponent's moves from matches he had played the day before. But rather than being a characteristic of chess ability, this kind of memory for the game is apparently unusual even for high-level players: the boy's coach noted that few players of any caliber could recreate their games move for move. It is likewise difficult to see how a high-IQ account of early prodigious achievement could explain one father's report that at age four his son learned to calculate three-digit sums mentally (so he could have the coveted position of "banker" during family Monopoly games), but had no idea of how to figure using paper and pencil.

In an ironic sense, by having become separated from the tradition of prophecy and omens and by being assimilated to the notion of high IQ, the prodigies of today have, in a strange twist, portended changes in the fabric of our culture: the rise to prominence of the technological society with its emphasis on logic and rationalism has left no place for prophecy or portent. The tradition of irrational signs or incomprehensible behavior survives in Western culture only at the periphery, for example, in science fiction and mystical branches of the world's religions. Those who gravitate toward the periphery do, indeed, take a different view of the prodigy, one that is sometimes unsettling to the families of unusual children.

For example, one family in my study hired a storyteller to instruct their child in folklore and folkways. When they took the boy to his first lesson, the woman greeted him with the request that he tell her about his experiences in "the Bardo." His parents looked at each other with non-comprehension curious to see how their son would answer a question on a topic he knew nothing about. To their amazement, their seven-year-old son began a discourse with his new tutor about his previous lives. (The Bardo, they later discovered, is the plane of being between earlier incarnations and future ones, as discussed in such mystical Eastern writings as *The Tibetan Book of the Dead.*) After several minutes the woman turned to the boy's bemused parents and inquired of them, "You *do* know who your son is, don't you?" When their reply was a cautious negative, she told them that he was one of "The Wise Ones." Some time later at the tutor's urging, they took the boy for an audience with a Buddhist Master. He told them that the boy was a Bodhisattva: he had chosen to forgo Nirvana, the highest level of spiritual development and sensibility, in order to provide guidance and example for those earthbound souls still following the Path.

In this book I would like to resurrect some of the original meaning of the term "prodigy," for I believe that the child who performs extraordinarily well in a highly demanding field is a distinctive, significant, and revealing phenomenon and cannot be explained by invoking the "high IQ" argument or any other relatively simple explanation. Such children do reveal talents and abilities "out of the usual course of nature." It is no simple matter to explain how the children I have studied are able to do what they do. Asserting that they are smarter than average, or even that they have a particular penchant for a specific area of activity, is insufficient. Such assertions do not provide adequate explanations for the report that, at age two, one of my subjects drew a person where one side of the body (which included facial features, arms and legs, feet and hands) was colored blue and the other, red, "because," he said, "it feels that way." It also will not explain how another child at age nine was described by one of his teachers as having the abilities and sensibilities of someone pursuing a Ph.D. in music. And I don't think it will explain the following incident, which a parent reported to me in a letter:

[My child] conceived a passion for languages which lasted from about 22 months to age four, [studying Hebrew, classical Greek, French, Italian, Russian, Spanish, Yiddish, German, Egyptian hieroglyphics, and Sanskrit]. . . . Shortly after he turned four, I noted that he had shown little interest in the material which his tutors selected for him. Instead, he was interested in pursuing the [personal] relationship which he had with each of them. I told him that if he was no longer interested in the language that was all right, but that meant we would stop the lessons and retain the personal relationships with the tutors as friends. He said that he was not really interested any more because he had figured out the answer to the question. Ever the straight man, I asked him, "What question?" "Oh," he said, looking at me with helpful attention. "I've figured out that there was a parent language for these languages (he listed the Indo-European ones) but not for these. It had 11 cases." I told him that scholars called the parent "Indo-European" and that I had been taught in college that it had ten cases. He said, "Scholars can be wrong. It had 11 cases!"

Seeking answers to extraordinary achievement in individual neurological activity will also fail to provide an adequate explanation. The task is to try to comprehend how it is possible for such marvelous and extraordinary abilities to exist without resorting to the general intelligence interpretation now in vogue, embracing a biological explanation that reduces the phenomenon beyond recognition, or abandoning altogether a rational perspective.

It is worthwhile to reconsider the possibility that the modern prodigy signals impending change. In this case, however, the change involves how we look at human intelligence, variability, and the conditions necessary for the expression of human potential. If we can understand better how and why the prodigy does what he does, we will have made some substantial progress toward understanding how talent can be developed in general. For while the prodigy's talent and progress is indeed out of the usual course of nature, the processes that control his development are not.[7] In short, the prodigy exhibits the very same kinds of developmental processes that the rest of us do, but because their abilities are so extraordinary it is especially revealing to observe these processes at work.

Generalists and Specialists

What is it, then, that makes the prodigy's accomplishments so different from those of other children? The answer lies in the fact that these children are special-purpose organisms, designed and geared to perform in a specific field of endeavor. The prodigy seems to be unique in having an extremely specialized gift that is expressed only under very specific, culturally evolved environmental conditions. In contrast, the high-IQ individual possesses generalized intellectual abilities that seem to permit high levels of functioning in a wide range of environments. Though both specialist and generalist may demonstrate impressive accomplishments they reflect radically different abilities, indeed different adaptive strategies in the biological sense. Mozart is an example of the specialist: while his musical gifts were indisputably protean, he has been characterized in other respects as a simple, intellectually unremarkable, and even boorish man. Leonardo da Vinci epitomizes the generalist profile: erudite, curious, gifted with a generally powerful mind, he mastered and contributed significantly to a variety of different domains.

Prodigies are, on the whole, extreme specialists. They are exceptionally well tuned to a particular field of knowledge, demonstrating rapid and often seemingly effortless mastery. While prodigies may or may not be talented in the sense of more generalized intellectual prowess, they do not demonstrate extraordinary performance across the board. Instead they seem extremely well matched to a particular environment, pretuned to grasp and master one particular area of endeavor. The prodigy is the most precociously specialized specialist that we know about. Indeed, the calling card of the prodigy is a tenacious commitment to do one specific thing at all costs: to see doing that thing as absolutely essential for satisfaction, expression, and well-being.

The importance of specialization to a society becomes ever greater as cultures evolve and become increasingly complex, with a dizzying array of new roles to be filled. The prodigy's extreme early specialization can be viewed as one way for nature to increase the likelihood of adapting to the rapidly changing world by creating individuals who are able to master and move about in a particular field exceedingly quickly.

Yet, increasing the complexity of life also increases the need for flexible, generalized intelligences. The individual with more generalized ability has the advantage of being able to get along productively in a wide variety of environments. Because "pure" prodigies are specialists in the extreme, pretuned and preorganized to seek expression for a set of highly specific capabilities, they may find themselves without some of the more general skills needed to negotiate a place in the existing culture. While the chances are good that generalists will find satisfying and productive areas in which to work, relatively few individuals who have extreme and isolated talent will have the opportunity to make use of it. The risks of missing one's special calling are greater for the specialist, but the benefits of connecting with it may also be much larger.

Nature's Gambit

Nature thus simultaneously operates two systems of talent development with the generalist and specialist types of intellectual adaptation. The former maximizes the likelihood that individuals will flourish under widely varying conditions, while the latter is designed to increase the likelihood that individuals will make maximum use of highly specific situations. However, the specialist strategy can be costly to those who are tapped for it, particularly from a personal and psychological standpoint. The premium on extreme, specialized, and often idiosyncratic talent that is fully expressed only under precisely regulated environmental conditions means that few individuals with extreme specialist tendencies will find the conditions necessary to maximize their potential: most extreme specialists do not, in fact, thrive. While the generalist is pragmatic and adaptable, the extreme specialist is dogged and unyielding. While the generalist relishes learning the rules and playing them to advantage, the specialist stubbornly insists that the rules be ignored or bent to his or her own needs.

Most individuals are a mixture of both specialist and generalist tendencies. Succeeding in most twentieth-century cultures requires a healthy dose of both. It is only under very rare circumstances that extreme specialists are afforded the luxury of expressing their unique potential. When these circumstances are propitious we find ourselves with a Mozart, Mill, Menuhin, or Millais in our midst. A child's early prodigious achievements are a sign that a number of unique circumstances have converged to allow complete specialized expression of powerful potential. The use of this rare, specialized potential is a form of high-risk, human venture capital that nature uses to hedge its bets on the future of humanity. Since the circumstances favorable to such expression are rarely present, nature's gambit is to sacrifice an enormous amount of potential talent for the occasional sublime match of child to field that yields the prodigy. By studying how such a match takes place we may better comprehend not only the prodigy but the more general processes involved in the development of potential.

Co-incidence

"Co-incidence" is the general process of development that is revealed through study of the prodigy. The exploration of this process is the major organizing theme for this book. I have used the term "co-incidence" to capture the melding of the many sets of forces that interact in the development and expression of human potential.[8] With prodigies the co-inciding of forces tends to be more sharply defined and their interactions more dramatic than in the development of potential in the average individual. It is therefore easier with the prodigy to see what these forces are and how they influence the child's developing mastery. However, the forces and processes of co-incidence operate in the same general way for prodigy and

nonprodigy alike. Thus, understanding something of the dynamic underlying the process of prodigious development will yield information about
the general development of ability.

It is the fortuitous convergence of highly specific individual proclivities with specific environmental receptivity that allows a prodigy to
emerge. This is an infrequent and unlikely event. The convergence is not
simply between two unitary, looming giants—an individual and an environment—but between a number of elements in a very delicate interplay:
it includes a cultural milieu; the presence of a particular domain which is
itself at a particular level of development; the availability of master teachers; family recognition of extreme talent and commitment to support it;
large doses of encouragement and understanding; and other features as
well. The explication of some of these forces is the primary focus of this
book.

FOUR TIME FRAMES

Understanding co-incidence requires consideration of at least four
different time frames that bear on the prodigy's appearance and development: the individual's life span; the developmental history of the field or
domain; cultural and historical trends that bear on both individuals and
fields; and finally, evolutionary time.

It is most natural to think about the prodigy in terms of the individual
life span. After all, a prodigy *is* a child, and in a very real way the history
of that child's talent is the individual history of the person who displays
it. Yet to focus on the person is to miss other frames that provide the
setting and sustenance for the development of the individual's ability.
Even my own field of developmental psychology, which is the most time
oriented of the psychological disciplines, has tended to view the individual's life span as if it unfolded without reference to longer time periods.
It is critical to keep in mind that a prodigy is first and foremost a person
living during a certain era, within a particular family, and with a wealth
of other, nonprodigious life experiences. It is important to comprehend
what the individual life course of a prodigy is like, how it is similar to and
different from the life experiences of the rest of us, and how the individuals fit into the eras in which they live and work.

The second time frame to consider is the "life span" of the domains
in which prodigies appear. The prodigy-to-be must encounter and master
a specific body of knowledge and skill within which prodigious abilities
will be expressed. The potential to perform at a high level in a particular

field may not be activated or developed if the field, which is itself structured and developing along a certain pathway, is not available in a way that is comprehensible to the young mind. Bodies of knowledge are themselves cumulative, distilled products of many individuals' efforts to master and extend a field. Fields change in both their substantive base and the forms in which the knowledge is codified. For example, physics as it is practiced and taught today is not the same field of seventy-five—or even twenty-five—years ago, having evolved away from a phenomenological toward a more mathematical emphasis. In turn, the capabilities, skills, proclivities, and talents required to understand physics at a high level today are probably somewhat different from those of a century ago. The individual's specialized capabilities must fit well with the accumulated knowledge of the domain and techniques for instruction in order for unusual performance to result. One wonders, for example, whether a mind like Einstein's in Galileo's day would have made a contribution to the existing state of knowledge about the physical world. Taking a reverse example, one might speculate whether the twentieth-century mathematician Ramanujan, who independently reinvented much of the mathematics of the past several centuries, might not have changed the course of mathematics had he been Newton's contemporary.

Thus, bodies of knowledge are themselves moving through time, but usually at a slower pace than individuals. Their own histories begin long before the prodigy-to-be arrives on the scene, and they continue to exist long after any particular prodigy is gone. In some cases, like Mozart's, the prodigy's talents will change the future development of a field; in others, like Felix Mendelssohn's, his accomplishments may only reflect its current status. In either case, field and prodigy share a slice of time and space that allows for the expression of individual potential through the joint existence of talent and medium.

The third time frame reflects broader historical and cultural trends that influence both individuals and fields and that are in turn influenced by them. A country may be at peace or at war, politically stable or undergoing revolution, in a period of prosperity or poverty, enjoy enlightened leadership or be governed by despots, may be relatively open to outside influences or closed to them, may encourage and embrace innovation or stifle it. These factors all in one way or another affect the cultural emphases and opportunities for learning. Perhaps more directly relevant to prodigies is that cultures vary in the importance they attach to the mastery of different domains at different times. At a particular time and place pursuing a specific field may be rewarded, ignored, or even punished. In the

United States today serious chess players find that the lack of institutional interest or support often undermines their efforts to sustain a commitment to the game. In contrast, the Soviet Union has developed a well-organized system for detecting, developing, and supporting chess talent. The reverse is true for entrepreneurial activities in the two countries. Thus, it is not enough to know that a child has great talent for a specific field, nor is it enough to know that a field is developed to a point where it is possible to engage and develop a given child's potential. Child and domain must be brought together under circumstances advantageous for sustained engagement. It may also be that certain kinds of prodigies will only appear and develop when a culture is itself organized to recognize and nurture excellence in that particular domain.

Finally, the fourth time frame is the evolutionary context within which all of the other aspects of the prodigy phenomenon play themselves out. Evolutionary forces operate on individuals through the biological processes of variation and natural selection, and on the accumulated products of collective efforts—that is, cultures and their artifacts—through more macroscopic processes. It is this broadest of time frames that provides the backdrop for the development and interaction of the other three. The presence and purpose of the prodigy must be examined against this broad framework of the evolution of human thought and culture. Prodigies, although awesome, are nonetheless a relatively regularly occurring phenomenon: a number of children with remarkable abilities are brought to public attention in each generation. Have they always been an integral part of the variation in human abilities? What kinds of roles have they played in the recognition, development, or advancement of knowledge? What kinds of long-term forces sustain the production and appearance of individuals bearing the potential for early prodigious achievements? The value and meaning of the prodigy for humanity as a whole must be considered within this very long-term perspective.

When the interplay among the four time frames is strikingly balanced and coordinated, a prodigy may emerge. The delicacy of the coordination feels as if the child, the field, the culture, and a moment in history conspired to bring about extraordinary individual achievement. Most of the time a much less well-coordinated set of forces prevails, and development occurs in the fashion more typical of children. In fact, the most satisfying explanation for the prodigy phenomenon I can offer is that these special children are, in essence, the product of the most delicate process of coordination imaginable among the different time dimensions—a beautifully choreographed co-incidence of forces. While co-incidence processes are operating all the time and affect all of us, in the case of the prodigy the coordination among individual, field, culture, and evolution is uncanny. This is why the prodigy helps explain both what the specific co-incidence processes are for him and at the same time how they work for all of us.

Prodigies and Genius

Are child prodigies geniuses? From the accounts of prodigies that appear in the media it would seem that they are. The families and teachers of child prodigies also tend to use the terms interchangeably to describe their charges. In fact, however, the two terms come from very different traditions and refer to very different phenomena. Some child prodigies do eventually come to produce works of genius, but most do not. The distinction between prodigy and genius should be clearly kept in mind. This book is about prodigies: children who perform at an extremely high level within a specific field at a very early age. Genius, on the other hand, implies the transformation of a field of knowledge that is fundamental and irreversible. A prodigy does not transform but rather shows unusual capability within an existing field. "You are not a genius," British mathematics prodigy Ruth Lawrence's tutor recently cautioned "until you have left your personal mark on your subject."[9]

Current IQ-based conceptions of giftedness have encouraged the tendency to assume that the terms "prodigy" and "genius" are interchangeable because they view all extreme forms of intellectual functioning in terms of IQ, a formulation which is based on statistical frequency. This model identifies the prodigy as a high-IQ child with a penchant for a given field. It views a genius as a child with an even higher IQ who can apply this extremely high general intelligence to whatever area of endeavor he or she chooses. The facts support neither definition. Prodigies and "geniuses" may or may not have extremely high IQs; furthermore, those who are credited with works of genius rarely make significant contributions to any and all fields they choose to study (physicist and Nobel Laureate William Shockley's amateurish psychologizing about the heritability of intelligence provides one clear example).

It is nonetheless fairly common to equate prodigies with genius, even in some of my own cases. And yet, there has never been a child genius in the sense that there has never been a child who has fundamentally reorganized a highly demanding domain of knowledge and skill. Nor by any means have individuals who have produced works of genius all been prodigies.

The prodigy's early mastery of a domain may put him in a better position for achieving works of genius, for he has more time to explore, develop, comprehend, and experiment within a field. Certainly some child prodigies have made major and lasting contributions: Mozart, Mill, Wiener, and von Neumann are a few examples of men whose early promise was realized in works of transcendent quality. But there is no guarantee that the prodigy's talents will move a domain forward. William James Sidis, Erwin Nyiregyhazi, Daisy Ashford, Fanny Mendelssohn, and Nannerl Mozart were prodigies who failed to make major contributions as adults. The kinds of abilities that allow for prodigious mastery of an existing domain and those that are necessary to transform the domain do not necessarily reside in the same individual. When they do, they most certainly reveal themselves at different times in the individual's own development. The road from early precocity to creative adult achievement is long, arduous, treacherous, and unpredictable.

For reasons that are not altogether clear, prodigies appear in some fields but not in others. In fact, there are relatively few fields in which they are found. While there are no estimates of the numbers of prodigies in various fields, the largest numbers in recent decades seem to be found in music performance and in chess. Other fields produce relatively few prodigies: occasionally a writing prodigy will appear, prodigies in the visual arts are extremely rare, and mathematics fosters far fewer prodigies than I thought would be the case when this work began. By the definition I have used to identify early prodigious achievement—performance in an intellectually demanding field at the level of an adult professional before the age of ten—there has never been a bona fide physics prodigy, or for that matter, a prodigy in any of the natural sciences. There are a number of fields that do not seem to produce prodigies by this strict definition, but in which individuals do show extraordinary promise and capability at relatively young ages. Although mathematics prodigies are rare, most individuals who will achieve great works in mathematics begin to express unusual talent in their teens. Also, the trajectory of achievement is extremely steep once the talent appears, reaching full power in very short order. If the notion of child prodigy can be extended into the teenage years, then mathematics and artistic prodigies are in reasonable supply. While the prodigy's unusual abilities do not assure contributions of genius, there nonetheless seems to be an intuitive connection between them. Indeed, prodigies are often called child geniuses. We will return to this issue in subsequent chapters as we examine more closely the qualities of children demonstrating early prodigious achievement.

The Plan of the Book

This book is organized into three parts. In part 1, the major co-incidence themes are briefly introduced (chapter 1) and the study of six child prodigies is described (chapter 2). Each of the children is introduced with thumbnail sketches in chapter 2.

Part 2 looks at the children in greater detail relative to the major dimensions of the co-incidence process. My aim is to share some of the subtlety and complexity that characterize the lives of these children— something we tend to lose sight of when considering the prodigy phenomenon from a theoretical vantage point. Chapter 3 considers individual talent in a child who does not entirely fit the image of the generally gifted student. His family's efforts to preserve his uniqueness and nurture his special abilities are described. Chapter 4 considers the second most important dimension of co-incidence: the domain within which the prodigy performs his or her "wondrous feats." Since the prodigy's achievements reflect an amazing complementarity between child and domain, it is important to understand some of the characteristics of these fields themselves and to speculate on why a particular field seems to lend itself to the appearance of prodigies.

Co-incidence has never, in my experience, worked without substantial effort by those closest to the prodigy. It is therefore essential to look at how families deal with the task of continuously trying to marshal resources, control decisions, and in general direct the process of preparation of the extremely talented child. Chapter 5 describes the experience of trying to respond to a child whose abilities and, therefore, needs are far in excess of what any family bargains for when they sign their contract with the stork.

The critical issue of mentors and teachers is the topic of chapter 6, which is a detailed examination of a critical turning point in one musical prodigy's young career: the transition from becoming a composer to becoming a performer. Chapter 7 considers some of the emotional and social aspects of the lives of prodigies, and as a backdrop for the more personal issues just considered, chapter 8 deals with broader, more indirect forces that nonetheless profoundly affect the development of individual potential: the particular place in which the child happens to be born and raised, the cultural and historical milieu, particular events and cultural or historical trends that impinge on decisions and experiences, all influence how (or if) an extremely talented child will be able to express his or her specific talent.

Part 3 moves back again to the broader level of interpretation of part 1. Chapter 9 addresses the prophecy tradition and describes several mysterious and unexplained experiences described by the parents of two of my subjects. Although these experiences should not be accepted without comment or caution, they nonetheless raise questions that have surrounded prodigies for centuries, questions for which we still do not have adequate answers. In chapter 10 the evolutionary themes are raised again, this time in greater detail. The metaphor in this chapter is that of a complex board game that has been played since time began but whose rules we are just beginning to learn. The prodigy offers helpful hints about what some of the rules of this game might be. Finally, chapter 11 draws forth the implications of the prodigy phenomenon for the fuller development of all human potential. The qualities and characteristics of prodigies, their families, and broader environmental conditions are reviewed for what they can tell us about conditions that might facilitate optimal development in other individuals. The prodigy's effort to harness the forces of co-incidence suggests some strategies, or at least orientations, for developing the diversity necessary for human survival and well-being. This tone of urgency reflects again the prophecy tradition. A brief epilogue in chapter 12 catches up with each of the children in the study, in some cases more than ten years after this work began.

2

A Study of
Six Prodigies

WHEN I first planned to study early prodigious achievement I envisioned undertaking a simple and circumscribed investigation: I wanted to test sixteen prodigies (four composers, four chess players, four visual artists, and four mathematicians) on a number of intellectual and psychological tasks. I quickly discovered, though, that there were two major problems with my carefully devised plan. First, bona fide prodigies were much more difficult to locate than I'd anticipated and when I did find them, the children didn't always accommodate my experimental design by hailing from the needed domains. Second, while it was reassuring to confirm that the children performed on the psychological tests as I had predicted, I felt as if my experiment provided little insight into the hows and whys of early prodigious achievement. I found myself continuing to visit these children and their families, seeking a richer and more detailed picture of the prodigy phenomenon. It was in this way that my original experiment evolved into a series of case studies.

Psychologist Howard Gruber once warned me that he thought it was impossible to do an adequate study of more than one case at a time. I took the comment seriously, as his masterful study of the development of

Charles Darwin's thinking has been a model for me to emulate.[1] Now, after several years of experience with six cases, I understand more fully what he meant. The six children in this study live in different towns and cities in the Northeast, making it difficult to maintain continuous contact with all but the one child who lives in Boston. Although The Spencer Foundation in Chicago has been generous in providing funds to visit each of the prodigies' families over the years, I still get only a fragmented view of their lives. At the most I have been able to visit some subjects several dozen times, others only six or seven times. Although the number of hours spent in contact with each child is substantial, it is nonetheless a tiny sample of experience that spans as many as seven or eight years of the child's development. And so it is with Gruber's warning in mind that I try to describe the course of development of each of the children in the study, knowing full well that I will at best capture a slice of their reality—a slice that I hope is nonetheless characteristic of the whole.

By and large the study has been done informally, through visits and interviews with the children themselves, their parents, teachers, siblings, friends and peers, and specialists in their fields. Sometimes I would visit them alone, more often with an assistant, and for the past seven years with my wife and collaborator, Lynn T. Goldsmith. Three of the children have been followed since 1975, and three others since 1978. We tried, where possible, to tape record our sessions, and the typed transcriptions of these meetings fill hundreds of pages. I also tried to make notes on my perceptions of the visit soon after an interview: interpretations of conversations, notes about the important issues emerging during the visit, observations of those interactions between individuals that seemed particularly noteworthy. These reports were done perhaps half of the time.

The children who came to be my subjects were not found in any systematic way. I began this project in 1975 by having an assistant spend the summer scouring newspapers and magazines for articles on exceptional children, contacting music and art schools and independent teachers for assistance and recommendations. It was not too difficult to find possible cases to study. What was much more difficult was to be certain before we made direct contact that the child was indeed likely to be a prodigy; we wanted to avoid the awkwardness and disappointment of contacting a family and then subsequently deciding that the child did not meet our criteria for early prodigious achievement after all. We succeeded in avoiding all but a few such situations by doing extensive background work before contacting the child or his family.[*] Essentially, this meant talking

---

[*]I use "his" because the children in this study were all boys. In principle and in fact there are girl prodigies as well.

with the child's teachers, reading reviews or finding other media coverage, discussing his performance with others professionals, and otherwise trying to build a clear impression of the child's level of achievement in his specific field. By the end of 1975 we had contacted and secured an agreement to visit two young chess players, Franklin Montana and Ricky Velazquez, and a composer, Nils Kirkendahl.* The chess players were each eight years old at the time, the composer a few months shy of his tenth birthday.

As colleagues in the field became aware of my work with prodigies, they sometimes sent us information about other possible subjects. Two of the remaining three children were located in this way. Billy Devlin came to my attention through Julian Stanley at Johns Hopkins University, who runs an ambitious mathematics talent search and talent development program in Maryland.[2] Adam Konantovich's family contacted me directly after learning about my work from Halbert Robinson, who ran a preschool program for very high-IQ children at the University of Washington until his death in 1981.[3] Billy was seven and Adam three-and-a-half when I first met them. Billy showed extraordinary mathematical talent at a very early age, while Adam was called "perhaps the most gifted child I have ever tested or heard of yet" by Professor Robinson. I met the last of the subjects, Randy McDaniel, when he was five. Like the Konantoviches, Randy's family contacted me after hearing that I was interested in gifted children in the hopes I might help them find a school or educational program for their son. When I heard that Randy had taught himself to type at three and was writing stories and little plays before he was four, I decided to investigate the situation more thoroughly. The child did turn out to be a writer and became the sixth subject in the study.

A few unexpected problems and situations came our way during the process of prodigy hunting. One was that we could find no prodigies in the visual arts. I had assumed that artistic prodigies were fairly common and that it would be possible to locate some for the study. We were, however, unable to locate a single bona fide young artist who was producing work of professional quality before the age of ten. In fact, it appears that prodigies in painting, drawing, or sculpture are relatively rare. Although Michelangelo, Picasso, Landseer, Toulouse-Lautrec, and Millais are often cited as historical examples of children with early prodigious talent in the visual arts, over the past ten years I have heard of only two children who might qualify as artistic prodigies.

The first is a rather puzzling case of a young girl named Nadia, who was brought to the attention of the psychological community by a British

*Unless otherwise stated, the names of children, parents, siblings, teachers, and schools are identified here by pseudonym to preserve their anonymity.

clinician in the mid-1970s.[4] Between the ages of three and six or seven Nadia produced drawings that without question would be taken to be those of a mature artist by most observers. Nadia's case is so puzzling because she was autistic; in no other area of behavior or skill did she function normally, let alone extremely well. She barely spoke, ignored virtually all social interaction, and in general showed signs of severe and deep emotional disturbance. In fact, Nadia seemed more of a "savant" than a prodigy, displaying a single extraordinary capability in the midst of a generally disturbed and abnormal mental state. Although Nadia's is a case to be taken seriously, it is still not clear how she might shed light on the question of how prodigiousness in the visual arts occurs.

The second case of an artistic prodigy came to my attention by chance. Some friends of ours were browsing in a bookstore in a small summer community in western Massachusetts and were drawn to a book published in China about a young girl named Yani who painted watercolors of monkeys. They thought we might also be interested in the book and brought it to us one night when they came for dinner. There was little question from the reproductions that this child represented a genuine case of early prodigious achievement in art. Her watercolors were of extraordinary quality and deserved to be called the work of an artist, probably from the time she was three or four. And most importantly, she was described in the book as a normal, healthy, happy nine-year-old.[5] Since our first introduction to her work my friend and colleague Howard Gardner has been to China and has talked with educators and artists about Yani. All agree that her talent is real, immense, and still developing. Not surprisingly, the Chinese community is eagerly watching and hoping to assist her progress. This one seemingly uncomplicated and promising case of a child artist is the only case I have heard of since I began studying prodigies.

I was also truly surprised that we could not locate a mathematics prodigy younger than ten years old during our initial search. Although we did find a child several years later who showed mathematical promise, even with Billy Devlin it subsequently became clear that his interests and proclivities were less toward mathematics per se than a more generalized interest in the natural sciences. It was also a great surprise for us to learn that although great work in mathematics is often done by young individuals, usually before age thirty, their work does not seem to begin in earnest until the early teens. Even historically, early prodigious achievement in mathematics does not seem to occur before the age of ten, although Gauss is always proposed as a possible exception. Sometimes, although more rarely, older individuals make significant mathematical contributions as well.[6]

It also happens that all of the children in this study are boys. This is not because I wanted to study boys particularly, nor is it that I believe that only boys exhibit early prodigious achievement. I ended up with boys partly because of the specific fields I chose to study and partly because, for better or for worse, boys have more frequently been identified as prodigies. Indeed, the kind of cultural selection and support that leads to such a gender imbalance in the identification of talent is one of the factors that enters into the co-incidence equation explored in this book. If I had chosen other fields to study—for example, certain sports or musical performance —I would have found girls to study at least as frequently as boys. I make no apology for this; I simply want the reader to know that it is not because of a belief in the innate superiority of boys that the current group of children happens to be all males.

Since I began my study I have become aware of several girls who certainly seem to be prodigies. The artist Yani is one of these. In addition, several years ago I met a fifteen-year-old girl from Washington, D.C., who plays a mean game of chess. She tied for third place that year at a World's Championship tournament for girls under sixteen. This is certainly a notable achievement, made more remarkable because she had learned the game only three years earlier. We happened to be guests on the same television show, and there I was able to talk with her and her mother about her chess game and how it had developed. I have no doubt from that meeting that she would have met my stringent criteria for early prodigious achievement had she learned the game earlier. She seemed to exhibit the other qualities that I have come to expect with prodigies: intense dedication to the field, extreme self-confidence, and a mixture of childlike and adult qualities. We have also recently become aware of a third young girl, a writer. She has been the subject of several local newspaper articles, and though we have only followed her development as it has appeared in the media, she and her family also seem to display the qualities we have come to associate with prodigies. Lynn and I have begun to make plans to follow some promising young girls in our future work; for now, the boys will have to do.

Another surprise was that, contrary to our anticipations, the six boys in this study are not all first-born children (although all but Billy Devlin are the oldest sons in the household). Racially, the prodigies are all white, but they come from several different ethnic backgrounds that influence their families despite at least a generation of assimilation into American culture. Only one of the children is Jewish, which surprised me. One is Spanish, one is Italian, one is of Finnish/Greek extraction, one is distantly Irish, and one is distinctly Scottish. In one instance the mother's ethnicity is unknown, as it simply never came up. In all, the prodigies represent a

diverse group, almost a small sampling of the Western immigrant na-
tionalities to this country over the last few generations.

The families are all middle class or upper middle class. The fathers and
mothers tend to be well-educated, professional people, and the homes are
all intact and seem stable and healthy. All of the marriages but one are first
marriages. By the standards of the 1980s there is almost a quaint and
old-fashioned quality to the families in the study, something which I must
say impressed me very much.

Although the children and their families are discussed in some detail
in later chapters in terms of various aspects of the co-incidence equation,
at this point a brief introduction to them is in order. Here are the children
and their families in the order that they became part of the study.

Our Subjects

NILS KIRKENDAHL

Nils was the first child recruited for the study. The first time I met him
he seemed typecast for the part. I must admit that I believed many of the
cultural stereotypes about the child prodigy, and Nils seemed to confirm
a reasonable number of them. He was slight, though not puny, fair and
bespectacled, a nine-year-old with a strong presence tinged with a dose of
arrogance. He was polite but reserved in conversation. Now, this should
not be particularly surprising, given that he must have been as wary about
a psychologist poking into the corners of his life as I was about encounter-
ing (and ostensibly having some psychological insights about) a real
prodigy in the flesh. But I must say that Nils did not appear self-conscious
or uncomfortable. When we spoke, he was slightly distant, as if he were
a trifle bored with the attentions of relative strangers. Nils did not, however, play the role of prima donna with his music teachers, whom he
treated with deference and respect.

I first met Nils at his composition teacher's studio in Boston. His
mother, Helen, would accompany him to his lessons, and sometimes also
his four-year-old brother, Loki. They had been making these regular weekend commutes for nearly two years, since Nils's developing talent out-
grew the resources of the New England city where they lived. His schedule included a full weekend's worth of music-related activities, including
some half a dozen different lessons and generally a concert or two as well.

Nils's musical education had been provided by local teachers until he reached the age of eight. He had first expressed a strong interest in music shortly before his third birthday. One day Helen had played a recording of the Tchaikovsky violin concerto and noticed that Nils seemed spellbound by the music. She asked him whether he wanted to learn to play the violin, and he eagerly replied that he did. Remembering that teachers using the Suzuki method would take preschool students, Helen promised Nils that they could see about lessons when he turned three. Nils's interest and enthusiasm continued, and Helen enrolled him in Suzuki classes shortly after his third birthday. According to Helen's report, by the end of the first year it was clear that Nils displayed an unusual talent that bore careful watching and nurturing. He seemed to have an intuitive understanding of the music, one which was strikingly different from the other children in the class. Nils continued with Suzuki lessons for another year and then graduated to a local private teacher. About three years later, by age eight, it was clear to both Helen and his violin teacher that Nils needed more advanced training, and a number of different lessons—composition, piano, violin, solfege (singing without accompaniment to provide discipline in sight reading and tonal development)—were arranged at various conservatories in the Boston area.

His composition teacher, Dr. Aaron, a man usually sparing of praise, described nine-year-old Nils to me as follows:

> Nils is just fantastic. He's too good to be true. He has no faults and that's terrible, it's frightening—marvelous, but frightening because you just can't believe that this is all going to happen. You can hardly believe that he is just going to continue to be as serious, as dedicated yet as unforced, as unselfconscious, as well-motivated, both in the sense of quantity and the sense of quality of his motivation, true dedication to his art, both as a composer and as a performer. I've never seen anything like that. . . . It is hard for me to see any way that I talk to him which is not exactly the way I would talk to the most advanced musician.

Although Nils had seemed to confirm a number of my stereotypes, he violated one of my strongest preconceptions about musical prodigies: his family did not live and breathe music. However, there were some serious musicians in both families. A great-grandmother studied the piano and Helen's uncle was a competent violinist. Helen herself studied piano and composition intensively for three or four years when she was in her early twenties. But in contrast to many families of musical prodigies, no one in either Helen's or Johann's families was exclusively, or even primarily, a musician. Yet for reasons that Helen is unable to articulate clearly, she had felt from Nils's earliest days that it was extremely important for her infant son to be exposed to a rich musical environment. And so she provided one by playing classical music all day long from Nils's first days home from the hospital. She apparently did not select particular musical pieces for specific pedagogical purposes, she just played records or the radio for all to hear. Today, music in the Kirkendahl household is much like the television in other homes—it is played almost continuously, providing a lovely background but often not attended to directly.

Helen Kirkendahl was a homemaker while her two children were young. She seems to reflect the values of her Greek heritage in her dedication to her children and her efforts to make home life as comfortable as possible. Clearly, she saw the education of her children as her single most important parental responsibility. This education took different forms for Nils and Loki, but it was serious business in both cases. There will be more to say later about what that meant for Nils. For Loki it meant teaching him at home through second grade by herself.

Nils's father, Johann, seemed relatively uninvolved in Nils's musical education and for several years was kind of a background figure in my perception of the family. I met him once, briefly, at a concert in the Kirkendahls' hometown, but it wasn't really until Lynn and I made a rather extended visit to their home that we had the opportunity to become acquainted in a relaxed way. What was apparent about Johann early on was that while he was largely uninvolved in the particulars of Nils's musical education, he and Loki seemed to have a special relationship. This relationship had no doubt developed in part because Helen was frequently off with Nils at concerts or lessons, leaving the two of them together. But in large part theirs is a natural comradeship built on a shared love of sailing and mechanical things. Johann is an engineer in a firm specializing in the development and production of aircraft engines and obviously takes much pleasure and pride in his work. He is very good at what he does and he also is resourceful—he has managed to finesse the move from technical staff to management characteristic of many engineering firms by fashioning, and selling to management, a special technical consulting position. He and Loki often discuss Johann's stickier technical problems, and Johann proudly reports that occasionally Loki is the one with the insight that helps to move the solution forward.

Johann left Finland for the United States as a boy. Although I do not recall the details of his family's emigration, I do remember that his father was an ice-skating instructor here for a time. Johann still has family in

Finland, many of whom work or relax on the water. He keeps in close touch with them and owns part of a sailing boat with some of these relatives. While Nils and Helen spend summertimes in intensive musical instruction, Johann and Loki often spend part of the time sailing Scandinavian waters.

FRANKLIN MONTANA

Franklin was a small, dark, intense eight-year-old when I met him at the Marshall Chess Club in New York. He was a no-nonsense chess player at an age when most boys were busy with sports and superheroes. One of my clearest memories of Franklin is watching him play an eight-hour tournament without moving from his seat while his adult opponents tired, snacked, looked over other tables, and even took time out to go to the bathroom. In spite of his father's ministrations, Franklin staunchly pushed aside sodas, sandwiches, and even candy as unwanted distractions.

According to Frank and Jane Montana this intensity is characteristic of their son—once he takes on a project he does it with a vengeance. Much to some teachers' distress, he is most frequently drawn to nonscholastic pursuits. He started a snow-shoveling business at age twelve, but unlike other adolescent entrepreneurs who simply let their immediate neighbors know that they and the family snow-shovel are for hire, Franklin blitzed his neighborhood within a mile radius with advertisements. He was so dedicated a worker that he was invariably late for school on snowy days, resulting in a miserable wintertime attendance record. A savvy businessman, he plowed most of his first year's hefty profits into a top-of-the-line snowblower.

In the case of chess, Franklin's parents reported that he seemed to catch on fire almost instantly. He first saw the game played by Fischer and Spassky in the World Championship matches in 1972. His father had a passing interest in chess, and like many others that spring he occasionally tuned in the much-publicized and dramatic event. Four-year-old Franklin began watching the matches out of curiosity (and probably as a way to get to spend a little extra time with his hard-working dad). His interest piqued, he asked Frank to teach him to play. Father and son dug up the Montanas' chessboard, and Frank showed Franklin how to set it up and make rudimentary moves. Franklin began to spend many hours with the chessboard. Jane recalls that Frank left on an extended business trip shortly after he and Franklin had begun to play together, stranding her—a nonplayer—

with a child who badgered her all day long to play with him; he couldn't be made to understand that she didn't know how to play the game, and his sheer persistence wore her patience thin.

That summer the Montanas took a membership at a local swim club. Jane would arrive at the pool for the day with her three children, beach bag stuffed with swimwear, clothes, sandwiches, drinks, suntan oil, and Franklin's chess set crammed between the water wings. Although he would agree to an occasional dip, he mostly hung out near the lounge chairs with his chess set. Finding partners was sometimes a problem. Frank was usually at work, and when he was home, he couldn't be counted on to play every single time he was asked. Franklin had also quickly realized that his four-year-old friends could not be coerced into anything that resembled a real game. They much preferred splashing in the water or running around boisterously. Franklin played and swam with his friends at the pool, but whenever he could he'd rustle up a game with anyone who would agree—most often one of the older kids. Before summer's end he was beating everyone at the swim club.

By the end of the swimming season he was inviting his friends' fathers to play with him. Never a shy or retiring child, he simply set off to find new partners when his dad was too busy or tired to play. Both thick-skinned and oblivious to criticism, Franklin didn't seem to notice the raised eyebrows he elicited when he invited grownups to a match. He didn't seem to notice their stunned looks either when he won. This is not to say that Franklin was modest about his winning. He would often scamper about delightedly and run to report his victories to his parents. But just as Franklin couldn't comprehend how some people didn't care about playing chess, he didn't understand that four-year-old boys rarely play the way he did.

By that fall he was taking private lessons with George Kane, a former chess Olympian who specialized in teaching chess to children, and his associate Bruce Pandolfini.* Franklin began tournament competition some two years later at age six, and by the time I met him, in 1975, he was one of the nation's top-rated players under the age of ten, with a B-level rating and about 1,400 tournament points.

Neither Franklin's older sister, Tricia, nor his younger brother, Keith, ever expressed more than a passing interest in the game that so consumed their brother. Tricia, Franklin's senior by about five years, developed her own set of interests and circle of friends that overlapped little with her

---

*Kane and Pandolfini are the real names of these two gifted teachers.

brother's. (I should note, though, that a number of years later Tricia offered to serve as Franklin's business manager in an effort to consolidate a number of his burgeoning entrepreneurial concerns.) Franklin and Keith, only two years apart, are closer friends and playmates and sometimes chief competitors, but Keith is no chess player.

It was Franklin's father who assumed most of the responsibility for getting Franklin to lessons and tournaments. A network television executive with a high-pressure job, his work often required late nights and business trips away from home. Frank was used to being on the go. He was a somewhat older father; although we never discussed his age directly, I would estimate that he was in his early thirties when Tricia was born, and closer to thirty-six or thirty-seven when Franklin arrived. He had fought in Korea, enlisting at seventeen by lying about his age. You had the sense that Frank Montana was seasoned—he'd lived hard and seen a lot, and it was the amalgam of working well under pressure and having seen the world that made him good at his job. He did not have much time in his days for relaxation, but when he did take time off he loved fishing or working in his garden. It represented a real sacrifice and labor of love for Frank to put the time he did into Franklin's chess career.

I never got to know Jane Montana very well. In fact, I only met her once or twice. Most of my contact with Franklin was at lessons and tournaments, with fewer of the more relaxed home visits than with any of the other children in the study. Since Jane tended to stay home with her other children, we had little opportunity to meet or visit. On those occasions that we did, I had the sense of a gracious, expressive woman who seemed to enjoy her children and her role as housewife and mother. She spoke with pride about all her children and offered candid and canny observations about their temperaments and interests.

Much of the discussion about Franklin and his family will be in tandem with an age-mate, Ricky Velazquez, who was also playing chess during the same period.

RICKY VELAZQUEZ

Ricky was also a B-level chess player at eight—an age-mate, passing acquaintance, and rival of Franklin Montana's. But while Franklin's play was focused and intense, Ricky was the Perle Mesta of the chess circuit. He had a flair at the chessboard, an ebullience and boyishness that was infectious. Ricky made his moves quickly, popping out of his seat as soon as he was finished to watch other boards, kibbitzing with anyone who was available and willing to visit. Sliding back into his seat, he would swiftly assess his opponent's move, briefly consider his options, make his move, and then be off again. He sometimes made hasty mistakes which cost him matches, but mostly, like Franklin Montana, he played exceptional chess.

He, too, had been playing chess for nearly half of his eight years when I met him, his interest also having been sparked by the 1972 World Championship games. Like Frank Montana it was Bill Velazquez who taught his young son the chess basics, and like Franklin's father on the other side of the state, Bill was almost as surprised by Ricky's passion for the game as he was with his son's extraordinary progress. Within the year Ricky was also taking private lessons, and showing well against local weekend players.

Ricky was also a gifted athlete, and by the time I met him, in 1975, he was already seriously playing Little League baseball. As both his athletic and chess talents blossomed, tensions between the two activities began to emerge. Although Bill had been primarily responsible for arranging Ricky's chess activities, he began to push Ricky to emphasize the physical sport at the expense of the intellectual one. Bill felt that playing baseball or soccer would help Ricky to be perceived as a regular, all-American kid, while chess activities would only isolate him from the other boys in town. Ricky's mother, Irena, didn't quite see things the same way. It was her feeling that Ricky would benefit more from the exercise of mastering a demanding intellectual domain than from spending afternoons in an organized sports activity. Ricky himself managed to wriggle out of the middle of their disagreement. He loved baseball and he loved chess, and somehow he found time to play both—and exceedingly well at that.

In fact, Ricky seemed to be one of those kids who did pretty much everything with seemingly little effort and great success. He was an attractive child, sturdily built, with dark hair and a slightly self-conscious smile. He had many friends, was comfortable around adults, did well in his schoolwork, and loved sports. There was both an ease and a sense of warmth and excitement about him that was unusual and infectious. In this respect, I think he took after his dad.

An executive in a multinational corporation, Bill was in his late thirties when Ricky was born. Alicia was born some three years later, and then Maria two years after that. Bill's family is of Spanish descent, although he was born and raised on the East Coast and does not speak even passing Spanish. Irena sometimes takes advantage of this; she taught Ricky and the girls her native tongue and has been known to select Spanish for discussions with them that are not meant for Bill's ears. Irena came to the United States from Spain in late adolescence. She still has close ties to her family in Europe and visits often, sometimes taking the children along to summer with their cousins.

The Velazquez household is a rather traditional and, in some ways, Old-World one. Irena sees her role of wife and mother as important and valuable and has been active in her children's school and extracurricular activities. Her children are polite and respectful of adults and also energetic and happy. Alicia and Maria seem proud of Ricky, less for any specific accomplishments than because he is their big brother. For his part, Ricky seems to take the kind of casual yet protective attitude toward his little sisters that big brothers sometimes do. The family is Catholic and church-going, and while religion did not seem to be a central theme in their lives, I had the sense that it was another factor contributing to the family's sense of order, tradition, and philosophy of life and living.

We will see in later chapters how Franklin and Ricky contended with the demands of chess in a culture that puts little value on a career as a chess player.

BILLY DEVLIN

The first time we met Billy he had obviously been expecting us. Lynn and I were met at the door of the house by Sue Ellen Devlin. While her younger son sized us up from behind her skirts, we exchanged pleasantries. He darted downstairs to the family room and burrowed into an impressive pile of books that were arranged with artistic casualness around the couch. "I'm reading a book about a rather curious particle," the seven-year-old announced. "It's called a quark." He pretended to read for a while as the adults continued their introductions and "getting-to-know-you" conversation; I'm not sure whether or not he decided that he had impressed us adequately, but he soon gave up his popularized account of the search for new subatomic particles and joined the conversation.

It was not as if we needed any assurances about Billy's ability. At age six he had taken the mathematical portion of the SAT and scored higher on it than I did as a high-school junior. He had been reading since pre-school, and seemed to have a penchant for the logical and quantitative, both mathematical and scientific.

Like most of the families in the study, Nelson and Sue Ellen Devlin were not prepared for such a powerhouse. Their older son, Nelson Kevin, some eight years Billy's senior, had grown up as a regular, average kid. They were surprised and somewhat taken aback to discover their second son was a child with a steel-trap mind and voracious appetite for information. Sue Ellen quit her laboratory job as a microbiologist to spend full time providing "enrichment" for little Billy and searching for school programs that would serve his unusual needs. While Nelson Kevin had been comfortable in their suburban public school system, Sue Ellen and Nelson finally decided on a local Montessori school for Billy that mixed younger and older children in the same classroom. School was supplemented with a range of tutors, visits to museums, and meetings with university professors, all orchestrated by Sue Ellen.

Billy was a small child, slightly pudgy, with light brown hair and new front teeth that were still too big for his mouth. In many ways he had yet to grow into his own intellectual interests just as his body was still playing catch-up with itself. He was an extremely confident child whose assertions were frequently tinged with a healthy dose of bravado. On that first visit Lynn had a conversation that we later came to recognize as characteristically overstated:

> Billy told me he had gone to visit a professor at a local university and had seen an electron microscope in the man's lab. He'd let Billy look at a number of different materials through the microscope. Suitably impressed, I told Billy that an electron microscope was a pretty fancy instrument and that I'd never actually seen one myself, only electron microscope photographs in books. Billy replied, "Oh yeah, it's really interesting. Everything looks brown through an electron microscope." I replied that I hadn't known that was the case. Billy assured me that *"everything* looks brown if you look at it from close enough." By now I was both confused and suspicious of the direction of our conversation. When I asked him whether he was sure of this, he replied confidently, "Yes." I thought to myself for a moment, "Here's a seven-year-old kid who's reading books about quarks. Maybe he knows something about the intrinsic spectral properties of particles that I don't." Somehow my better judgment prevailed and I reminded myself that although Billy might be a budding Einstein, Gauss, or Newton (and I most certainly was not), there were nonetheless still some things I knew more about than this seven-year-old—an extraordinary seven-year-old, to be sure, but still a little kid nonetheless. Fired with new self-confidence, I fished a blue eyeglass case from my purse and handed it to Billy, asking him if it, too, would be brown if he looked at it from up close enough. He kind of mashed it against his eye for a moment, looked squarely at me and announced disingenuously "Yes, it does."

On the other hand, the bravado and confidence were not entirely misplaced: Billy most certainly did some extraordinary things. His math tutor sent the following progress report to Julian Stanley of Johns Hopkins University after less than six months' work with his six-year-old charge.

> Billy has completed Chapter 1, Book 0, of *Elements of Mathematics,* at a pace he essentially set. The chapter was completely covered, including the test, in eighteen one-hour sessions. . . . This is only slightly more class time than the goal of fourteen sessions suggested for selected junior high school students covering the same material. His score on the test on Chapter 1, which he completed, mostly in writing, in about 45 minutes, was 65 out of 70.

Half a year later, Sue Ellen wrote to me that "Billy was seven years old [at the end of] January. Since Nov. Billy has been increasingly interested in physics and in a 2-week period, at his leisure at home and school, read among other books of interest, *College Physics* by Edwin White, which was I believe some 1070 pages. . . . He is very easygoing and to see him on the playground or out playing ball, one would not suspect his intellectual pursuits."

But whether or not you could detect it from afar, Billy certainly was not your average six- or seven-year-old. He seemed to have a passion for collecting and ordering things. He also knew many details about various fields: natural science, science fiction, geography, arithmetic, and mathematics. Sometimes his interests were more mundane and boyish. In 1979 the two Devlin boys proudly led us on a tour of their mammoth beer-can collection, carefully catalogued on their dad's computer and lovingly arranged and stored in the basement. I was pleased sometime later to contribute a fairly exotic can of Israeli beer that we solicitously saved for him for the whole of our sabbatical. Getting it home undented was not easy.

Despite the difference in their ages and Billy's preoccupation with intellectual matters, Billy and Nelson Kevin seemed to enjoy a genial relationship. Nelson Kevin wasn't much interested in schoolwork and didn't try to compete with his younger brother. During his teens, Nelson Kevin's friends were the center of his world. He was better coordinated and more athletic than Billy and took pride in these accomplishments. This is not to suggest that Billy wasn't game for competition: I remember watching Billy and Nelson Kevin skateboarding down their driveway, wondering how many more trips it would take before Billy skinned himself from head to toe.

It may be that the age difference helped to minimize outright competition between the two boys. The Devlin family is the only one of the six in my study where the child I followed was not the oldest son, but in some

ways the eight-year differential between Nelson Kevin and Billy effectively created two separate, single-child "families." For Nelson and Sue
Ellen, each boy was so developmentally distinct that their needs and interests may have only barely overlapped.

In Billy Devlin we will see how a child who appeared to be a prodigy
in one field (mathematics) actually turned out to be something else, and
who, in the process, taught us a good deal about both prodigies and the
fields in which they are found.

ADAM KONANTOVICH

I don't recall having any preconceptions about Adam before I met him
in 1978, only an immense curiosity about what a three-and-a-half-year-
old would be like who was reported to read, write, speak several languages,
study mathematics, and compose for the guitar. Lynn remembers wondering whether he'd be wearing diapers. (He was not.) In fact, at first sight
he was like any other young boy: he was a round child with a chubby face
and long, wavy auburn hair, dressed in a colorful T-shirt and Health-Tex
overalls. He lisped a bit when he talked.

But he talked more like a bright ten- or twelve-year-old, conversing
in an elaborated way about things that interested him. He liked to play
with words, making "proto-puns" and jokes that combined words with
physical activity. In fact, one of the things that struck us most about Adam
during that first visit was his exceptional sense of humor. He had a wry
quality and—if it is possible for a three-and-a-half-year-old—a dry wit
that almost more than anything else we saw that day seemed extraordinary
for a child of so few years.

This sense of humor, often coupled with tidbits of esoterica, has been
an abiding characteristic of Adam. One of my favorite examples is from
a few years later, when five-year-old Adam and his parents were visiting
in Boston and we all decided to go on an outing to the Science Museum.
While at the museum we went to a puppet show for preschoolers about
humpback whales. Adam readily joined the other children at the puppet
theater, while we sat in the back of the room with the rest of the adults.
He seemed to participate in the drama of the show much as the others
there, offering spontaneous comments now and then, as did some of the
other children. He readily participated in audience activities, stretching his
arms above his head when invited to breathe like whales, calling to the
whales, and so on. Adam was the only child who answered the performers
when they asked who had tried to kill the "hero" of the show, a baby
humpback whale. (Adam: "The evil Colin!") Later, the performers asked

the only rhetorical question of the performance: whether anyone knew what humpback whales ate. Given the ages of the children, it seemed to us that most of the kids would be lucky to know that the humpback was a particular type of whale, let alone anything about its eating habits. Adam, however, didn't miss a beat when he quickly replied, "They eat krill." Lynn and I thought perhaps he'd read a display mentioning krill in another part of the room as we'd walked in for the performance, but when Adam continued, "they're small shrimp, but they're not microscopic!," we decided he really knew. At the end of the show Colin's magic whale-killing telescope was ruined, and the performers asked the children what he should do instead of hunting whales. Adam volunteered that he should clean houses for a living.

On our first visit to the Konantoviches we were struck by the fact that Adam's home seemed to be as unusual as he did. He has grown up in an exceptionally child-oriented environment, both physically and psychologically. With the exception of Fiona's office, which was more or less off limits, the Konantovich home was designed to stimulate and engage Adam's interests. Furnished in bright colors and contemporary Scandinavian furniture, the rooms were arranged to give Adam the maximum amount of space to explore, experiment, and relax. The Konantoviches wanted Adam to feel that the house was his, too, and had "childproofed" and "child-appealed" it so that Adam would be comfortable, interested, and safe. On our first visit the house was crammed full of Adam's toys— brightly colored stacking rings and cars, stuffed animals, shapes and beads, science kits, and "flash cards" of French and Hebrew letters and simple vocabulary words. And books. The walls in the living room were lined floor to ceiling with bookshelves (as were the two bedrooms upstairs): I estimated their personal library to be at least 3,000 volumes in 1978—I daresay it has at least doubled since then. Since that first visit the range and level of materials have changed as Adam has grown, but the emphasis on providing an exceedingly rich, varied, stimulating, and aesthetic environment most certainly has not.

Nathaniel and Fiona had always hoped to have a bright child who would approach learning with joy, spontaneity, and excitement. Before Adam was born they had agreed that they would try to raise their child by paying careful attention to his or her interests, needs, and requests, be they intellectual, social, or emotional. They were not prepared, however, for a child who challenged their parenting resources and stamina—and their fundamental notions of ability and development—before they had even become used to their new parental roles and responsibilities.

According to their pediatrician, Adam was exceedingly mature neurologically at birth. This assessment, however, did not prepare them to expect that Adam would begin speaking words, and then gramatically correct sentences, at three months of age. Fiona and Nathaniel brought young Adam back to the pediatrician and asked him to help them understand these unprecedented accomplishments. The doctor observed that Adam's development, both neurologically and behaviorally, continued to be exceedingly precocious, but he could offer no further explanation or advice. By six months Adam was carrying on complex conversations, and he was reading simple books and correcting his mother's spelling by his first birthday.

If Adam's extreme precocity was difficult for Fiona and Nathaniel to assimilate, it was nearly impossible for child-care providers. Although both Fiona and Nathaniel had originally intended to continue working full time after Adam's birth, they found that they could not obtain adequate child-care for their extraordinary baby. Rather than leave Adam with someone they could not thoroughly trust, the Konantoviches rearranged their work schedules so that one parent could always be with him. Nathaniel, a science professor, tries to organize his teaching schedule so that he has much of the afternoon free. Fiona is a psychotherapist in private practice. She works mostly in the evening, when Nathaniel is available for parenting; when she must schedule appointments during the day, she tries to arrange for Nathaniel to come home to watch Adam. Adam also learned very quickly about his mother's need for quiet during her work hours, and well before the age of two could be counted on to play quietly and unobtrusively by himself when clients were in the house.

The Konantovich family, warm and generous and fun-loving, is the most dedicated, persevering, and intellectually active trio I have ever had the opportunity to observe. Fiona and Nathaniel's dedication to parenting and their unending quest for stimulating and supportive environments that will respond to Adam's needs are discussed in more detail in chapter 5.

RANDY McDANIEL

As happens with some regularity, in the fall of 1978 I received a telephone call from a mother who had been referred to me by the consultant for the gifted in the Massachusetts State Department of Education. It seems that Jeanne McDaniel was having difficulty finding an appropriate school for her son, Randy, a six-year-old with unusual writing abilities. The family had moved around the region and was now willing to relocate once again if a school could be recommended. I have never been comfortable recommending schools to people, for several reasons: recommendations imply endorsements, which I don't feel I could or should make; furthermore, selecting a school setting is far too complex a decision to be made without knowing the child in question; and it is not my role as a researcher to evaluate school environments. I wanted to be of help but could do no more than make a few vague suggestions. But I did ask Jeanne to tell me what Randy had been doing that seemed unusual, and, based on her reply, I decided that this was a child I would like to see at closer range.

Jeanne reported that Randy had been writing little stories, plays, short essays, and poems since he was three, when he taught himself to type; he had been pounding out the material ever since. His father, Darren, a writer/journalist himself, had taken care of Randy during his earliest years while Jeanne worked full time as a schoolteacher. They lived in a semirural area about an hour away from Boston but were planning to move to the city in the hopes of facilitating Randy's education, particularly his social development with peers.

We arranged for a meeting, and Jeanne and Randy rode to Boston on the bus, Jeanne with a folder of Randy's writing, and Randy, with excitement and some trepidation. Jeanne told me that as they were getting off the bus Randy had wanted to make sure for the fourth time that this Dr. Feldman was not, in fact, a new dentist. Our meeting was fairly short. Randy eagerly showed me some of his work, including his "Superheroes" play, reproduced below verbatim, which was written when he was five.

Superheroes

Introducing the superheroes!

SCENE I

The Daily Empire Building

Syperman and Batman are standing on the roof of the Daily Empire Building when they hear an explosion in the distance.

Superman says: "Batman, what is that noise?"

Batman replies: "I don't know, but look at that heavy black smoke in the sky. Ihope nobody was hurt, Duperman. We'd better go over and find out."

Superman jumps into the air and glies over Metropolis, landing on the sidewalk next to the exlposion area. As he arrives he sees Bigfoot also landing.

XSuperman XXXXXX says: "Help me find out if anybody has been hurt, Bigfoot."

Bigfoot and Superman enter the burining building. They hear cries coming from a doorway at the end of a smokey corridor. Bigfoot says: "Ahhhrrr!" "Kyasaar."

"Yes,: says Sueperman. XXXXXXXX You're right, CCCCC Bigfoot. People are trapped in that room. We must get them out of there."

Bigfoot runs to the end of the corridor and smashes the door with his shoulder. As the door breaks, people come runningout of the smokey room.

"hank you Bigfoot," says a man. "Look," says a woman, "Superman is here, too. Thank heavens they came in time."
Just then, another explosion rips through the building, and cries for help are heard by Bigfoot and Superman.

XXXXX "The cries seem to be coming from the second floor," Superman says. "I'll go outside and jump up through a window."

Superman abd Bigfoot run to th3 sidewalk. As they emerge from th4 building, they see another superhero, wonder woman, arriving on the scene.

Wonde woman takes out her lqriat and athrows it high into the air. It catches and holds on the edge of the second-floor balcony. Wonder woman climbs hand over hand up the lariat rope and hurdles the rail of the balcony. Then she rusahes into the burning building.

Watchingt from below, Superman and Bigfoot are concerned about the danger to Wonder woman.

"Let's jump up there and help herx," Superman saus.

"Kyaaar," Bigfoot agreees.

The two mighty ssuperheroes jump to the second floor and rush into the smokey burning building.

Then XXXXXXX they see out of the smoke an old mankkkkkkkkkk kkkkkkkhhhhhhhhhhhhhhhhhhhhhhhhhhhhhhhhhhhhhhhhhhhhhhhhhhhhhhhh hhhhhhhhhhhhhhhhhhhhhhhhhhhhhhhhhhh
   hhhhhhhhhhhhhhhhhhhhhhhhhhhhhhhhh
man. He's a bad guy. mHe doesn't have a gun. He kills only with his hands. He is trying to killla ll the superheroes and has set XX this fire and explosion so that the superheroes will come to the rescue and then he will kill them.

Now XXXX he has XXXXX three of the superheroes in the same burning room.

"You are at my mercy," he says in his hideous voice.

At that very moment, Superman takes a deep breath and blows out through his lips, creating a wind so strong that it carries the evil man out over the balcony and up into the air, over the clouds, a d finally sends him into the XXXXXX middle of Lake Michigan. CCCXZXZXZXZZZZXSYZXZ XZXXXZXXXZXXXZXXXZXXXZXZXZXZXZXZXZXZXZXX But that is not the end of the story.

SCENE II

(Ghotham city)

Superman and Bigfoot appear on the scene.
Superman says;;:Wev'e got to climb that (playboy) building, Bigfoot.
Bigfoot says;:CIA. CIA. CIA. CIAAAA"!
They climb the building.
That, ladies and gentlemen, was written by Randall McDaniel. Thank you.

A small child with sharp, almost birdlike features, Randy had darting, twinkling eyes and a flamboyant manner. He was more than ready to show off a bit and acted the parts of his play with gusto. Later, on many occasions, Lynn and I were to be treated to the acting out of his own works, musicals, and Monty Python comedy routines. Randy seemed to be a real ham, a performer looking for an audience. I have also come to associate Randy's appearance with that of Basil Rathbone's portrayal of Sherlock Holmes (although it is difficult to imagine Mr. Rathbone as a six-year-old). Randy has had an abiding fascination with all things British, and badgered his parents for a cape and Holmesian hunting cap while most boys his age were lobbying for Superhero underwear. In fact, until quite recently Randy has even thought of himself as a Brit somehow misplaced in America.

Randy's family did find a school in Boston, The Learning Place, and they moved to the city late in the fall of 1978. During that year I had a number of opportunities to observe Randy both in and out of school. In the years since, our families have become close friends. It is hard to know how much the sheer fact of propinquity has led to our friendship, but for whatever reasons we have seen more of the McDaniel family than any other one in the study. Our role with them has been as much friend as observer, and the line between research and friendship has long since blurred. The same has been true to some extent with all of the families, but especially so with the McDaniels.

Like the Konantoviches, the McDaniels have only one child. Theirs is the only second marriage in my study, and Darren has two grown daughters from a previous marriage. Darren was in his early forties when Randy was born, and Jeanne in her early thirties. Physically, Randy resembles neither his mother nor father very closely, but is viewed by both Darren and Jeanne as a melding of the two of them—the embodiment, through his specialness, of the rightness of their relationship and of the life course they feel destined to follow. Indeed, in many respects the McDaniels' attempt to provide Randy with the best education and support system has been for them a test of their ability to understand the forces and factors governing their own lives. We will take a closer look at how they have gone about dealing with his particular talents in chapter 3.

These, then, are the subjects of my study. The talents of the prodigies are remarkable, and the families they are part of are remarkable as well. Some of the prodigies are no longer doing what they started out to do as talented children. Some have not yet found their final paths. At least one seems to be well on his way to a career in the field in which he was first identified. It will be the task in the following chapters to try and unravel the threads of their lives to make some sense out of how things have gone so far.

PART II

The Co-incidence Process

3

Talent and Transition in a Writing Prodigy

O F ALL of the factors that must co-incide to yield a prodigy, individual talent is the most obvious and, in a sense, most necessary. While my intention is to focus on the range of forces that contribute to the realization of prodigious potential, clearly the children's talents are striking and extreme. If these children themselves were not truly gifted, they would not emerge as prodigies. Most of us, even if we are placed in environments that greatly support and facilitate mastery of a particular field, would not have shown prodigious abilities. While it is important to remember that a child cannot realize his or her potential without the other factors comprising co-incidence, the individual potential for prodigious achievement itself is obviously a critical precondition.

Randy McDaniel: Child Writer

This chapter is about talent in a child writer, and the role that talent plays as a critical factor in co-incidence. Randy McDaniel is the purest example of prodigiousness I have studied in the sense that his talents appear to be the most specialized of the six. The fact that his talents were primarily literary is especially interesting since, for the most part, writing is not a domain where prodigious achievement occurs. Serious child writers are uncommon for at least two reasons. The field itself has few organized supports or strategies for instruction in the craft. I strongly suspect that Randy's unusual talents would have languished had his father not been a writer himself. On the nontechnical side, child writers may be rare because children normally lack the kind of experience, insight, and understanding that writers are expected to convey in their works. In general, the absence of writing prodigies makes Randy's case particularly interesting. As we shall see, his other major area of talent—music—will begin to play a greater and greater role in his development as time passes.

Being unusual by virtue of being a very young writer has influenced Randy's life in a variety of ways. His strong proclivity for language, both spoken and written, showed itself quite early. Yet, among the prodigies, Randy has had more than the usual share of skeptics. The reason seems to be twofold. First, although Randy's performance in other academic areas is strong, it is not as accelerated as his linguistic skills. Second, because child writers are rare, there seems to be more suspicion and distrust of Randy's talent than if he were a chess player or mathematician, for example. The relative absence of support or instruction for writers of all ages has also left Randy more isolated from a community of fellow practitioners than some of the other children we have followed. It appears that for writing, more than for any of the other areas our subjects have chosen to pursue, continued development of early promise in the field requires extreme, internally generated dedication and purposefulness because there are few cultural rewards. Randy's sense of purpose and resolve to be a writer has had to be at least as strong as his talent. Certainly all of the children we have followed can be characterized as strongly motivated to exercise and develop their extraordinary talents, despite the obstacles or attractive alternative activities that may present themselves. But the extent to which extreme internal motivation is demanded for continued progress depends on the extent to which the field itself receives outside cultural sources of support and encouragement. Of those fields we have observed, writing seems to be the least connected to an external network of instruction, fellow travelers, and rewards from the larger culture. Although Randy's early talent was strong and quite specifically directed toward the written word, and despite the fact that his special abilities have been a central organizing force in his family's life, it has been a continuing struggle for him to stay with his writing.

EARLY DAYS

In retrospect, Jeanne and Darren are not surprised that their son has shown unusual abilities, for they consider him to be the product of their own unique and powerful relationship, one they have always thought of as a spiritual union. They see Randy as simply another strong expression of their life together; he was born on Easter Sunday in 1972.

Randy was born in the Midwest, but several weeks later the small family moved back East to the region where Jeanne and Darren both had grown up. They rented a farm not far from Jeanne's family, where they spent five "golden years." Darren, ever conscious of the spiritual dimension of the McDaniels' experience, mused that "on the farm we were blessed. We were aware of the spirituality of our family all the time." The family was self-sufficient, happily insular, and graced with beautiful surroundings.

The special quality of Randy's relationship with his father stems from this time as well. Darren had been placed in charge of five-month-old Randy's care so that Jeanne could return to her teaching job at the beginning of the school year. After many years as a journalist and newspaper editor, Darren was delighted to stay home, work on the novel he had been incubating, and look after Randy. The setting was writer-perfect: a 150-year-old farmhouse set in pastoral peace, a loving wife heading off to improve young minds every day, and a baby sleeping in his cradle to round out the picture. However, Darren soon found that Randy had no intention of cooperating in his novelist's fantasy. Randy did not behave anything like a baby should. He hardly slept at night, let alone during the day. Randy was walking by six months, and he far preferred his father's company to a seductive arrangement of toys on the far side of the typewriter. Furthermore, Darren found Randy exceedingly good company. He began to spend less of his time writing and more time teaching and playing with Randy. It is not insignificant that Randy's favorite games and activities were ones that Darren himself enjoyed. Looking in at the family from the outside and retrospectively, I suspect that Darren might have abandoned his novel for the pleasure of his young son's company and education in any event, but Randy's attraction to the same kinds of activities that moved his father may have clinched the deal.

Randy had been interested in words and their tonal qualities from the very beginning. Jeanne reported that Randy delighted in a neighbor's renditions of nursery rhymes, laughing and moving his arms and legs to the rhythms. He also had clear favorites, being particularly partial to "Hey Diddle Diddle." He loved stories and had taught himself to read at two-

and-a-half. Darren told us how one morning about half a year later, while downstairs reading the paper, he heard typing upstairs. Engrossed in the news, he wondered absently what kind of TV program Randy could be watching that featured a typist. When the distracting staccato of the typewriter had continued for several minutes, Darren put down his newspaper and went upstairs to coerce Randy into turning off the television. But instead of finding his son engrossed in a Sesame Street vignette about secretaries, he found Randy himself sitting at the typewriter hunting and pecking out a short communiqué. To the best of Darren's and Jeanne's knowledge Randy had never before used the typewriter, although he had certainly spent many hours watching both parents compose at it. Three-year-old Randy was delighted with this quick, efficient, and neat mode of writing and has used the typewriter ever since.

Over the course of the next few years, Darren became Randy's primary educational resource, both for writing and for other studies. Darren's pedagogical style was somewhat idiosyncratic—a blend of classical and pop—but it seemed to captivate Randy and pique his curiosity. They would watch educational television together daily, and Darren's lessons would take off from there. The "Nova" series was one of Randy's favorites, combining scientific subjects with a presentation characterized by clarity and panache. When he was two-and-a-half, Randy saw a television show on the stars and planets that mesmerized him. Eager to pursue the subject further, he and Darren embarked on his first "study." They ransacked the library for information about modern conceptions of the heavens as well as the history of astronomy. They went to museums, decorated Randy's room with posters, made models and comic books, wrote stories. From the solar system Randy moved to a study of mythology. He is reported to have read Darren's college textbook on the topic and wanted to know everything he could know about mythological figures and their adventures. One study led to another, with Randy's own tastes leading the way and Darren responding with a potpourri of resources. A few months after Randy's sixth birthday, Jeanne summed up Randy's early educational experiences as follows:

> Randy began reading on his own at the age of two to our surprise. His first "study" was the planets and the solar system. He went on from there to the dinosaurs, musical compositions, the orchestra, the lives and works of the composers, the macabre (Dracula, Frankenstein, and other monster-types), the history of the comics and its heroes and a variety of dramatic literature. He had read Ibsen's *Peer Gynt* and knew the Grieg score by the time he was four. By knowing

the music, I mean that he had memorized the score almost instantly, as he does everything. *Cyrano de Bergerac* and *Romeo and Juliet* are current favorites. He writes daily. Because of his frustration and some limitation of fine motor skills, he began to type when he was three and has been using our IBM Selectric since . . . He has not had any particular leanings mathematically, but his understanding of the universal questions of time and space have always had a fascination. Though he refused to learn 2 + 2, he was thrilled with a calculator and very pleased to be able to add two million and two million. Just by chance a few weeks ago, he discovered the Morse code and learned it in a few hours.

The glue that held all of these disparate activities together was Randy's orientation toward the written word. He wrote constantly, tirelessly, about everything he studied and anything that whetted his curiosity. He wrote about God and about his dogs, about himself and about fictional TV characters, about fishing with his grandfather, and about becoming famous as an adult.

Randy seemed to use his writing to exercise his delight in words. Rather than sharing thematic content, the early writing is mostly an exploration of word texture and ambience. The particular content of the piece often seems secondary, as if its purpose was merely to provide a vehicle for the language. Sometimes a conversation or activity became the basis for a story, other times it might be a television program or a book Randy had read. In other respects Randy was like a serial novelist or formula writer, using a central character in a number of slightly varied adventures. In the tradition of Dickens, Conan Doyle, and the creator of the Hardy Boys, F. W. Dixon, Randy produced two separate series. The first borrowed the "Dr. Who" character from the BBC television series, showcasing him in a number of intergalactic adventures. The second featured a Victorian sleuth of Randy's own creation named Komar Lorkes.

Given Darren's profession, it would be easy to explain Randy's passion for writing as a manifestation of his father's ambitions. Perhaps Darren did see some of himself reflected in Randy. But the McDaniels are sophisticated and reflective individuals, aware of the psychological dramas in which they each might play a part. Moreover, their mutual commitment to each other and to Randy has always been the central force in their lives. Darren's relationship with his son is complex, and Darren is as aware of its different dimensions as anyone. He is not simply pushing his son to realize his own unfulfilled dreams. Above all, he is a loving father dedicated to facilitating Randy's well-being.

SCHOOLING

A clear indication of this commitment to Randy's welfare was the family's move to Boston in the fall of 1978 in order to enroll Randy in school. By Randy's sixth birthday it was clear to both Jeanne and Darren that their local schools—both public and private—would not be able to meet Randy's special needs. They withdrew him from first grade, Jeanne quit her job, and she and Darren tried teaching him at home. By the middle of the fall they both were beginning to feel that Randy's educational and especially his social needs had exceeded the resources of "The McDaniel School." It was less their own limitations as teachers and advisers and more that they recognized that Randy was missing the social stimulation of a school environment. The insularity that they had carefully protected and cherished no longer seemed so clearly in Randy's best interest; Jeanne began to take the steps that were to bring the halcyon days at the farm to a close.

I originally met the McDaniels during Jeanne's search for a school setting that would meet Randy's growing educational and social needs. Jeanne had begun searching further and further afield for an educational environment that would challenge and support Randy. Even more important was to find a place where he would be understood and appreciated for what he was. She first contacted me in the hopes that I would have a recommendation, and while I'm afraid I was of little help in finding a school, we did come to establish a strong relationship.

Jeanne and Darren's commitment to Randy's development was such that they were willing (if, understandably, somewhat reluctant) to relocate and shoulder the considerable financial strain of private school. When they married, Jeanne and Darren quite consciously decided not to become trapped by the acquisitiveness they saw driving much of the country. They felt strongly that a preoccupation with financial success often led to a moral and spiritual impoverishment. They were unwilling to make the trade. In practical terms, this has meant that they have made professional decisions that are compatible with their philosophy and values, although less financially rewarding. And while the McDaniel coffers have rarely been overflowing since I have known them, they are unstinting in providing materials and experiences they feel will benefit Randy. So, while the problem of finding the right school for Randy was not easy to solve, they did solve it, at least for a couple of years. This, by the way, is about as long as most solutions seem to work with prodigies. Educating a child as talented and idiosyncratic as Randy is more than most schools can handle for very long.

Persistent sleuthing led Jeanne to locate a small school in Boston called The Learning Place. Although it was not a school especially for gifted or talented children, it was a place where Jeanne felt Randy would be accepted and at home. Darren was ambivalent about leaving the farm and moving the family, believing that their special closeness and connectedness might be lost if they left. Despite his reservations, however, he accepted the decision that seemed so important to his wife and son. It was not so much the specific school that Darren objected to but rather the thought that their idyllic existence was about to be irreversibly transformed—as indeed it was. As Randy entered the world of the schoolboy, the fierceness of his attachment to his parents began to diminish. The family was no longer self-contained or self-sufficient, and Randy began to explore his new connections with both hesitation and delight.

Shortly after the McDaniels moved to Boston Jeanne invited me to observe Randy in his new school. As I wandered through The Learning Place on my first visit, Randy McDaniel appeared and introduced himself to me, remarking, "My mother told me all about you." Somewhat taken aback by his directness, I replied that his mother had also told me all about him. He introduced me to his best friend, Aaron, and a group of four or five of us moved toward an area of the large schoolroom that was used for games. Aaron, Randy, and Joshua began playing three-dimensional tic-tac-toe, while another child and I sorted two incomplete decks of cards to make one full one. I was able to watch Randy and his playmates while I lost a game of fish to a little hustler named Annie.

Randy seemed very much at home in The Learning Place and definitely enjoyed his time there. Randy's teachers felt that his performance in nonliterary subjects like arithmetic and science was not particularly exceptional but did note that his orientation toward language was highly unusual and extremely well developed. When given the opportunity he wrote stories and plays with abandon, texturing his prose to create ambience in a most masterful manner. He was also an eager performer, reciting his own works as well as entire record albums from memory (he had a particular penchant for musicals and comedy routines). The children and staff at The Learning Place seemed to take Randy's talent in stride, according him no particularly special privileges, but appreciating his strengths as "what Randy does." For his part, Randy was not arrogant or condescending toward those around him. His teachers described him as a caring and sensitive member of the community, a "fine human being." School head Tom O'Brien summed it up when he said, "Randy is a character, but we love him."

RANDY'S WRITING

Randy had written literally thousands of pages by the time he was eight, and the examples of his work presented in this section are but a tiny fragment of his oeuvre. Nonetheless, I think they are characteristic of his writing at different ages and reflect the kinds of themes and language typical of Randy's writing. The first example was done when he was barely five years old; the second is more recent, written at the end of 1981, when he was nine. I choose these two examples because they seem to me to represent genuine expressiveness in writing. Neither is a polished piece; neither would be taken to be the work of a mature writer, but there is something of substance in both. The first example, "The Life of Randy McDaniel," is presented as written, with slight alterations to maintain the anonymity of the people and places mentioned:

I was born in Chicago, Illinois, where I first saw the glimpse of a beautiful woman. She was called Jeanne, and she was my mother for years to come. I usually called her Mom most of the time. Isn't that what most sons call their mothers? Also, I had a father named Darren, and he once worked in the Boston Herald [a newspaper]. In that time, it was as it is today. He works at the Herald now, it used to be called the Boston Herald Castaway. Now it is called the Boston Herald American. There's one man that screws up Dad's life in the Herald. He says his name is Fred. I don't pay much attention about what he says about him. Mom and Dad were very astonished at what I had done some days. I turned on the televison [*sic*], ate my first piece of grill [*sic*] cheese, and various other things. One time, he went to Boston very early, after I had been born, and came back a week later. A while after that we moved to Tracy, where I met my grandfather. He's really called Manfred Scalia. And also I met my grandmother. Then I moved to Princeton [the farm] and there I met Floyd, Mary, Gary, and Grace. Gary often [went?] with me and Gary [?] on fishing trips. When I first went fishing, I wasn't skilled, so I didn't catch anything. I had a good time there. There I had two dogs, Ginger and Zep. I loved them. Then a man named Mr. Peek, sold the house to somebody else. Then we left Princeton. Now we live in New Brighton. This is where [grand]Pa lives. I go by my house once in a while, looking for Zep. Ginger is at another house. One time we had Zep stay here for a few days, but it didn't work. I hope we move soon, and stay there. This is what happened in my life.
P.S. If any of my children friends see this, when they grow up, they

will read it to their children over and over again, because of me, their long-time friend. THE END

There is much about Randy's "biography" that is what one would expect from a five-year-old. He lists his family and friends and describes a series of events ("then . . . then . . . then . . ."). Sometimes pronominal reference is ambiguous, and much of the sentence construction is quite simple. Yet there are also ways in which this story is quite unusual. Although some five-year-olds might be able to dictate a story of this length and complexity, Randy typed this without assistance and with few errors. It is a fairly long story, and more coherent than one might expect from a child this age. Some of Randy's sentence construction is quite sophisticated, and the language he uses is not always what one hears every day at the preschool playground. So, too, some of the special quality of the farm is captured here, some of Randy's sadness at losing his two dogs, and certainly the difficulties of moving from place to place. I think that his rather strange, aphoristic postscript, which invokes the importance of friendship and some sense that Randy will be special to at least a group of childhood friends, is an early articulation of Randy's longstanding belief in his own uniqueness.

Four years later Randy wrote the following poem. He did so in response to one written by Joshua, his friend and classmate at The Learning Place. Joshua had never laid any claims to Randy's territory as the school's resident writer, and yet he had written a beautiful poem. In fact, even by Randy's reckoning, it was probably better than many of the fluffy stories that had recently been occupying Randy's time and energy. Randy was surprised and jealous. After all, although Joshua was a good friend, Randy was the writer. Jeanne and Darren reported that Randy produced the following piece soon after reading Joshua's poem.

UNTITLED

Really writing nothing one lone man in a spaceship
   He wanders around, asking me questions
  and people reply,
    "The ultimate fantasy is reality."
    "Without words is the greatest dream."
    "The spirit is self-explanatory."
    "Opinions mentioned cannot be spoken with words."
Good poem, he adds, goofing off at the door, trying to get
people's attention. The wrong thing to do, says the
traveler with the silly hat

and the devil
shadowplay in the other one's sun
   With the spirit
   And there's little Randy
     Standing in the grass
       watching the air
     Self-explanatory, says the school principal. I'm not
impressed.
Who in the world
     is?
Nobody. No world
     not

       a world
There is none.
Don't keep reminding me, the man said. Add question mark.
       you must remember to write this book
       right
         but this is the nothing book, Davey
         and you can write it any
       way you want it.
All right, says the man in the spaceship, fingering his nose
  People say he sucks his thumb every
         night
There is the devil
  Standing between two big toes
  Without any expression on his face
  Waiting for the final decision
    That is all
All that is written as a poem.
But I don't like poems, the retarded (oops, I'm sorry) retainer
(again) retired
    Army sergeant says
      That's because you were in NASA
         Randy replies
    Don't call me my mother
      Waiting for the clouds to come
        The dog barks heavily walking down the moonlight road
        By himself
          One lone sergeant in a tank
           Asking people questions
      They reply
      "Are eternal."
        ARE.
      We ARE.
      They ARE.
        Everyone ARE.

Is, Randy, IS.
We ARE.

Randy M.
The Dedicated
[1981, age 9]

Again, the quality of the writing is remarkable, although not yet fully mature. Some of the poem is difficult to interpret, some passages just seem to fizzle. But there is strong feeling here, feeling that would be apparent whether one was aware of the motivation behind the poem or not. Randy used the poem as a vehicle to reassert his position as the Number One Writer among his peers, although I don't think he ever showed the poem to Joshua. What was important was to write something *for himself* that was good enough for him to feel that he still had the talent if he chose to exercise it. Randy himself seems to come in and out of the poem: goofing off, standing there, waiting for reaffirmation. I also appear, unbidden, as someone who will judge his quality as a writer (and he was right, I guess). Again, there is an aphoristic, mystical quality to the poem, sandwiched in between a spaceman, a military man, and a few more recognizable characters, including the devil. This is a serious piece of writing, and it expresses some things that were true for Randy, that reflect his thoughts and feelings in a poetic manner. I would not suggest that this example of Randy's writing qualifies him as a professional poet, but I would argue that his writing here serves as a serious vehicle of expression, made possible by his mastery of language and the technology for using that mastery well.

The importance of the technology of the typewriter to Randy's writing should also not be underestimated. Jeanne had noted on several occasions that, when very young, Randy's underdeveloped fine motor skills slowed him down significantly when he tried to write longhand. When typing, his imagination could take flight; writing, he often felt frustrated and earthbound. He simply could not manipulate paper and pencil well enough to express himself adequately with these tools. As an example of the difference between Randy's handwritten and typed compositions, contrast the biography and poem above with two letters Randy wrote to us in 1980. The letter to Lynn was part of a school exercise written in March 1980, when he was a month shy of his eighth birthday. It is difficult to imagine that this childish note was penned by the author of the short biography or the *Dracula* play that appears at the end of this chapter (see pp. 67–69). Furthermore, the biography and play predated the letter by nearly three years. The differences between the letter and the typed pieces

Thursday, March 6, 1980

Dear Lynn,

How are you? How is David?
I am doing good in school and I'm
not getting beaten up.

How is David's book doing? I forg
got when it's going to come out. By
the way, did you like the program abou

2.
gifted kids you saw when you came
to my house?

←------Well, I've got to go now. See
you later.

Signed,

P. S,: All the kids are writing letters
today.

Have
  a
  Happy
    Baby

November
20-odd, 1980

~~???~~ Hope you are having fun!
      Cecilia Ann is a rather nice name, and
I am glad another being is now in existence.
The baby must be very nice, and by the
time this letter reaches you, it will probably
  be weeks old.
     Hope the baby likes Sherlock Snoopy!
The clothes are ~~???~~ for further needs.
·Once babies are one, they like dressing and
undressing dolls. This is just to help.
          Love to all

can largely be attributed to the differences between the typewriter and the pen as instruments of expression. Writing longhand only became comfortable for Randy after his fine motor coordination improved. His note to us in November 1980 welcoming our new baby illustrates his progress in this new medium.

The biography and poem are samples of writing that are intended to convey something specific about Randy and his own experiences. A large portion of his work is not directly about Randy himself. Examples are the *Dracula* play and the "Dr. Who" story, which are reproduced at the end of this chapter. These are both selections from series he has written. I sometimes think of these as examples of Randy's "pulp novel" side. In the tradition of the continuing serial, Randy has spent significant periods of time churning out such plays and stories with assembly-line regularity, making what seemed to me slight alterations in plot and story line. (And yet Randy knows—and loves—each separate piece intimately, launching into eager expositions with dramatic flair at the slightest indication of interest.) What distinguishes these series, aside from the sheer prodigiousness of volume, is Randy's ability to establish a tone, an ambience, through his use of language. It is a general lack of interesting plot or character development in such pieces that leads me to suggest that Randy's writing is by and large more stylistic than substantive, more a technical tour de force for his age than a source of expression of his most significant emotions and thoughts about his experience.

Yet there should be no question that they are extraordinary works. It is hard to imagine that a child not yet five years old could have fashioned such a play, loosely based on the Dracula story. It is not a mature piece of writing, but Randy was able to structure a convincing dramatic situation and to demonstrate reasonable command of the requirements of playwriting. For example, one must introduce the characters, set the scene, and provide stage directions. These he does. One of the most original and interesting aspects of Randy's play is the mocking humor of the dialogue. Some of the descriptions of the characters also show promise—for example, of Harker, a real-estate agent hoping to make a large commission on the Count's castle. The evocative quality of the language is also striking in certain respects, although not overall. For example, the dialogue for Mr. Hawkins, the real estate broker, and the gypsy woman seem entirely in character; the Count's accented English is also precisely what we have come to expect from the "hideous fiend." There is also unusual understanding of the structure of a play, good use of humor, and a certain lightness of touch. This play is not profound, but then, not every play should be deep and significant. There are time-honored forms of writing that are meant solely to entertain, and it may be that Randy will continue to write in a lighter vein. Certainly by volume, such writing is his primary activity.

For Randy, *Dracula* was one of a number of works about superheroes. His enthusiasm for "Dr. Who" continued unabated for the better part of three years. He has probably written a hundred "Dr. Who" stories, each one based on the character from the television series. The story appended to this chapter is the first part of an eleven-part (forty-five page) "book" called "Dr. Who and the Ice Planet" (see pp. 70–75). By age six Randy clearly demonstrated a sophisticated understanding of the proper format for organizing and producing a book. Each book included a cover drawn by Randy, a table of contents, and mock permission from the BBC to base his stories on the TV show.

As with his earlier *Dracula,* the Dr. Who story is relatively long on action and short on character development. There is the same tendency to use humor in a sarcastic and mocking manner and some obviously imaginative situation development. I cannot say for certain that Randy's stories are entirely different from those in the actual "Dr. Who" series: there are simply too many of them to compare, and I am not an aficionado of the genre. Randy reported that his plots were of his own creation, though clearly based on characters and situations from the TV and paperback series. When asked where he got his story ideas, Randy was quite willing to acknowledge that his familiarity with Dr. Who came from reading everything he could about the character and never missing a broadcast. While his stories may bear similarities to the originals, they do not seem to be simple rehashings of plots he has seen or read. The settings and predicaments seem to be ones of his own creation.

My sense is that Randy has indeed written new "Dr. Who" stories, ones that preserve some of the essential elements of the original series: the protagonist's dry humor, affinity for "jellybabies," and somewhat outlandish garb; the exploration of the unknown; battles with evil; "magical" movement through time and space; cliffhanger endings where dilemmas are unresolved. These stories are without doubt unusual writing for a child of seven or eight, although his treatment of some of the structural features of storytelling could not be taken as fully developed. His stories are often short on beginnings, middles, or ends: they seem to proceed through the stitching and weaving together of adventuresome vignettes rather than through the exposition of a problem, its elaboration, and eventual resolution. In this respect, Randy probably chose well when he selected the "Dr. Who" series to emulate, for the premise of time and space travel allows for abrupt transitions in the original plot as well as in Randy's adventures.

I also find Randy's expositional skills weaker than his dialogue in these stories. This emphasis on dialogue squares with other observations of his penchant for the spoken word: assuming foreign (particularly British) accents, reciting comedy routines from memory, or providing running newscaster-type commentary of daily activities. Randy's strength as a writer seems to come more from his evocative use of language to set tone and to create a style rather than in his ability to tell a really good story.

There is no doubt that Randy possesses a true and extraordinary gift for language. Remember that Randy began his "Dr. Who" series at an age when most other children are grappling with first-grade readers and writing short, stilted descriptions of school outings. Though far from fully mature, even as a six- and seven-year-old his gift for writing was indisputable.

WRITING AS A DOMAIN

Randy's writing, although clearly advanced, would not be taken for that of an adult writer. In this respect his work is different from that of some of the other prodigies. Nils Kirkendahl, for example, was playing the same music and was judged by the same standards as older performers. His compositions were similarly judged. The chess matches of our chess players were based on the same rules of play as games played by adults. In fact, many of the young chess players' matches were against adult players two and three times their age. While Randy's writing was without a doubt extraordinary, it is apparent that it was done by a child. As impressive as it is, it is still the work of a young mind. In part, I think that Randy's writing can be recognized as a child's because the demands of the domain of writing itself make it virtually impossible to master the field as a youngster. It is not that Randy's achievements are not exceptional, but rather that writing is a domain in which true early prodigious achievement according to my criterion—performance in an intellectually demanding domain at or very near the level of an adult professional before the age of ten—is extremely rare. John Stuart Mill is said to have written short essays during his preteen years that were extraordinary in their scope and maturity, and a little girl by the name of Daisy Ashford published a best-selling novel in her ninth year.[1] Yet, on the whole, writing is a domain that seems to require greater age, and presumably greater maturity, for the production of works that stand the test of time.

Writers are expected to illuminate experience, to tell about wonders imagined as well as seen, and to reflect with insight and wisdom on the meaning of things. In this sense writing is much more demanding than

chess, where the parameters are more clearly defined and the structure of
the domain more consensual. Musical performance seems to occupy some
middle ground. The basic structure of a piece—the score—is set and established, but the individual must bring both technical and interpretive expertise to the piece to make it come alive. I am not suggesting that there is
no development after childhood in either chess or music, just that both
fields lend themselves better to adult-level performance by children than
does the domain of writing.

Despite this, we have seen that Randy McDaniel was occasionally
able to express powerful thoughts and feelings in his writing. Much of the
time, though, Randy seemed to prefer creating action and fantasy stories.
And indeed, Randy himself claims that, by and large, there are few significant themes to his work. Darren believes otherwise and has sometimes
tried to convince Randy; but I have seen Randy hold his ground, saying
that Darren is reading his own ideas into Randy's writing, ideas that Randy
neither intended to include nor perceives to be there even when Darren has
suggested that they are.

THE ROCK BAND

At about age eight, Randy developed a prepubertal fascination with
the Beatles and redirected much of his energy into becoming as much of
a Beatle as possible. Initially this took the form of an intense interest in
song lyrics. Soon Randy was strumming away on a $25 guitar. Randy
marshaled a group of classmates into a rock band, serving as manager and
promoter. It was just about this time that John Lennon was killed by Mark
David Chapman, and Randy was deeply affected by this tragic event. It
seemed to move him emotionally even more strongly toward music and
away from nonmusical writing.

Up to this point neither Lynn nor I had noticed any particular talent
or inclination toward music in Randy, although his parents had reported
that he loved listening to recordings of classical music as a very young
child. (Darren had himself been a child musician with a beautiful singing
voice.) And in characteristic style, Randy became totally involved with his
new project. There was some continuity with his earlier enterprises (the
Beatles being an English group, for example), but some important depar-
tures as well. The two most important were the fact that his work with the
Beatles' music was almost altogether social rather than solitary and that
Darren's involvement was primarily as an appreciative and encouraging
observer rather than as a mentor.

Randy assembled his group on his own initiative. Tapping his school chum Joshua for membership turned out to be crucial to the process, since Joshua's stamp of approval made the project a legitimate one in the eyes of the rest of the school. Randy served as lyricist, promoter, producer, and creator of "album" covers. This undertaking was different from all previous activities in that Randy began to become enmeshed, if only vicariously, in the complex social world of the rock musician.

Though Randy's interests expanded to include music, it must be noted that he has never gone through a period when he did not write. Band or no band, it was a rare day when he did not sit down at the typewriter and bang out an hour or two's worth of writing. The themes have varied, the material has varied, the quality has varied, but the words have nevertheless cascaded out of the typewriter. Randy does seem to have the personal discipline required of a serious writer.

I remember especially well a visit to the McDaniels in the summer of 1980, when they were vacationing in a rented trailer at the beach. Lynn and I had joined the family about noon. After lunch we all went to sit on the beach. About an hour later, Randy got up without comment and went back into the trailer. From the window overlooking the bay, we heard the steady peck, peck, peck of his portable (he typed then, as now, with one finger). More than an hour later he emerged, again without comment, ready for a swim with Darren and me. It was all very matter-of-fact.

For about a year, Randy's prose writing seemed to wax and wane. There seemed to be danger in Randy's new interest in music: it was enticing him away from serious writing, and, in the process, Randy was losing his "specialness" and joining the world of the ordinary. In the summer of 1981 we invited the McDaniels over for a picnic, a walk in the woods, and an evening's conversation. Several days later Darren wrote us an exuberant letter, marking the event as an important one for Randy—perhaps the beginning of his most recent period of major productivity as a writer. As it turned out, within a few months it was to be the Beatles and record covers, lyrics and songs and mock performances once again, but for a while, at least, Randy returned to "real" writing. Our time together had apparently served a catalytic purpose for Randy. As Darren described it:

Sunday will go down in history as one of Randy McDaniel's break-through days. He bubbled all the way home, talking about your house and your cat and then, without pausing, going on to outline the theories on which his writing is based—"no discipline, because it's simple for me," and therefore no rewrite; no talking about stories in advance because "that makes it boring when I write it!" When we got home, he went to the typewriter and worked till eleven, producing 18 pages, rich in detail, and with hardly a typing error. It's been the same all week. I pick him up at school at three, we go to the Burger King for a hamburger as he lectures like a professor about the Victorian style, the rhythm of the sentences, the descriptions of London and the details about even the minor characters. Then back to the typewriter, stopping only long enough to watch the news, in which he's developed a new interest. After a latent period of more than a year, he's the old Randy again, but now at a higher level.

TAKING CONTROL

It is common in my experience with prodigies that they come to a place where it is necessary to assert their independence from their parents. It is probably part of the general transformation of adolescence, but it is complicated by the extremely active role often played by parents in the lives and work of their prodigious children. For Randy this separation perhaps started a bit early, when he was barely ten. He seemed to use the band to assert his independence from his parents and to join the social world. This was in fact what Darren and Jeanne had encouraged through their critical decision to leave the farm.

The decision to shed some of his "outsiderness" has not been made lightly, however. An essential part of Randy's life and a large part of his self-image was and is based on his being different. We did a local television news show together in 1979, and Randy sadly noted that his school was trying to force him to be like the other kids, to make him fit. Howard Gruber has argued that the truly creative person must always stand outside of society, that he must feel some alienation from normal social life in order to maintain the independence of judgment and the sharp sense of purpose required to sustain a major creative effort.[2] Randy distinctly reflected this quality; indeed, he wore it as a badge of his giftedness. He was defiant, determined to maintain his distance and uniqueness. One way of doing this was to closet himself in his room every day and write. As he grew older, I think that he internalized this sense of uniqueness in a positive way that allowed him to participate in the social world of his peers. More than any other activity, Randy's band served to soften his defiance, and perhaps to take the edge off his dedication to the literary life.

And while the band has been dis-banded for several years now, some of the effects remain.

Some of what has happened for Randy McDaniel was quite healthy and expected, some perhaps less positive—particularly the way he began to disengage from his apprenticeship with Darren. Naturally enough, Randy's idolization and dependence on his father began to wane, but did not always ease into a caring and friendly style. It is not unusual for adolescents to develop an arrogance that extends to their parents: Mark Twain once remarked that as he grew older his father's intelligence increased astoundingly. It should not be surprising that we sometimes found Randy to be impatient with Darren's interpretations of his writing. Darren, for his part, sometimes persisted in asserting that he glimpsed the true power and meaning of Randy's literary contributions. Randy's assertion of independence is a normal and important part of growing up, but it seemed to us to have thrown the family off balance for a while. I think that all three of them think it is important to preserve the sense of specialness they feel as a family. I see this period of Randy's early adolescence as one of delicacy for the McDaniels, as it is for many families. How they come out on the other side will have as much to say about Randy's future—and their own—as anything else since Darren and Jeanne decided to join forces.

Co-incidence

How do the factors that enter into the co-incidence equation look for Randy McDaniel? Like other children in the study, Randy strongly asserted his talent at a young age. And like many prodigies, Randy's first teacher was his father. He was particularly fortunate, however, that Darren (and to a lesser extent, Jeanne) were themselves high-level practitioners of their craft, able to instruct and guide Randy's writing. This has proved to be particularly important in Randy's case, since the domain of writing offers little systematic or formalized instruction for aspiring young writers. I believe that it was because Darren was himself a writer, thoughtful and conscious of the expressive power of language, that Randy's own orientation to the written word was able to flourish.

There seemed to be times, particularly at school, that his extraordinary expressive abilities actually created difficulties for Randy. Although a strong and highly able student, he was not particularly moved to train his talents on tasks requiring logical, deductive reasoning. And while he would engage his parents in discussions about the structure and meaning of mathematics as a discipline, he had some difficulty grasping arithmetic as taught in elementary school. Looking at Randy from the viewpoint of their own curricula, some of his teachers saw Randy's talent as anomalous, outside of the skills that really "counted." It seemed less important to them that Randy never needed spelling instruction—he could spell words like "apprentice" and "masquerade" when he was four—than that he didn't always prepare the most meticulous science project in the class.

It must have been disconcerting for Randy's teachers (and perhaps for Randy as well) to contrast his ability to write, memorize, and perform entire plays or recordings with his difficulty in solving simple arithmetic problems. Although one would expect that teachers would immediately recognize Randy's talent for language as extraordinary and unique, it seems that his lack of orientation toward logical or scientific tasks somehow lessened Randy's gifts for some of his teachers. The effect of this skepticism was, I think, to make it more difficult for Randy to maintain his own sense of being special and unique. Although his schoolwork was almost always of high quality, there were some teachers who perceived other children as more "gifted."

Randy's talent may be less obvious to some because it does not necessarily assault the senses at every turn. More than a year ago his mother commented on this aspect of Randy's "giftedness":

> The tendency, once "giftedness" has been established, is to define it solely as a cognitive ability. The kind of logical developmental gift that Aaron [an academically gifted classmate] has was thought to be an indication of the "truly gifted," whereas Randy's reluctance to show any interest in numbers, chess, or mind games was looked upon by many as a weakness. "Well, sure, Randy can read and write [detractors say], but he's not *really* smart."

For the pure prodigy, the isolation of a talent may be an advantage if that talent survives the pressures of childhood and adolescence. When a talent does not compete with other possible lines of activity, it should be less difficult to make the commitment to it alone. Although Randy's talents are primarily literary, there are still some competing abilities and interests that he will have to deal with if he is to become a writer. Writing has been the center of his life for several years, but Randy also loves to get up in front of an audience and perform. He loves the attention and approval he gets from the immediate response of an audience. His gift for memorizing routines and his flair for performing have led to many opportunities to entertain; he has also appeared in dramatic productions in the Boston area and he shows real talent for acting. Finally, his enthusiasm for music, which showed itself very early when he became entranced with Grieg's *Peer Gynt,* has reasserted itself in a preoccupation with pop music, especially the Beatles. In fact, his lessons on the guitar and his singing and song writing threaten to crowd his writing time out of his daily routine.

Several of these talents and interests may be incompatible with the solitary, sedentary life of a writer. Randy basks in the immediate response of people to his performances, while the distant rewards of writing may have less appeal for him. Writing is a lonely craft, requiring tremendous self-discipline and demanding an exceptional ability to delay reward. Although the magnitude of the required discipline and sacrifice may seem to diminish as Randy grows older, it is not surprising that as an adolescent he would have a tendency to seek out experiences and activities that are more immediately affirming. That Randy may have the talent to allow himself the choice of one direction or another is the critical issue for co-incidence. The single-talent prodigy is most likely to pursue mastery in a single field; the more talents there are competing with the target one, the more likely that they will split the resources and time available. This seems to have begun to happen with Randy McDaniel.

The co-incidence between child and domain is a central factor in the making of a prodigy. The domain in which Randy's talent first expressed itself is unusual. Writing is a field that has produced few prodigies, and when they have appeared they have rarely become significant writers in adulthood. There certainly are people for whom writing is a lifelong passion, and even those who feel compelled to write although they have little talent for it.[3] Nonetheless, sustaining early talent as a writer is extremely difficult and rare. The discipline itself is only loosely organized, with little that is formalized in the way of stages or levels of mastery. Consequently, there is little instruction available for developing the craft. Despite Darren's attention as a committed and talented teacher, the domain itself offers little in the way of a pedagogy, or clear-cut guidelines for charting the student's progress. Darren could provide examples of high-quality writing in a variety of styles and with different content, and he could discuss Randy's own writing with his son. But in terms of refining his own skills, Randy was largely on his own. Indeed, Darren and Jeanne believe that they should not provide critical reactions to his work.

For children especially, the importance of mentors and supporters cannot be overemphasized, and these are rare in the field of writing prior to adolescence. Randy, of course, had his father as a continuously attentive and encouraging teacher from the first years of his life. This no doubt contributed to Randy's love of writing and his desire to do it well. But for most prodigies in most fields, the child's first teacher, often a parent, is replaced by a more advanced professional instructor. This is more difficult to arrange for young writers. For a child like Randy, who began to write at age three, there are few mentors to serve as appropriate role models through the second phase of the child's preparation. In short, it is likely to be very difficult for a child to find the resources necessary to further a writing talent that appears very early.

The critical points in any developmental process are the transitions between stages, and Randy is fortunate to have parents who are resilient and flexible in their responses to the changes of interest and direction taken by their unusual son. As always, Darren and Jeanne have been sensitive and responsive to the complex changes that have occurred in Randy himself, encouraging him to explore whatever areas capture his interest. It is not always this way. Glimpsing talent, parents can intervene in their children's lives in ways that are intrusive and even destructive. They sometimes decide that their child is going to be a great gymnast, physician, or architect (as Frank Lloyd Wright's mother did) without so much as considering whether the child has any talent or interest in the chosen vocation. When parents are lucky or insightful or both, such pressure can yield extraordinary results. And sometimes it takes determined parents to steer their child through the shoals of distraction and on toward great adult artistry. It has been reported that cellist Yo-Yo Ma sometimes resented being made to practice while he was growing up,[4] but his transcendent playing may depend, in part, on just that imposed discipline. As with most other aspects of the process of development, there is no certainty about what the right course may be for any child. Regardless of the specific path taken, for the prodigy's talent to flourish the parents must demonstrate constant vigilance, dedicated efforts to choose and sustain resources, and a willingness to change course when the situation demands it. The McDaniels have shown these qualities, and because of their efforts in encouraging Randy to give his interests free rein, his course is actually less clear than it was several years ago. It takes remarkable faith and more than usual restraint to pursue such a course.

Randy has had to recognize that the price for pursuing a serious writing career is very high. It is unclear if he is willing to pay that price even if his talent might justify the sacrifice. Being a child writer seems to be more difficult, or at least more lonely, than being a musician, chess player, or mathematician. These are matters we will take up in the next chapter, where we consider why some fields seem more suited to the appearance and development of prodigies than others. But consider just these two points: as in the visual arts, writing requires both technical mastery and originality; also, preparation and guidance through the early years are relatively unstructured. It is almost as if the field has had to deal with child prodigies so rarely that it has not produced an organized way of responding to the phenomenon. For Randy McDaniel, the domain of writing, if not writing itself, has its problematic aspects. Only time will tell if Randy will seek to coordinate his own talents and proclivities with the personal and social demands of writing as a career.

Samples of Randy McDaniel's Writing*

D R A C U L A

A screenplay by Randy McDaniel

XXXXbased on the novel
by XXX Bram Stoker

CAST OF CHARACTERS
>   DRACULA, a vampire
>   JONATHAN HARKER, a real estate agent
>   MR. HAWKINS, a real estate broker
>   A GYPSY WOMAN
>   TOWNSPEOPLE
>   MAN" 's CRY
>   WOMAN
>   BATS OFFSTAGE
>   DRIVER

Scene I

A real estate office in London.

MR. HAWKINS: Come in, Harker. I've got a very important assignment for you.

*Reproduced, as originally typed by Randy, are his *Dracula* play (written at age four-and-a-half) and "Dr. Who and the Ice Planet" (written at age eight).

HARKER (taking a seat): Will I be traveling, sir?

MR. HAWKINS: To Transylvania, Harker, XXX to see a certain Count Dracula. He is in urgent need of a large estate in England. I'd like you to go and see the man and take care of the particulars. You might find him an odd sort of chap. Lives in a castle on the side of a mountain, sounded very curious on the phone . . . ah well, there's big money involved, Harker, do your best lad.

Scene 2

A hotel in Bucharest. Harker is shaving when he hears a knock on the door.

HARkER:XX(hears door knock) cCome in . . . (door opens)

gGYPSY:I have come to warn you that Count Dracula is a very strange man.

HARKER: Oh, nonsense. Who are you and what do you want?

XXX GYPSY:iI Aam a old gypsy, and I know many things. Count XXXXDracula is a vampire.

aAnd there are only a few things that can stop them. Take this garlic, my son, and this cross. Either one will stop that hideous fiend. . . . you will know the truth of what I am saying when you see that Dracula casts no X reflection in the mirror. Take this small mirror and see for yourself. . . .

HARKER: tThank you. When he takes one look he'll go wild.

Scene three

At the gate of Castle Dracula. Driver xxxxx takes Harker's bags into the Castle and disappears. Harker waits at gate, which finally opens with a loud creak.

HARKERXX: xxxxxHello, is anyone there?

DRACULA: Velcome to Castle Dracula, my frant.

YOU must be able to rexxrecognize me. I am Count Dracula.

HARKERX: Very good mexx meeting you,Count.

COUNT DRACULA:YOU must be hungry after your long journey, my frant.

HARKER:I am very well, Count.

COUNT DRACULA:Then come in (Bbows), come in.

HARKER:I will, Count.

COUNT DRACULA:Very Vell then come in(bows again)come in.

(hHARKER goes in) HARKER:Is this the dining room?
COUNT DRACULA:Yes.
hHARKER:I shall go in.
ccCOUNT DRACULA:I will foloww you.
9(HARKER goes in and takes a seat and so does cCOUNT DRACULA
but HARKER SEsees that he does not touch his food)
I have already eaten, my friend.
harHARkER:So you have,Count.

(after eating)
COUNT DRACULA:You must be tired, my freind.
hHere is the door to your room. Are you tired?
HARKER:I am,Count.
Vell thxxxxx COUNT DRACULA:Vell you can go.
(COUNT DRACULA exits and so does HARKER)
9(morning HARKER Iis shaving)
COUNT DRACULA(Fentering0)Good mornig,Mr.Harker.
HARKER:(not seeing him) gGood morni ng,Count. . . .
9(hHARKER turns around and the count sees the blood flowing. HE
tries to get his blood and drink it. tThey fight. B ut HARKER throws
him down.
COUNT DRACULA flees while HARKER IS strugulling to get out.
tThe count bolts the door shut.)
e(Evning) HARKER ISin his room.
He suddenly thinks he sees the count climb up the tower wall.
It is the count. He climbs in.
(A few days later) HARKER knows that DRACULA CLIMBED up the
wall only beacause he wanted to get to his coffin.————xxx So he tied
his bed sheets to form a long rope. HE put it down and out he went.
and now he was in the courtyard.
But how xxxx could he get up there?
He saw hand-holds and foot-holds so up he climbed.
til he gets to the window! hHe climbs in.
And now he sees the coffin of Dracula!
So he opens it. and there lies Dracula, sound assleep with his eyes
open. HARKER has to hurry to kill Dracula becausei it's almost the
full moon. Finally he finds a wodden curtain rod. He takes it off. And
he plunges it trogh the heart of Dracula. aAnd then the body disolves
into red dust. aAnd that is the end of Dracula.
THE END

Doctor Who and the Ice Planet

Based on the BBC television serial THE PLANET OF ICE
by arrangements with the British Broadcasting Corporation

CONTENTS

1

A Frozen World

Everywhere, there was ice and snow. An endless stream of white covered
the surface of the planet. Icy hills, adorned with frozen bushes, littered the
landscape. Here and there an evergreen tree, but all the rest was white x
and cold.

There was a buzzing noise, and a tall figure appeared out of nowhere.
He had brown hair and blue eyes. A blue cowl was on his neck, vaguely
covering a red vest, white shirt and red tie. A black cape was tied around
him, and he had blue pants on.

Beside him appeared a tall man with a square jaw and curly hair. He
had a heavy red jacket on, and red pants on.

In front of them appeared a slim, dark-haired attractive girl with a
loose yellow jacket on, over a green snowsuit.

On both sides two figures materialized. One was a man-like robot
with a metal sign on it—AL. It was a red, yellow, white and blue robot.
The XXX other figure was a dark-skinned, wide-eyed man with tattered
clothing and sharp teeth.

The first man was the mysterious traveller in Time and Space known

NOTE: This original story includes characters from the BBC series "Dr. Who." It is published
with the permission of BBC Publications and the British Broadcasting Corporation.

as the Doctor. The others were Harry Sullivan, Medical Officer from UNIT onx planet Earth, Sarah Jane Smith, a journalist from Earth, AL, a bodyguard XXXX robot, and Beastly, a jungle man with animal powers.

The Doctor smiled. Having travelled like this before, he was not XXXXXX surprised. What amazed him was the cold, icy landscape before him. AlXXXX-ready he felt like he was catching frostbite. He wasn't really, however.

Sarah pulled tight the collar of her jacket, and asked, "What's going on Doctor? What happened?"

"Well," explained the Doctor, "the people on Space Station Nerva wants X to colonize this planet . . . for what reason I don't know . . . and I volunteered to investigate it."

The TARDIS, the Doctor's Time and Space machine, had landed on a Space X Station, where the humans had been put to stay, because the Earth had been destroyed. Now they were looking for a planet to colonize. However, this place seemed very unlikely.

"And what planet is this?" asked Harry.

"I'd like to know too," said Beastly.

"Zigar!" cried the Doctor. "The greatest crystal deposit in the entire universe! Do you know that we're standing on a crystal mine!"

"No, I didn't really," said Sarah. "But what about the TARDIS?"

"They'll send it down from Nerva later, "said the Doctor. He stopped. There was silence.

"Well," said the Doctor, "let's start!"

Something caught Sarah's eye. It was white and shiny. She picked it out of the snow. It was a crystal. "Doctor," she said, "look-aa this!" The Doctor turned. "Ah!" he cried. He snatched it out of Sarah's hands, and XX examined it for a minute. "A frozen liquid crystal! It could feed half of the galaxy!"

"What does that mean?" asked Beastly. "It means—"began AL. "It means X that you should find some more," said the Doctor. AL turned towards the Doctor. "I was going to say that, Master."

"Well, I did, so there!"

"My data banks are completely accurate, Master."

"Well, don't cry about it!"

The Doctor turned to find Beastly running towards a patch of very high and very icy hills. "Where are you going?" called the Doctor. "I'm going to see what's over this hill," said Beastly over his shoulder. "All XXXXXX right," said the Doctor. "Just be careful!"

Harry appeared behind him. "Let's look around the area."

The Doctor xturned to face him angrily. "Look what you did! You made x me forget what I was going to say."

"Sorry."

"Now . . . what was I saying?"thought the Doctor. "Ah,yes, I was going toxx say, 'Let's look around the area.' "

"That's what I said."

"Really?"

"Yes."

"Well," said the Doctor, "Let's have some jellybabies and tea and talk X about it."

He turned to face Sarah who was already digging with her hands. The XX Doctor smiled. "What you need is a shovel, Sarah," he said. He took out a stick that instantly grew into a shovel. "Thanks,"said Sarah, and she XX continued.

But the Doctor was still not satisfied. He turned to AL. "AL, help her. Me and Harry are going to look around." All right?"

"Yes, Master."

"Good. Come on, Harry."

The Doctor set xxxoff in great strides, and Harry xxxxxxfollowed him,running after him.

Sarah laughed,and continued with her work.

Since he was used to climbing to great xxxxxxheights, Beastly had xnoxxxx trouble climbing to the top of the icy hill. Wringing his frostbitten hands, he slipped on a snow patch, and his head fell into the snow. Shaking his head, he rose, and leaned over the hill's edge. Suddenly below, a white claw appeared. Beastly was unaware. Suddenly, the claw struck him, pushing him off the ridge. Screaming, Beastly fell into the snow.

* * * * * * * * * *

The Doctor and Harry were just looking around and walking, and XXXall XXX they could see was ice and snow, so it was quite unexpected when they ran into a rather large snow fort, a perfect square, with 15-foot high snow walls. "A snow fort," said Harry. "Wow!" "Very interesting," said the Doctor. "WEll, I think I'll call this the Ice Square."

They went walking on. Something suddenly caught his eye. It was another crystal. "Hey, Doctor, another Ice Crystal!"

The Doctor turned. "Oh, yes, this place is a miinnnn. . . ."

Harryx whirled. The Doctor had fallen into a pit, 50-feet down.

"I've seen these before," said the XXXXDoctor.

"Are you all right?" asked Harry.

"Yes, I guess," said the Doctor.

"All right," said Harry. "I'lll. . . ."

Harry tumbled fell on top of the Doctor. "Aaaagh," said the Doctor.

Harry rose, and the Doctor followed-suit. He looked around the Ice Pit. "This is incredible!" he cried. "It's . . . this whole planet . . . is incredible!"

"It is, isn't it?" said the Doctor. "I wish I came here before."

"Yes,I think you should have too,"agreed Harry.

"Sssh!"said the Doctor suddenly.

Harry heard a powerful wind, but was xrather puzzled. "What is it?"

"There's a storm brewing," said the Doctor. "That could be danger-ous."

"How?"XXXXasked Harry. "How can it be lethal?"

Suddenly snow crystals began to fall. "I'll tell you why," said the Doctor. "Those are coming from the sky a million times a second. They'll XX cut us apart or bury us alive!"

Harry turned pale. "What are we going to do?"

"Try and find a way out of here." The Doctor ran to the wall of the XX Ice Pit.

A crystal fell on him. Blood spurted for a moment from the XX back of XXX back of the Doctor's neck, then—nothing.

"Are you all right?" asked Harry.

"Yes," said the Doctor. "Just a little wound."

Suddenly, a wind started blowing. "It's fierce," said the Doctor. "Too X fierce. We've got to find a way out of here."

A voice came from behind him. "Help, Doctor!" The Doctor whirled. The X crystals were falling more rapidly now, and the wind was pulling Harry XX into the shower. There was almost no hope of him surviving.

The wind began pulling at the Doctor. He resisted long enough to see X Harry tumble to the ground, and also see a shower of crystals fall on top of him. But he could no longer resist. The wind hurtled the Doctor into the air, carrying him away into the sky.

Sarah looked around. She and AL were still alone. The others were still not here. She looked at AL. "They've been gone long," she said. X

"Correction, Mistressx," said AL. "Four hours, twenty-two minutes, seven xx seconds."

"All right, all right," said XXXSarah. "Lwt's go look for them."

"Inadvisable," said AL. "The Master has not reported in yet. We are unsure whether it is not dangerous."

Sarah's fearsome independence was not threatened. "I'll go by myself."

There was a pause. Then AL said, "Let us go."

Sarah smiled, and they went off.

When they got xxto the Ice Hills, Sarah looked up. "It's too high," she said. "I won't get up there." AL said, "Get on my back." Sarah did, and XX suddenly XX they were in the air. It was a second when they landed.

"Thanks," said Sarah. "Thanks not necessary," said AL. "Now we will—"

AL broke off as Sarah gasped. "What is it? What is it? Danger!"

"Look!" screamed Sarah.

Over the ridge and on the other side of the hill, was the body of Beastly. He might have been dead.

The Doctor fell with a thud right in the snow. "Ach," he said. As they said on Aridia, "Ochtenbergerkratchnt." He looked around. He was in the X middle of a frozen Ice Forest, with frozen trees and bushes, and very soft snow. Cracking a piece of snow open, he picked up the contents.

"The food source of the galaxy! The riches of the Universe!"

There was an angry roar. The Doctor whirledX.

XXSixty yards ahead of him was a large white city. It was covered with snow, a camoflauge probably, because he never saw it before himX.

As if mocking him, angry roars broke out around him.

4

Domains That Produce Prodigies

B ODIES OF KNOWLEDGE are the accumulated and distilled works of many contributors, both prodigies and others. A field cannot exist as a dynamic entity without human effort, participation, and purpose. A linear accelerator is not physics, a museum is not art, and a chessboard is not chess. We know that certain fields seem to provide relatively fertile ground for the appearance of prodigies and others do not. As we saw in the preceding chapter, Randy McDaniel's specific talent for writing is one that we rarely find during childhood. There are many possible reasons for this, and we considered some of them with Randy. In this chapter we look at the prodigy phenomenon not from the point of view of the child with talent but from the perspective of a body of knowledge that must be mastered. In particular, we consider the idea that bodies of knowledge themselves evolve and change with time as a result of transformations as small as the founding of a theater in a remote village and as major as the publication of the double helix model of DNA or Freud's account of unconscious motivation. Domains can be thought of as having their own developmental histories that must be understood before the phenomenon of the prodigy can be adequately explained, for the prodigy and the domain are two expressions of complementary developmental processes. They are interdependent yet distinct manifestations of human intellectual history.

Of course, the time scale for the development of a field of knowledge is much longer than the life span of a single individual. In most cases, the fields in which prodigies appear have long histories. Chess has been played for several centuries, music goes back to the very beginnings of human history, as does visual art; mathematics has been evolving over more than twenty centuries. The same can be said of dance, athletics, and literature. Their histories are much longer than the life of any one individual. Yet a long history does not ensure that the field has experienced much development. For a field to develop it must have sustained major qualitative changes in organization, structure, technology, and practice.

As a domain develops and forms a stable set of structures of knowledge and practice, it also builds up a set of levels of expertise. Individuals differ in the degree to which they become masters of the existing knowledge structures, the existing canons of practice, or the deeper understandings made possible by the mastery of a field. For a domain to be developmental it must have several such levels to master (although a specific required number of levels is not known), and those who aspire to become masters must move through them in sequence. Thus there is a certain orderliness to a developmental domain, a certain known path from novice to master that every aspiring student must traverse.[1] If this were not the case it would be impossible to guide or teach, to prepare curricula, to write textbooks.

Is there reason to believe that development, not just change, has been occurring in domains in which prodigies appear? Prodigies in fact appear only in developmental domains, that is, in those domains that have themselves experienced major changes or reorganizations over a period of several generations of practice. Not that all developmental domains produce prodigies; philosophy has a very long developmental history, but prodigies have occurred rarely. But if a domain has prodigies associated with it, it is virtually certain to be a domain that has a developmental history.

When we see a prodigy we are actually seeing a kind of coordination of a child with certain specific capabilities and a domain with certain complementary demands. The interaction between prodigy and domain represents the coordination of two developmental histories—that of the individual and the domain—during a critical period of time. One can imagine a rapidly moving rocket hitching a ride with a planet for a while, since they both happen to be in the same orbit and each is served in some way by the other. The presence of the satellite may bring the planet needed resources; the planet makes it unnecessary for the satellite to exhaust its power just getting from one point to another.

Unfortunately, although we know a bit about developmental processes in normal human beings, we know very little about the developmental processes that are involved in the formation and transformation of bodies of knowledge and skill. There is no discipline analogous to developmental psychology for the study of bodies of knowledge as developmental phenomena. Fields such as history of science, philosophy of science, and history of art are close, but these traditional disciplines are not particularly psychological in their orientation.[2] That is, they tend to focus on events, mature works, static states, and additions to the knowledge base without delving into the psychological processes that gave rise to, catalyzed, and ultimately transformed these fields. Nor has there been much insight into how developmental changes occur in the key individuals in each field, whether prodigies or not. Indeed, the idea of development is itself a relatively recent one, having no major place in the intellectual history of Western culture until Darwin's theory of evolution brought the notion of such change to center stage. Our first task, then, is to try to describe more clearly just what a domain is, then to see what the more specific features are of domains in which prodigies are found.

Qualities of Developmental Domains

Since a prodigy must perform in a specific field it is worthwhile to consider what characteristics determine that a field may be ripe for prodigiousness. I have already said that the first set of requirements specifies that the field or domain be developmental; the second set specifies some additional qualities that make a given domain particularly suited to participate in the appearance and expression of prodigies. There is no such thing as a prodigy without a domain through which the possibilities present in the child are unveiled.

ATTRACTIVENESS AND ACCESSIBILITY

For a domain to serve this catalytic function, that is, to release capabilities in children or adults, it must be perceived as attractive—must intrigue, provoke, and energize a response. Domains do this by their tendency to draw upon specific talents. It is likely that all human beings have differentially strong attractions, proclivities, and tendencies to find and construct meaning through the various symbol systems available in a given culture during a given period of time. Not all children are equally drawn to words, to music, to gesture, to numbers, to maps.[3] Some children are more attracted to machines, others to living things. Domains are the repositories of such inclinations—culturally preserved, dynamic artifacts of the different ways in which human beings have tried to understand themselves and their world.

A domain must allow for differences in achievement both within an age group and across age groups. If a domain draws upon a specific subset of human capabilities, then those who are inclined to find expression through that domain will tend to do so more, and probably better, than others less inclined or talented. Those for whom the domain represents a unique opportunity for expression are likely to be the best performers. Sometimes differences in inclination and talent show themselves early. Most often talent is identified at some later point. Performance in children is rarely judged in relation to the highest or most sophisticated known levels established for the domain. In the case of a prodigy, these two frames of reference tend to coincide. The prodigy not only shows more talent than other children of the same age, she or he is able enough to be judged in terms of the most demanding criteria for performance in that field regardless of age.

Domains differ in their degree of accessibility. Some, like Piaget's universal stages of cognitive development, are eventually mastered by almost all children. Other domains are more restricted, and these domains afford relatively few the opportunity to reach their more advanced levels. In fields like ballet or philosophy, for example, only a small proportion of humanity has the opportunity to experience the highest reaches of the domain. For such domains, talent, opportunity, and hard work play a critical role in determining how far a person will go. Typically, the most advanced stages of a domain are only achieved by adults who have spent many years in active pursuit of excellent performance. In a few domains, it occasionally happens that in record time unusually young individuals move to the most advanced levels, traversing a distance that usually takes a decade or more of study. These are, of course, domains that allow for the appearance of prodigies.

PERFORMANCE STANDARDS

For a domain to be developmental, let alone to be eligible for prodigy making, standards of performance must exist. One cannot progress through the levels of a domain unless there is a set of reasonably stable and clear criteria of excellent performance. This is the second characteristic of a developmental domain. The field must be sufficiently understood by teachers, critics, audiences, collectors, and the like to devise and maintain standards of high-level performance. Domains vary in terms of the clarity of their criteria and how widely they are shared; mathematics seems to have very clear and widely shared criteria, while the visual arts and literature vary more widely, with less consensus regarding standards of excellence. It is not essential that there be perfect agreement on exactly what constitutes a valid decision about talent. For example, if art critics agree that a piece of work is worthy of consideration as a serious artistic achievement, it is not essential that they agree that it should be purchased for the permanent collection in the Metropolitan Museum of Art.

Developmental domains themselves go through periods in which their standards undergo change. This may mean that during a certain period it may be more difficult to be certain of what constitutes quality. The past decade or so has seen substantial diversity among music critics in evaluating new works, perhaps more so than at any previous time. Something similar may have happened after the turn of the century in painting, when Cubism and, somewhat later, Abstract Expressionism were making their way into respected critics' minds. Changes in criteria and periods of instability may profoundly affect who will be credited with doing the most important work at a given moment and what the most valued work will be like. Little is yet known about these matters. It would certainly help to know more in our efforts to comprehend the prodigy. To the extent that standards change, are less clear, or consensus is lacking, it is harder to evaluate the talent and promise of a potential prodigy.

LEVELS OF MASTERY

Along with standards of excellence for evaluating performance, a domain is also characterized by distinctive levels of mastery. The fact that some professions, trades, disciplines, and crafts have created formal rankings for achieving different levels of practice is one indication of orderliness or an attempt to impose order on a complex field of endeavor.

The skills that mark each level of each domain will vary, but there may be some qualities that commonly characterize novices in all domains. Whether given a special title like "plebe" or "rookie" or "novitiate" or more informally labeled, virtually all domains recognize the newcomer as having a special status. The novice has made a commitment to try to master a domain but has not been seriously engaged in the process long enough or intensely enough to be judged. Yet there are wise teachers who can tell a great deal about the promise of a novice even very early in the formal training processes. I have heard tennis coaches claim that they can tell in ten minutes whether a child has a natural gift for the game. I have heard attorneys claim that they can tell within a month or so how well a new associate will perform in the practice. In music, stories of early and intense engagement are legend: Lorin Hollander's almost instant acquisition of the musical notation system, Yehudi Menuhin's rejection of a toy violin because it "did not sing" are well-known examples. Thus, although everyone starts as a novice, not everyone begins with the degree of engagement or rapid accomplishment that marks the early experience of the prodigy.

For those who continue past the initial phases of mastery, there next comes a period of apprenticeship with a master of the discipline.[4] Here again, differences arise in how people perform. A few children, for example, who have not shown much interest or talent during the novice phase blossom into passionate learners under the attention of a charismatic mentor. This may be especially true in the natural sciences, where mastery may be less rapid until some kind of bond between teacher and student develops.[5] Once the spark has been ignited, the student may sustain a lifetime of motivation on the momentum built up in a critical formative experience, typically during the adolescent period. Charles Darwin seems to have been a case of a relatively lackadaisical child intellectually, with little to suggest that he would do anything well, let alone revolutionize biological science. It was at Cambridge, under the tutelage of botany professor J. S. Henslow, that the first strong signs of his proclivities and talents emerged. For the moment it is not important to dwell upon the constraints imposed by different fields on the individuals aspiring to master them. We simply should recognize that in virtually all fields that produce prodigies, and of course in many fields that do not, there are distinct phases through which one passes toward mature performance. For certain fields and for certain individuals, the period of apprenticeship is critical. These early phases of mastery seem to be particularly critical in the fields in which prodigies appear.

The time required for an apprenticeship varies both across domains and among individuals. It can range from as little as a year or so in certain trades (for example, electrician) to many years in certain professions (for example, surgery). The duration of apprenticeships is one of the variables to consider when attempting to gauge the degree of an individual's promise or the amount of information and skill requisite to mature performance in a complex field. At some point, a transition from apprentice to journeyman or independent status must begin. The transition need not be abrupt, nor need it be marked formally. But if a person is to become a recognized practitioner, that practice must begin to be increasingly independent. In musical performance, students begin to give recitals almost from the beginning. As the student matures musically, these recitals become more and more public. Graduations and special occasions, as signs of movement to new levels of professional mastery, may be marked with public performances. Finally the student is perceived as ready to begin a professional career as an orchestra member or a concert soloist. The decisions about public performance are most delicate ones, and how they are made has much to do with a musician's likelihood of becoming successful, an issue we will consider in detail in chapter 6 where we discuss violinist Nils Kirkendahl.

Although the process marking movement through levels of expertise tends to be well structured in musical performance, it is much less so in the visual arts. Rarely is it clear that a student is on a track toward professional artistry until at least the beginning of intensive art training during the late teens. The real test of the transition to high-level practice usually comes after formal training, when the aspiring artist takes a loft or studio and tries to earn a living by making art. In other fields the way toward independent practice may be more or less structured, but there must be such a path, with reasonably clear criteria for assessing advancement through successive levels of mastery, if a domain is to be considered developmental.

If a person remains engaged in the pursuit of mastery of a domain, and if that pursuit is successful, his or her work will reflect ever greater distinctiveness and control over the more difficult aspects of the field. Each field has its own special challenges, well known to those within, sometimes not understood by those on the periphery. For a gymnast, it might be the iron cross or the vault that must be surmounted. For the ice skater it might be a double lutz jump or triple salchow. In mathematics there are certain well-known problems that challenge the aspiring master and others that remain to be solved. When a youngster meets such challenges, recognition within the larger professional community often follows. Mi Dori played the Bach "Chaconne" for master teacher Dorothy DeLay (their real names) when she was eight and, with DeLay's imprimatur, established herself as a prodigy to be reckoned with.

That each field has such winnowing challenges seems likely, and that they serve somewhat similar purposes also makes sense. A few fields have

specific criteria for awarding status to those who have met various challenges, but most are not so well marked. On the whole, the clear distinctions tend to be at the heights of a field rather than at critical points
between early progress and master-level practice. Official ranking as a
chess master means that one has achieved a certain level of play against
recognized competition. Sport fields are similarly organized at the higher
levels of practice. The Nobel Prize recognizes outstanding achievement in
several scientific and humanistic fields, and the Japanese Living Treasures
program acknowledges excellence in various traditional crafts and trades.[6]

Some especially challenging tasks and practitioner's techniques lead
to the creation of jargons unique to particular fields. At the very least,
specialized vocabularies help maintain the distinctiveness of the field;
they may also help keep outsiders out and insiders in, or afford the opportunity of telling one from the other. Contributing to this vocabulary
may be a sign of having made a creative contribution to the domain, as,
for example, in the naming of medical disorders (Reye's syndrome,
Turner's syndrome), inventions (Cray computer, Jacquard loom) or physical laws (Mendelian genetics, Gibbs' free energy) after their discoverers
or developers.

DISTINCTIVE METHODOLOGIES

In addition to a series of ever more sophisticated levels of mastery and
a set of distinctive concepts, developmental domains are also characterized
by a special set of methods, techniques, technologies, and/or sources of
information and organized support. For a domain to be mastered, its methods and media must be mastered as well. Some of these demands are
primarily physical. For example, my subject Nils Kirkendahl had composed pieces at age nine that he was not capable of playing because he
could not yet reach from one end to the other of the full keyboard of a
concert piano. In another situation, it may be a forlorn hope for a person
with a limited perceptual capacity to excel in a domain that requires full
sensory participation. I once listened to two adult potters discuss a piece
of sculpture they had seen. The less gifted potter saw fault lines in the
structure, while the more talented potter knew at once that these were
marks from the molding process, which indeed they were. Both potters
were equally familiar with the technique the sculptor had used; he was a
colleague and friend of both. One of them, however, saw more clearly and
understood better than the other; there is no other way to say it. I should
add that the two potters also agree on who is the more gifted, even as they

argue heatedly over whether one actually perceives things more acutely than the other.

While I do not want to overestimate the importance of sheer physical capability in the achievement of excellent performance, I discuss it because it is one of the first reasons offered to explain why there are prodigies in some fields and not in others. When considering that few visual artists create distinctive works before ten or twelve, while many musicians (both performers and composers) do, it is often argued that the physical demands of painting or drawing prevent children from performing well. This is not a plausible argument, since children play the piano, violin, and even the drums very well before age ten; it is unclear what kinds of demands on visual artists for fine motor control might exceed the demands on musicians. A more likely explanation is that the technology and techniques for composition and performance are more organized and accessible to the young musician. There are also clearer criteria for excellent performance. Drawing or sketching well is the closest analogue for the artist to playing well, and this is less an indication of prodigiousness in art than playing well is in music.[7] In some fields the special techniques are conceptual and abstract, perhaps making them less accessible to the young mind. Pure mathematics is an example of such a domain.

Still other fields seem to depend more on experience than on specific knowledge or practiced technique. A patent attorney rarely reaches peak performance until after forty: levels of mastery in the field are poorly charted; little about actual practice is made explicit in books, courses, or seminars; and the practitioner is dependent on the availability of a mentor and an arena in which to refine requisite skills. The same might be said about disciplines such as philosophy, literary criticism, or psychiatric practice. Where the central challenge of a domain depends so much on the actual experience of living in the world with other human beings as well as on a base of specialized knowledge and skill carried by a select few, the likelihood of a child showing advanced skill at an extremely early age is drastically reduced.

EDUCATION

Virtually all domains have associated with them formal or informal pedagogies—the techniques, skills, and tricks of the trade taught in schools or by teachers. Books, libraries, museums, agencies, service organizations, and, of course, the actual institutions responsible for carrying out the practices of the domain all have the purpose, at least in part, to transmit knowledge to aspiring newcomers. The pedagogical traditions and techniques associated with particular domains also affect the likelihood of early prodigious performance. For example, if there is no tradition of children being involved in the domain—as in medicine, for example—instructional techniques are unlikely to be easily adapted for children. Where children have been involved in the field and where there are special accommodations for them (as in the case of child-sized violins and teachers who specialize in instruction expressly for children) the domain will afford easier access.

Domains that are most accessible to mastery by children are generally ones requiring relatively little in the way of prerequisite knowledge or understanding. For example, in order to be a linguist, it not only helps to be conversant with several languages, but one must be able to analyze this body of knowledge for common and distinctive principles. Even were a child to have a gift for languages, the time needed to master a sufficiently diverse sample of languages is considerable. Not until then, it may be assumed, would the actual work of the linguist begin. Sometimes a child appears who has a gift for speaking languages, but he or she is rarely a linguist before adolescence and rarely if ever does original work until well into his or her twenties.

CULTURAL SUPPORT

In addition to all of its other characteristics, a domain, if it is to produce prodigies, must be valued and supported within a given culture. Only in those fields where we value extraordinary achievement do we look for it. Only where there are rewards and incentives for excellence do we encourage children to strive for it. Mihalyi Csikszentmihalyi of the University of Chicago has argued that a prodigy is a cultural invention, pure and simple.[8] This may take things a bit too far, but the point itself is well taken. However great the raw talents a child brings to a domain, they will be developed only if the culture provides opportunities for practice and encouragement for excellence. The fields available at a given moment for a given child to explore include only those that are culturally valued. Cartography was a domain that until the beginning of this century produced precociously talented mapmakers. In fact, in one book written about prodigies more than fifty years ago, a mapmaking prodigy was included.[9] Were such a child to show this talent today, little effort would be made to develop the gift. We will have more to say about the relationship between culture and prodigies in succeeding chapters, especially chapter

8, but it is important to recognize that cultures select and emphasize the value of various domains, thereby constraining who can be conceived as a prodigy at a particular time.

SUMMARY

The qualities that make domains developmental may be summarized as follows. A domain must afford a range of performance both within and across ages that is sufficiently great to reveal qualitative differences in talent. There must be products of performance, either in concrete form or conceptually, that can be evaluated by means of a coherent and relatively consistent set of standards of excellence. The domain must recognize reasonably clear levels of achievement ranging from those of the novice to those of the seasoned master. The domain, to be distinguished from other fields, needs to exhibit a set of distinctive concepts that pertain to some of its special qualities of performance, such as a "four-wheel drift" in auto racing or "chiaroscuro" in the graphic arts. Domains must also have pedagogical traditions. These may be of varying degrees of formality, but some form of self-conscious transmission of knowledge is essential. For pedagogical purposes as well as for the purpose of communicating the unique meaning expressed in each domain, special technologies or techniques are evolved and used in a given field. Finally, a culture or social group must value and reward achievement in a field if it is to be maintained. This is particularly true in relation to the appearance and preparation of prodigies.

It may seem as if every field would qualify as a developmental domain. This is not at all the case, although much of what is valued in human achievement may be so characterized. But in fact, the bulk of human labor is probably not performed in fields defined by the characteristics we have just outlined. Although there are no doubt exceptions, most manufacturing jobs, bureaucratic tasks, office work, unskilled labor, soldiering, and many service positions are not linked to developmental domains: range and variability of achievement are not one of their key features. These kinds of tasks are carried out in ways that permit little development of skill, under the direction of a few whose work may be developmental in the sense that I have used it. Indeed, any operation that requires massive atomized labor is going to be mostly nondevelopmental. It should be recognized, then, that the kinds of performance highlighted in this book are not available to most people as ways of earning a living. This may be unfortunate, but it is important that we not overestimate the proportion of human work that may be characterized as the pursuit of excellence in developmental domains.

Fertile Ground for the Appearance of Prodigies

Prodigies appear in developmental domains—but not all developmental domains. An analysis of the features of a domain that attracts prodigies might help us understand why they appear in these and not other fields and, perhaps more usefully, might help us guess which fields may lend themselves to prodigies in the future.

ACCESSIBILITY

First and foremost, a domain must be accessible to a child. This means that a child, even a very young child, can grasp its meaning when exposed to the practices of a domain. It is unlikely that children will understand banking and finance, for example, as we are reminded in the movie of *Mary Poppins*. The potential excitement and challenge of "a tuppence wisely spent" were totally lost on the two Banks children, who saw the bank as merely a cavernous building with nothing much going on. On the other hand, music touches even very young children, as parents of infants will attest. All of our own children, for example, frequently quieted to singing or recorded music when little else would soothe them. They continue to love to sing and dance. Both Nils Kirkendahl and Randy McDaniel were reported to have strong preferences for classical music from their earliest days.

Both the artifacts of the domain and its activities play a role in accessibility. There are stories of young children who, having seen a set of chess pieces, were utterly fascinated by them and simply had to know more about the game.[10] The spectacle of an orchestra performing in classical repertoire was mesmerizing to Yehudi Menuhin before he was two. Accessibility is also one of the reasons why jobs like firefighter and doctor are compelling to children. They are accessible to a child's sense of meaning. How could the sedate practice of law compare with the color, drama, and excitement of police work? The more abstract and removed from the experience of children, even children who are very gifted intellectually, the less likely that a domain will be the source of prodigies.

ORGANIZATION

Prodigies are more likely to appear if the knowledge base of the domain is highly organized formally and highly concentrated symbolically. Music, chess, and mathematics share this feature, while visual art does not. The symbols for music and chess are drawn from a relatively stable set of elements, related to each other in relatively clear ways. Of course what is done with these symbols varies, especially in mathematics, where they are drawn from geometric and logical as well as numerical symbol systems. The more restricted the set of symbols, and the more restricted the number and variety of rules for relating them, the more likely the domain will be accessible to and usable by children. Poetry and literature are based on a very restricted set of elementary symbols (the alphabet), but the rules for their use in creating poetry, stories, plays, or novels are complex and loosely organized. This lack of formal organization would not lead us to expect writing to be a domain rich in prodigies, and indeed they are quite rare. Some forms of poetry, by my account, should be a bit more accessible to children than other styles of literary expression, and this indeed seems to be the case. Although there are few literary prodigies of either kind more children produce poetry rated as craftsmanlike and expressive than quality short stories or novels or plays. So, too, child writer Randy McDaniel produced some of his best work in poetry.

PHYSICAL CAPABILITY

The physical demands of a domain also influence the likelihood of prodigies appearing, or even of non-prodigies progressing through successive levels of mastery. Domains have physical requirements for high-level performance as well as intellectual ones. To take an obvious example, but one that is personally painful, it makes no sense to aspire to play center for the Boston Celtics basketball team unless one is at least six feet ten inches tall (I played center for my junior high school basketball team at just under six feet—and then stopped growing). As with many young girls, my wife, Lynn, wanted to be a ballerina, only to learn that her feet were not designed for standing on pointe. One wonders how many stories like these have played significant roles in the lives of people. If the methods for detecting and directing the enthusiasms of children were more sophisticated, fewer blind alleys and devastating "failures" might occur. On the more positive side, it is probably a good thing that domains vary in terms of the physical abilities they demand. The great psychologist Piaget taught us that development has its own pace, neither to be speeded up nor slowed down. It is critical to understand the optimal moment of engagement for various domains and for children of varying talents. Sports and dance, because their physical demands are so central, would appear to be promising sources of knowledge about these aspects of the match between individual and domain. Indeed, there no doubt exists within domains a great deal of informal lore about the role of physical capability that needs only organization and correlation to be of better use.

DOMAINS FOR FUTURE PRODIGIES

We have already noted how cartography has declined as a producer of prodigies, but we have not yet considered where new prodigies might be found. A domain that fairly well screams its availability for prodigies is computer programming. It may even be that, given a somewhat liberal definition of prodigy, several have already emerged. There are instances of teenagers who have devised sophisticated programs for a variety of purposes, including accessing supposedly secret data banks. The computer is a quintessentially accessible domain; the power of the machine is there at the touch of a button. No special physical abilities are called for to operate even the most powerful computer. There is relatively rapid feedback about the success of a programming effort, and the results of running the program are very visible and can be very dramatic. Furthermore, the symbol systems and rules governing the domain are closely constrained. The major problem of access may be the number and variety of computer languages. Different languages are designed for different computational purposes; this may require learning several languages for programming different kinds of problems. Still, the prestige, rewards, and cultural preoccupation with computer technology will no doubt continue to focus attention on skill in this area. This combination of qualities of domain and culture suggests that we may be entering a period in which child prodigies will emerge in the field of computer programming. This is especially interesting because it would be an example of prodigies in a field that has not existed for very long, perhaps for only three or four decades. In terms of the history of the domain itself, this seems to be the minimum time necessary for prodigies to appear; but appear they will, at least if the relevant characteristics of domains match my description of them.

Less obvious as a source of prodigies, but possibly more important, will be those domains that are of great importance to humanity but that have been undervalued, particularly those that have been traditionally considered as "feminine." I am thinking of domains that emphasize moral and ethical development, realms of human endeavor that involve the understanding of others' points of view, cooperative enterprise, negotiations, and compromise. These domains are less well defined because there have been fewer efforts to formally chart their levels, create technologies, or build formal pedagogical traditions. Spiritual dimensions that focus on the best human qualities of care, concern, charity, peace, and sympathy with others represent underdeveloped capacities in our children, at least insofar as they are recognized as worthy of cultural recognition and reward. Such qualities have begun to gain recognition as feminist and minority groups have "raised consciousness" in various fields. Newer theories of intelligence such as Howard Gardner's "frames of mind" also have helped catalyze changes in cultural values by broadening the scope of abilities contributing to intellectual functioning. Gardner, in particular, posits both interpersonal and intrapersonal intelligences, which draw on many of the kinds of abilities and sensitivities described here.

Because these domains are less well formed as developmental fields, one may expect that prodigies will be rare, and that when they are found, they will be somewhat older than prodigies in some of the more traditional domains. On the other hand, since ethical or moral prodigiousness may reveal itself in common, everyday situations, the opportunity to detect such prodigies may be much more widespread than in other domains. It may also be that some of the Eastern disciplines that focus on the spiritual, emotional, and universal qualities of existence will find their way into Western culture in ways that help structure and define these more diffuse domains. I will have more to say about these possibilities in later chapters, but we should recognize that prodigies are found only where we look for them, where we comprehend them, and where we care enough about high-level performance in a domain to regard the signs of extraordinariness as somehow critical to the continued well-being of society.

A domain, after all, is a human construction. It may have a separate existence from a person, and is without question larger and more diverse than any single human being can experience or encompass. Yet it is still the case that a domain has no significance except as it is practiced by passionate and committed human beings dedicated to mastering its secrets and fired by the possibility of extending its range and power.

Conclusion

In this chapter we have been looking at the prodigy from the point of view of the field or domain within which the child demonstrates prodigious behavior. We have learned that most fields of endeavor in which human beings labor do not produce prodigies. Only those domains that are developmental are candidates for early prodigious mastery. A pattern of prodigy appearance, steep trajectory toward high-level mastery, and length of peak effectiveness while working in a field seems to differentiate one prodigy-prone field from another.

I have also suggested that some fields that we think produce prodigies do not do so, or at least produce fewer than expected. And when prodigies do appear in these fields, they are older than children who perform at equivalent levels of mastery in other fields. The reasons for this seem to lie in the particular characteristics of the field's organization and its pattern of transmitting knowledge. Mathematics is perhaps the most surprising example. In mathematics, prodigies are virtually never found before age ten or twelve, whereas in chess they are not that rare by age five or six, and in music performance by three or four. The visual arts seem to have produced few prodigies in the past several hundred years, although by the late teenage years and early twenties some visual artists have done remarkable work, and writers are extremely rare. If we want to extend the boundaries of childhood to include the teenage years, then these distinctions would perhaps be less compelling. But if developmental psychology has taught us anything, it is that there are distinctive mental qualities that change with age, with major reorganizations taking place at roughly eighteen months, six years, and around twelve years of age.

It remains true that within the fifteen or twenty years of time encompassed by this liberal definition of childhood, prodigiousness appears at widely different times. Some of the time variation is due to the ability of a culture to respond to an extraordinarily talented student, some to the field itself, and some due to the nature of the abilities necessary to do the work of a particular field at a high level. Still, the fact remains that prodigylike behavior in different domains varies as to time of appearance, types and stringency of criteria used to identify extreme talent, and time elapsed between early remarkable performance and mature mastery of the domain. By studying prodigies in various fields, we can learn about the fields themselves and how they function within society.

Domains must be relatively coherent for prodigies to show up, although just what "coherence" means is difficult to say precisely. Thinking about the relation between fields and prodigies has suggested some possible lines of attack on two other questions: how a field encodes, stores, and transmits its information to those who would master that field; and, also, how a field itself develops—the phases it goes through as it becomes more complex, differentiated, and coherent. Our knowledge of these and other qualities of fields can lead to predictions about those domains where it seems reasonable that prodigies will appear. For example, prodigies may emerge in a field for the first time; or there may be a renaissance of prodigies in a domain such as spiritual or moral leadership when a culture begins to value and encourage excellence in the domain. I hope I have made clear that knowing about prodigies helps us know not only about children who are awesome in what they are able to do but also about the culturally prepared niches within which these prodigies' awesome feats are performed. If the prodigy phenomenon leads us to ask questions about the nature of knowledge and how it is organized into domains, then the prodigy will have served a vital purpose. This is, of course, not all that the prodigy can tell us, but it may prove as valuable as any we might propose.

With a talented child and a domain that is accessible and appropriately developed, we have two key ingredients for a prodigy to appear. Whether it actually happens depends on several more factors. Especially for those fields in which the process begins early, as, for example, in music, chess, and many sports, there is one co-incidence factor that is absolutely critical—the child's family. To the family falls the responsibility of recognizing the child's burgeoning talent, responding to it by providing experience with the cultural domain through which that talent can express itself, and organizing and managing co-incidence forces so that the child will be able to use the full power of the talent.

Under certain conditions families become even more important, as in the two cases discussed in the next chapter. In these families, the children were seen as having untapped talent, but not in the usual form that it takes in prodigies. As we will see, although the two children represent opposite extremes, their families agree on what it takes to bring forth and develop the full potential of children.

5

Families: Catalysts and Organizers of Co-incidence

IN THIS CHAPTER we look at how two families have dealt with encouraging the potential of the children they are raising. In the Konantovich family, the appearance of exceptional intellectual capability was a surprise, yet they were not wholly unprepared to respond to it. Although they believed in the value of intense early stimulation to maximize development, they found themselves challenged almost immediately to extend their horizons in order to respond to their child's extraordinary intellectual demands and abilities. In the other family, the Lemkes (their real name), their child is no prodigy, and they made no assumption that their son possessed any kind of extreme ability. Indeed, it took an act of supreme faith to believe that there was any mental activity whatsoever in Leslie, the child the Lemkes raised. I am presenting these two dramatically different cases to illustrate how central the family is to the process of developing human potential. In the case of the Konantovich family, the talent their child Adam possessed was genuinely extreme, and their response to this talent has been correspondingly extreme. In the case of the Lemkes, they simply saw it as their responsibility to search for and bring forth Leslie's hidden capabilities, although there was virtually no indication that Leslie had any capabilities at all for more than a decade and a half! For them, an extreme response, although a very different one, was also demanded. In both cases, the role of the family in the boys' development could not possibly be overestimated.

For the most part the parents in my study of prodigies were not looking for prodigies among their offspring. Once an extreme talent burst forth, however, they tried to respond to it. This was the case for the two families to be discussed in the present chapter, and in this respect they are typical of prodigies' families, but more intensely responsive. Although the Lemkes do not have a child prodigy and are not in my study, the qualities revealed in their approach to child rearing help to sharpen the issues about raising extraordinary children. The Lemkes in particular, although not involved in raising a prodigy, are an inspiration to anyone who might think about raising children.

Even in families where there is a tradition of exceptional ability—for example, in music or chess or mathematics—the appearance of extreme talent that can lead to a prodigy can come as a shock. This is because, in certain cases, the mastery that children display comes so suddenly and with so little warning that it seems to be beyond comprehension and to require a rapid and intense response by the parents. In the more successful instances, the parents of the prodigy-to-be are shocked only temporarily and find that they can marshal the resources necessary to develop the child's talents—and continue to do so indefinitely. Such was the case of the family of Lorin Hollander, now a successful concert pianist in his forties. Hollander remembers the moment that his father, a violinist and Toscanini's concertmaster in the NBC Symphony, discovered that his son possessed extraordinary musical abilities:

When I was 3½, I went with my father to a rehearsal and heard them play a Haydn quartet. I was profoundly moved by the music. When I came home, I wanted somehow to put down what I had heard. I found some drawing paper and began to draw spirals. My father asked me what I was doing, and I began to sing him back the piece, which I remembered perfectly, and told him that I was trying to write it down. My father said, "No, you silly boy, we already have a way of writing music," and he brought out the score to show me. I fell into the music; that's the only way to describe it. Within four minutes I knew the notes, the clefs, everything. A car horn sounded outside and, just for fun, my father asked me what note it was. I immediately answered, "F sharp." He took a spoon and clinked a glass. "B flat," I told him. Then he and my mother realized they had a prodigy on their hands and they started to run around to people to find out what to do.[1]

While not every prodigy enters the world of his domain in quite so dramatic a fashion, most of my subjects did astound their parents.

Once the talent appears, it would be difficult to overestimate the amount of time, energy, commitment, and emotional support required from one or more members of the child's family. In most of the families I observed, one parent has been more involved in the child's education than the other. Sometimes it was the mother, sometimes the father, but in all cases the demands on the parent of educating the prodigy put a strain on the family and a drain on its resources, financial and otherwise.

In this country it currently falls to parents, or occasionally to other relatives or friends, to do the heavy work of prodigy preparation. As parents have always done, they go about the complex task of developing a prodigy intuitively, and with little knowledge or support from the rest of society. In democratic countries like the United States, it is basically the parents' decision and responsibility to encourage talent. Greater knowledge about the process of identifying and developing talent might give parents incentive or encouragement to consider a "curriculum" for their young child, but the responsibility remains largely theirs. A lot depends on whether parents see the fulfillment of their responsibilities as requiring that they do all that is possible to facilitate their child's development, and to give up much of their own ambition and recreation in the bargain.

In the context of this culture, families are therefore crucial early catalysts in the co-incidence process. They are responsible for initial exposure directly or indirectly (for example, through television program selection, records, concerts), and for responding to the first signs of powerful affinity for a domain. At whatever age these affinities show themselves, it will not be long before most parents will have to confront the fact that their own knowledge of the domain is inadequate to the needs of their child. Outside help is absolutely essential. At that point, their functions expand to include selection of teachers and mentors and management of the child's preparation.

The period of exclusive parental introduction and instruction is brief but critical. The opportunity to become engaged—to fall in love—with a field must be offered to the child. Once properly introduced to a domain, there is relatively little that most parents can do directly to further the development of their child in the field. Within a few months, for example, both the chess players in my study were beating nearly everyone in sight. Even in musical families, where parents are themselves performers or composers, the likelihood is overwhelming that outside resources will be required to help prepare the child for whatever is to come. In other domains that are less clear in terms of their fertility for prodigies, it is correspondingly less clear just how much exposure and at what level it is necessary to stimulate the connection between prodigy and domain. Still, once known, it is likely that before very long parents will need to search for proper and appropriate teachers, schools, tutors, mentors, camps, or clubs where the child's talents can be further developed. The task of the family is to organize, coordinate, manage, and monitor the process.

Whatever the family's history of commitment or tradition within a given field, the major decisions about the education of a prodigy fall heavily on their shoulders for the first several years. If the child's talent shows itself extremely early, say before the age of three, parents may understandably be reluctant to give over the education of their offspring to a cadre of teachers. Even when training is done by others, it still falls almost exclusively to the family to foster the social and emotional aspects of the young prodigy's life. Although the prodigy may outstrip other family members in specific achievements, there are many realms in which he is still a child and needs the support, wisdom, and nurturance of family life. This is an issue we will take up in detail in chapter 7.

Whatever the mix of prodigy-related issues and the more usual child-rearing responsibilities, there is no question that the families of child prodigies are burdened as well as blessed: raising a child with prodigious talent requires levels of energy, commitment, sensitivity, and patience far exceeding those that most of us possess. The prodigies' family lives are in some ways analogous to the experience of families of handicapped or disturbed children in that the appearance of a child with unusual, extreme talent seems to violate parents' expectations of what their children's abilities will be. The families in my study were all surprised (and even taken aback) by the extreme and early talent their children have displayed. It is in this respect that the discovery of extreme talent is similar to the discovery of a physical or emotional handicap. It is almost as if there is a certain range of ability that parents expect their children to fall within. When a child shows signs of going beyond that range, in either direction, a kind of panic sets in. I do not mean to equate the anguish, guilt, sadness, and turmoil that must accompany the realization that a child is handicapped with the emotions that accompany raising a prodigy, only to suggest that there is a common need in both situations to accept the fact that the price for successful parenting will be much higher than expected.

Furthermore, according to the theory of co-incidence, from time to time talents will appear that are not well matched to existing domains nor to the range of possibilities that a specific pair of parents can comprehend. In such cases the process of identifying and channeling talent will be even more difficult and potentially frustrating. In 1972 the great Olympic gymnast Olga Korbut asserted in a television interview, "If gymnastics did not exist, I would have invented it," thereby giving expression to her deeply felt sense that her talent demanded an outlet. Reflect for a moment on what life might have been like for Olga had she found herself with such a specific talent in a different time and place, where gymnastics was unknown or unvalued. Perhaps little Olga would have invented something like protogymnastics, or perhaps she would have found some other form of kinesthetic expression. Otherwise she might have felt unhappy and unfulfilled and may never have known why. There are undoubtedly children who have been blessed with extreme talent but who, unlike Olga Korbut, have not been lucky enough to find a domain through which their talents can be expressed. The kinds of demands such children make on parents may resemble those of handicapped children even more closely; they may feel frustrated, angry, unhappy, and unfulfilled without understanding why.

It should not be surprising that parents, families, and the children themselves sense without necessarily knowing it that the development of their talent is set against great odds. In fact, if there were a fuller understanding of just how steep the odds really are, it is doubtful that many would even try. It is part of the American myth, though, that everyone has a chance for success if he or she just works hard enough. A film on television recently showed a young athlete who, when cut from a professional football team, is encouraged to try his hand at the decathlon—and goes on to win the Olympic gold. Sylvester Stallone's *Rocky* movies depict the story of a punk from South Philadelphia who works his way to the world boxing championship. Novels with the rags-to-riches theme abound and frequently enjoy extended tenure on the best-seller lists. In actuality, the likelihood of a single individual achieving the sort of successes portrayed in these popular vehicles is virtually nil. Fortunately the myth does not give an accurate account of the odds.

In socialist countries such myths are not as necessary, at least in certain fields, since excellence in these fields is a matter of official policy. There is less need for families to motivate individuals to throw themselves into doing particular kinds of work exceptionally well; doing well in a designated field is what is expected of a patriotic person. The state has its own way of encouraging certain kinds of co-incidence—for example, by institutionalizing screening for talent, offering instructional programs, and providing attractive incentives to individuals for practicing within the domain. But because it supports only a small number of domains, and because it is interested in only a very few, the state may provide an even more restrictive framework for the expression of individual potential.

Part of the price of the prevailing Western view that everyone has a chance is that the burden on families in our society is especially heavy. It is no wonder that it becomes a matter of national concern when "the family" seems in any sort of jeopardy: the family bears the brunt of responsibility for childrearing, with very little assistance from the state. In the Western context in particular, the individual's family is as crucial a force as any in the co-incidence equation. It is primarily the parents' responsibility to integrate the child's disparate experiences into some kind of coherent whole, for it is generally the parents who, more than anyone else, are concerned with the child's overall development and well-being. As advocates and advisers, parents of prodigies face a startling array of responsibilities: they must secure and orchestrate special instruction, consult and counsel on decisions (both large and small) related to special training, watch for signs of fatigue, lack of interest, stress, or disquiet in their children, provide emotional support, and seek to maintain as "normal" a life for their children as they can. Without this kind of sustained commitment to the nurturance of talent, it simply will not flourish. Parental devotion to the development of prodigious talent has been the strongest constant across the cases in my study.

The Konantovich Family

Among the families of gifted, talented, and prodigious children I have known, I have not encountered anything like the Konantoviches when it comes to dedicated, persistent, and resourceful pursuit of educational resources for their child. In fact, I came to know this remarkable family as a by-product of one of their many efforts. They had visited the late Halbert Robinson's preschool project for gifted children in Seattle, hoping that his school for academically talented youngsters might be a fitting place to continue two-year-old Adam's education. When they reluctantly decided that it was not really what they hoped it would be, they turned their attention toward Boston as a place where Adam's educational needs might be met. Apprised of their decision not to relocate in the Northwest, Hal suggested that they contact me if they were considering moving to Boston.

By the time Adam was two he was already straining his parents' ability to keep up with his educational interests without outside assistance. For the first year or so Fiona and Nathaniel managed to provide most of his educational experiences themselves. In fact, they had worked out a detailed and practical philosophy for the rearing of children before Adam was conceived, a point of view about parenting they plan to publish someday as a book. Although they expected to produce a bright and responsive child, they had no inkling that their son would prove to be a child of almost unprecedented ability. But one thing is crystal clear. Nathaniel and Fiona do not believe that people should bring children into the world until and unless they are prepared to give fully of themselves once that child has arrived. And they have lived out this belief even when it has been physically, emotionally, and financially draining.

RAISING A PRODIGY

Certain themes have run through our conversations about pedagogy and child-rearing, themes that Nathaniel and Fiona practice as well as preach. Although they may not represent a fully articulated form of the Konantovich educational strategy, I do not think I violate their ideas about responsive educational practice in any major way by presenting these themes as the backbone of their philosophy. Their central pedagogical canon is to provide frequent and varied stimulation for the child. In early infancy this stimulation would engage different sensory modalities, and might take the form of bright colors, interesting shapes, visually active displays, a variety of sounds both musical and nonmusical, and large doses of interpersonal interaction. Furthermore, this stimulation should be constantly under the supervision of an observant and sensitive adult (parent) so that it can be optimized through variation and so be maximally responsive to the child's needs and interests.

Fiona, a serious folksinger, has described, for example, how she sang to her eleven-hour-old son during his first breastfeeding. She noticed that he was sucking in rhythm to her song, so she changed from a $\frac{4}{4}$ allegro moderato tempo to a slower, $\frac{3}{4}$ lento: he did as well. In this way, rhythms became a regular way for Fiona to communicate with her newborn and she used them as a springboard for other forms of musical embellishment.

Stimulation past early infancy should also take a variety of forms. From our observations, the Konantoviches engage Adam in ways that involve a heavily verbal presentation, a tendency to introduce domains or issues through abstract concepts (this is apparently in response to Adam's own preferred style for learning), a startling range of examples designed to pique curiosity and interest, the encouragement of experimentation (both mental "thought experiments" and actual ones), introduction of interesting facts, and the effort to gain access to resources—both written documents and human experts—to pursue interesting questions.

We quickly discovered, for example, that there is no such thing as a casual tramp through the woods. On our first walk with Adam, Fiona, and Nathaniel into the forest preserve near our home, we spent the better part of an hour barely penetrating 100 yards into the woods: Fiona would see a cluster of particularly interesting ferns which we all stopped to inspect, and the three Konantoviches launched into an extended discussion of reproduction in different plant types. Two steps later, Nathaniel would find some decomposing something-or-other, and he and Adam would speculate about how long it had been decaying, what kinds of chemical reactions you would find going on, and how long the entire process would take. Then Adam would spy an interesting species of bird and describe its nesting habits. Nearly every experience provided the potential for lively and interesting discussion. All the Konantoviches have curious and inquiring minds, and Nathaniel and Fiona are energetic about using naturally occurring events to explore, reflect, and wonder.

The Konantoviches also tend to present material to Adam at a very high level. This meant simplifying as little as possible and also using an adult vocabulary to converse with him from his earliest days. (Lynn once received what must be close to the ultimate compliment from Fiona for not "speaking down" to five-year-old Adam as nearly everyone else did.) One of the results of this particular strategy is that by four or five years of age Adam's own vocabulary was in many ways indistinguishable from that of a well-educated adult, though his language was sometimes somewhat stilted and formal. It was also sometimes disconcerting to hear high-level discourse in the squeaks and lisps of a preschooler.

The third major emphasis in the Konantovich educational strategy is that child-rearing should be child-centered: parents should be available to children virtually all of the time. Physically, this has meant that only rarely is Adam out of either Nathaniel's or Fiona's direct care. (This evolved partly because the child-care alternatives they tried proved totally unsatisfactory. As Adam grows older this situation is changing, although the Konantoviches still spend much more time together than do most families.) Practically, this means that Adam's requests for attention or information are, on the whole, of the highest priority. Short of being interrupted during important conversations or during Fiona's time with clients, Nathaniel and Fiona have come to see one of their major roles as being available and responsive to Adam.

Fiona and Nathaniel are the first to admit that this is not always easy and that "parental burnout" is sometimes lurking around the corner. As Adam has grown older and (like all children) less egocentric, they have tried to encourage him to recognize that his parents are not as energetic as he, and to try to give them a little rest now and then. I remember Fiona relating how Adam as a two- and three-year-old would be up from eight in the morning until two or three at night, continually chattering away, making observations, and asking questions about this and that. Although Fiona could by no stretch of the imagination be classified as a low-energy individual, she began to find Adam's schedule oppressive and finally explained to him that she was finding it extremely difficult to keep up with his nineteen- and twenty-hour days. She reported that Adam, somewhat surprised and taken aback, asked why she hadn't told him earlier that his nocturnal habits were a burden. He promptly began going to bed by 10 P.M., and several days later he asked Fiona solicitously whether she was feeling a bit more rested!

Perhaps the most important aspect of the Konantoviches' child-rearing has little or nothing to do with responding to Adam's omnivorous intellectual demands, and that is that they are virtually always loving, gentle, and patient parents. They treat their son with respect yet authority, with affection yet firmness, with humor and happiness. For all their attentiveness to Adam's needs and interests, Fiona and Nathaniel are easygoing and playful with him: there is always much laughter, cuddling, and teasing in the Konantovich household. While Nathaniel and Fiona acutely feel the responsibility of educating such an extraordinary mind, they agree that, first and foremost, their responsibility is to raise a social, self-confident, psychologically healthy young boy. Continual and varied stimulation, physical and psychological availability, and access to material at a high level of sophistication, all within the context of a loving and caring relationship, are major building blocks of the Konantovich educational strategy. Certainly their efforts have been rewarded with a strikingly unusual child.

By the time the Konantoviches had been to Seattle and back and had contacted me, they felt that Adam was in desperate need of a broader range of educational and social opportunities than those they could provide themselves or through private lessons. Adam was barely three years old when we began discussing the possibility of the Konantoviches using the resources of Boston as their educational base. Nathaniel and Fiona were looking for a wide range of activities to address Adam's intellectual interests and needs. Until then they had been supplementing their own efforts at instruction in particular content areas with a variety of tutors: the burdens of locating and interviewing suitable candidates for these positions was tedious and frequently frustrating, and as often as not the relationship between Adam and his instructors was short-lived, with the tutor turning out to be lacking in sensitivity to Adam's interests, his youth (for despite his intellectual precocity, he was still emotionally and behaviorally a very young child), or his particular style of learning and thinking.

According to Fiona and Nathaniel, Adam's style of learning is particularly idiosyncratic and unusual; they have more recently described him as having a nonlinear, theoretical and holistic, essentially non-Western cast of mind, which often makes classic American teaching styles less effective with Adam than they are with other children. He is apparently unwilling to master facts and experiences as would be typical, inducing general principles from these already assimilated particulars. Rather he attempts to grasp things holistically and theoretically, and once he has acquired the general framework, fills in the more concrete facts. Fiona once described Adam's mental approach by noting:

> He has an intuitive sense, it seems to me, of the theoretical holes in any subject and while he often delays learning the "nuts and bolts" of a subject area until he has gained some theoretical mastery, he can make creative use of the basics to investigate what he has been working on at the theoretical level. Once he does elect to learn the basics, he does so with breathtaking speed and phenomenal retention, correlating with theory and questioning basic premises as he does so. (Letter, May 1979)

From what I have seen, Fiona's description is accurate, except that in my view Adam seems to avoid subjects when he feels he cannot master them quickly. I would not say that he is eager and willing to jump into any field at any level: he is actually quite selective about what he wants to learn and in what way. Nonetheless, Adam's general learning style may well conflict with the usual theories of intellectual development, which claim that the direction of cognitive growth is from specific to general—from direct experience to abstractions based on that experience. Jean Piaget's theory of intellectual development, for example, is of just this sort. If Adam's mind indeed works in the way that Fiona characterizes it, then it presents an anomaly for what we think we know about intellectual development. This may account in part for his reluctance to perform in situations that seem contrived or alien.

By age four he had already begun to investigate a wide range of topics, some fairly superficially and others with great intensity. In general, these seemed to cluster into several broad categories: symbol systems (cartography, languages—"Basic" for the computer, French, German, Russian, He-brew, Sanskrit, Greek, Egyptian glyphs), music (composition and perform-ance), science and mathematics (zoology, chemistry, physics, computers, geometry, and algebra). He had strong and abiding interests and prefer-ences, and while he generally accepted his parents' guidance and judgment about his readiness to tackle new fields, he would rarely give up on a subject that caught his fancy. Fiona recounted the following incident to an astonished group of professionals attending a conference on giftedness and creativity.

> At age one, the PBS broadcasts of the Boston Symphony would hold Adam spellbound for their entire length. He said that Seiji Ozawa was his favorite person in the whole world. Just about on his first birthday, he watched in rapture while a violinist played a prominent passage during one of those broadcasts. He said "Oh! What is that?" I told him it was a violin and he asked to play one. I said that his body was not ready yet. He asked when it would be and, thinking of the Suzuki method, I told him when he was three he would be able to play the violin. The matter was not mentioned again until a few days before his third birthday. He came into the kitchen and said, "Fiona, I'm ready!" I said, "That's nice, dear. What are you ready for?" Adam reminded me that I had told him he could play the violin when he was three. We began a long and frustrating search for the right teacher for him. He was composing in his own hand, had perfect pitch, was fascinated by the music to which he was exposed.[2]

THE BOSTON EXPERIMENT

One of Nathaniel and Fiona's most pressing educational concerns for Adam was social—he had no real playmates or friends and was relatively unskilled in negotiating the social world of the preschooler. There were few neighborhood children to play with, and those who were available were either too aggressive or too uninteresting to Adam to maintain an ongoing relationship. Fiona and Nathaniel had already tried Adam in several local private schools but these had also proven unsuccessful. They had even tried valiantly to start a school of their own for gifted children, but none of the other families they approached was willing to make the commitment of time, energy, and financial resources that the Konan-toviches saw as critical to the success of the enterprise. They are, to be sure, not your average suburban family.

It was therefore in large measure the possibility of a suitable school arrangement for Adam that encouraged Fiona and Nathaniel to pursue the notion of relocating in Boston. The school was The Learning Place, which Jeanne and Darren McDaniel had come upon for Randy the previous year (see chapter 3). Although Adam was some three years Randy's junior, I thought he might also thrive there in the environment created by Tom O'Brien and his coworkers.

What made this school unique was its basic gentleness and ability to instill a sense of caring and respect for every person there, regardless of age or status. It seemed like a perfect setting for children like Adam or Randy who were unable to deal with aggressive and insensitive treatment from other children. Adam simply was not prepared to handle the usual bumps and jolts of the classroom, especially one populated with energetic, ego-centric preschoolers. Anyone who has spent time watching life in school-rooms cannot but be impressed with how much verbal and physical ag-gressiveness usually occurs in them.[3] But just as important as the aggression itself is the fact that most children are amazingly good at rolling with the punches. For Adam the hurts and injustices of other children's behavior cut too deep to be brushed aside. Tom O'Brien's genius was to have created an environment where tolerance, restraint, and an emphasis on each child's special strengths prevailed.

Although The Learning Place did not normally take students under the age of six, Tom O'Brien thought that they could make special accom-modations for Adam. As it happened, he and Randy McDaniel ended up in the same class, and we were able to watch them together for the remain-ing six months of the school year.

Fiona and Nathaniel's Boston experiment also became an effort to gain four-and-a-half-year-old Adam access to the resources of Boston's uni-versities. Actually, the situation was not wholly unprecedented: almost exactly seventy years earlier a young man by the name of Norbert Wiener was enrolled at Tufts at age ten because his father, a professor of languages at Harvard, thought that the pressures and publicity attendant on studying at Harvard would be too much for his son. And the decision was a wise one. When Norbert graduated from Tufts at twelve he began graduate school in zoology at Harvard but was firmly encouraged to leave after his first year. Even with a quite credible B.S. under his belt Norbert had not been ready for Harvard (nor had Harvard been particularly ready for him). I thought the same might well be true for Adam. In fact, we were not actually considering that Adam be formally enrolled in any college. What we had in mind was an informal agreement for Adam to use the resources of the universities, to spend time with willing students and faculty, and to otherwise be enriched by the university community.

I thought that Tufts would be ideal for this purpose because it was small, relatively easy to penetrate, had an excellent child study center for consultation, and of course was where I happened to work. My sense was that if Harvard or MIT (where Lynn worked) were what Adam needed, it would be easy enough to tap those resources without getting involved in formal agreements or even informal arrangements beyond those with the individuals or organizations involved. Later on we were able to work out something along these lines with the MIT Computer Center, which allowed Adam to hang around and use the machines and talk to the staff.

By January all the pieces of the Boston experiment were in place, and the Konantoviches transformed themselves from the designers of the experiment into its subjects. The sheer logistics of the situation would have discouraged most families, but Fiona, Nathaniel, and Adam carried on cheerfully during that half a year in spite of the most demanding schedule.

Since they were only temporarily trying out their arrangements before committing to a relocation, they continued to live in another city and commute to Boston. Fiona and Adam (and Nathaniel, when his schedule permitted) drove or flew to Boston, where Adam attended classes at The Learning Place on Thursdays and Fridays. They stayed the weekend to go to the MIT Computer Center, the Science Museum, and to take in a variety of cultural offerings, and then returned home for three days of lessons, tutorials, field trips, or appointments. If you wondered about my earlier statement that Adam's education was expensive, you are probably beginning to get an idea of where the money went. Interspersed into Nathaniel's school vacations and summer terms the family went on trips to Scandinavia, to folk singing and dancing festivals in North Carolina, Michigan, and Vermont, and to Philadelphia where Fiona and Nathaniel had both studied and still had friends and colleagues. If it sounds like something of a whirlwind, it was, and still is, although more than five years have passed since they gave up on the Boston plan.

During this period we were of course able to see Adam and his family more often than before or since. His development certainly seemed to continue at a remarkable pace. I remember one visit to our house in May 1979, when Adam was five. I sat off in a corner with Adam and put together a cardboard Buckminster Fuller model of the earth that they had picked up at the Science Museum earlier that day. We were putting together the base of the model and I asked Adam if he knew what shape it was. Adam replied, "Pentagon." I remarked that it was really two pentagons, one at the top and the other at the bottom. "Sure, it's a pentagonal prism," my five-year-old companion remarked casually. I laughed out loud, and also gulped, and we continued putting the model together.

These visits were probably the best times we had together. Occasionally the family would stay overnight with us and we would enjoy leisurely breakfasts and long conversations. Most of the time Fiona and Adam stayed with Linda, Adam's teacher at The Learning Place. This arrangement was itself an indication of how interesting and attractive Adam is and how far people were willing to go to try to make the environment optimal for him.

One thing I remember about Adam during these visits to our house was that he did not like to be touched or picked up by anyone other than Nathaniel or Fiona. The three of them enjoyed an exceptionally warm and physically affectionate relationship, and while Lynn and I felt that we were also considered good friends and the object of significant caring and warmth, Adam himself did not much care for physical contact with us. I could understand not wanting to engage in physical activities with me, but Lynn has such a gift with children that this struck me as very surprising. With Randy McDaniel, for example, Lynn became a favorite cuddling object, and Randy was as much attracted to being with Lynn as to being a subject of my studies. With Adam this was not the case, or if it was, it was so in a very different way. He clearly did not want Lynn to tickle, hug, or tease as his parents did. Adam kept his distance.

As for the school and the rest of Boston's resources, the Konantovich family seemed to revel in them—at least for six months. Whatever happened at The Learning Place must have satisfied them because they sang its praises highly. In our own observations of classes at this unusual school, we saw a rather informally structured environment where students were usually free to come and go, but where a teacher was always monitoring the activity, more or less the way a good open classroom would operate. It was, of course, especially interesting to us to be able to watch two of our subjects at the same time, although, as it happened, they were not close friends. Certainly their relationship included the taint of rivalry, both in terms of their particular areas of strength and in friendships. Both Randy and Adam were sometimes drawn to one-upsmanship, as revealed for example in a humorous exchange Lynn observed between the two boys just before the end of the year. Randy and Adam were playing a game where Randy named a color for a sausage and Adam would say whether a sausage of that color existed. For example, Randy would say "blue sausages" and Adam would reply "no such thing." "Green sausages." "No such thing." "Red sausages." "There is such a thing . . ." A bit of an argument ensued when Randy tried "black sausages" and Adam replied "no such thing." Randy called him for an error, arguing that sausages are black when they are burnt.

By the end of the school year it had become clear to Fiona and Nathaniel that moving to Boston was not to be: The Learning Place seemed to be in a transition toward becoming a somewhat different and more traditional school and would no longer provide the kind of environment that was best for Adam's personal and social development. They reluctantly and painfully concluded that Adam would have to be educated in the matter of getting along socially somewhere else. Because of their own restricted schedule, Fiona and Nathaniel had also been unable to set up the kind of mentorships and tutorials we had originally envisioned in the Boston proposal. In fact, the only sustained experience Adam had that spring was to go to the MIT Computer Center every week and work on the computers.

Lynn worked at MIT and had been able to arrange for Adam to have access to the LOGO computer lab. The Konantoviches did take Adam there over a period of several months, but ultimately things did not work out well. The reasons for this were unclear.

The people around MIT computer laboratories tend to be high-level computer experts, but they also tend to be idiosyncratic, egocentric people, and they are not generally given to spending their time with five-year-olds, even exceptional ones. Furthermore, experts are not necessarily the most sensitive or innovative *teachers.* There were few who could (or would) bridge the gap between their own level of mastery, technical language, background, and expertise, and that of a gifted but still inexperienced computer programmer like Adam. MIT is basically for people who have already proven that they can do technical thinking at an advanced level and who are in the business of honing and refining their skills, pushing at the edges of their chosen fields.

Some of the "hackers" who inhabited the computer lab took an interest in Adam, but none in a sufficiently sustained tutorial manner. Adam's work on the computer was decidedly advanced for a five-year-old, but not dramatically so. On one of Adam's first visits to the lab Lynn watched him work on programming the LOGO "turtle" to draw geometric shapes. LOGO is written especially for children to help them easily engage in the programming process.[4] So far as Lynn was able to tell, Adam had many of the same difficulties drawing geometric figures as other children do, but it was difficult to tell what the causes of those difficulties were. He tired of the turtle fairly rapidly, preferring to spend the rest of his time performing more verbal manipulations with the machine, like writing a program to fill the screen with the word "Adam." Perhaps all that can be said of his grasp of computer programming was that it was neither instant nor intuitive, but that he showed no reluctance exploring the machine or what it could do.

As it happens, Lynn was also able to gain the benefit of some observations of Professor Hermina Sinclair, a close collaborator of Piaget's, who happened to be at MIT during one of Adam's visits to the computer lab. Lynn asked Mimi if she would give us her impressions of Adam, which she did. Here is an excerpt:

> As far as dealing with LOGO is concerned, I saw nothing very surprising, that is to say, nothing I wouldn't expect some bright (but not wildly exceptional) 7–8 year old to master in fairly short time. However, Adam does work very quickly, and very accurately, none of the annoying (to the children) mishaps such as forgetting a space, etc. happens (or only rarely). (Personal communication, 1980)

Professor Sinclair went on to say that she found her visit frustratingly short and that her curiosity about Adam was not at all satisfied by that brief encounter. As Adam was no longer visiting Boston regularly by the end of that school year, the opportunity for further observation did not present itself. This is a real pity, since Professor Sinclair is one of the world's wisest and most insightful observers of children. We would probably know a good deal more about Adam if we had been able to put the two of them together for a few more hours.

The honeymoon in Boston lasted only six months, and when it was over it became much more difficult for us to see Adam and his parents. No one is entirely sure why the experiment failed, but the causes were multiple, complex, and intertwined: the texture of daily life at The Learning Place was changing dramatically; the vast intellectual and academic resources of the Boston cognoscenti were more difficult to tap than we had originally expected; and I, too, contributed to their unmet expectations. I had hoped to use Adam as an opportunity to test a model educational plan for extraordinary children that had been brewing in the back of my mind for some time, using Tufts as a coordinating center and resource bank for gifted children in the greater Boston area. The libraries, computer facilities, and laboratories were to be made available for his use, student and faculty tutors were to volunteer as mentors to supervise his studies, and a student liaison was to work with Adam, his parents, and Tufts to coordinate the actual plan for how he would spend his time in a given week, month, or year. When the time came to actually implement such an effort, however,

I found I had other concerns and responsibilities that kept me from giving the project the attention it needed. Add all of these factors to the particular idiosyncracies of the Konantoviches themselves, and it seems that the experiment was doomed to failure before it ever began, although obviously none of us had seen it that way initially.

The Konantoviches certainly cannot be faulted for lack of effort. Their commitment to facilitating and developing Adam's promise is as extraordinary as Adam's talents themselves. Something very powerful moves them which is not quite the same as what moves the rest of us: a sense of mission, a responsibility for assisting their son to develop his abilities so that he will be able to take his place in the world. They are often as amazed and awed by Adam as those who know him less well. Yet, as his parents, they cannot briefly marvel at his uniqueness and the power of his mind and then turn their attention back to more pressing personal concerns. They are constantly pushed and challenged to keep up with Adam's voracious appetite for knowledge and instruction. The role of the parents in selecting educational experiences, monitoring progress, and providing psychological support is protean in any family with a child prodigy. For the Konantoviches, the unique range and depth of Adam's abilities has multiplied this responsibility to staggering proportions.

Some years ago I made up the term "omnibus prodigy" to try to describe Adam. He was different from the other children I was following in that his talents were not bounded within a single domain, nor did he seem to have the combination of general academic ability plus an extreme special talent that characterized some of my other subjects. I thought that the term "omnibus prodigy" served to capture the fact that his gifts ranged across several domains and defied simple categorization.

In fact, in some respects Adam did not really fit into my theory of prodigies at all. I had been looking for children with a single isolated area of great talent within an overall typical mental structure. Adam's gifts were not only not singular, they were, at least by his parents' description, deep, powerful, symbolic, theoretical, and without the usual boundaries. If I had been more wedded to my theory at the time, I would have simply thrown him out of my sample or at least dismissed his case as anomalous, and gone about tidying up the theory of prodigies that I was working on. When I heard that Halbert Robinson thought Adam was perhaps the most gifted child ever tested on the Stanford-Binet, I decided that I could stand having a messier theory. Less facetiously, I sensed that any theory worth its salt should be able to say something about talents like Adam's as well as about the more specific and "modular" ones I was used to.

Excerpts from a letter from Fiona to Tom O'Brien at The Learning

Place illustrate the scope of Adam's interests, the thoughtfulness and care his parents gave to planning his educational experiences, and also some flavor of their energy and dedication to assisting Adam in his intellectual explorations:

Dear Tom,

After our conversation a few days ago, I tried to give coherent shape to my notions of what an education for a person like Adam ought to include. As I stressed to you on the telephone, these thoughts are only a beginning of what a curriculum for a child of his sort ought to be since I am neither a philosopher who is familiar with the phenomenology of human thought, an educator with a familiarity with professional practices, a student of the domains of human knowledge nor an omnibus genius. But I am a thoughtful parent who has observed Adam's learning close at hand and, of course, a professional in a related field so I have a few hunches to begin with. As a basic premise, I take as a truth that Adam will absorb content and fact effortlessly when that content is interesting and relevant to a wider learning experience. . . .

In light of this, it seems clear to us that his requirements in teaching personnel are for persons of the greatest degree of professional competence so that the theoretical as well as the specifics, the developmental, historical, the possible as well as the known and the scope as well as the praxis of any field can be a part of his work with these skilled mentors. We are also talking about persons at this level of competence who like and can enjoy the emotional state of small children. A tall order to be well filled, we think, by a fairly small number of persons likely to be concentrated where persons of professional eminence and intellectual playfulness, in the finest sense of that word, abound; if anywhere, in a university community.

In terms of the areas of study which are, or will likely soon be, important to Adam, several stand out at once. The possibilities for fruitful study in this area [of symbol systems would be] enhanced if he were to be able to work systematically with someone who was involved in the structure of language, of communication, of the shape of human communication phenomenology, of philology, etc. . . . Clearly the entire area of mathematics requires attention by those who lay out his education. But the other route which takes him into mathematics is the path of dimensions. Shapes, relationships, geometry, topology, curved and flat space, all these evoke not only his serious learning, as we customarily think about it, but evoke that high level of playfulness which penetrates past easy answers, wears out and upsets teachers of ordinary competence and delights the special mathematician. . . .

Musically, Adam would benefit greatly by working with a person skilled in composition, in music theory, in ethnomusicology (to prevent the development of Western musical myopia), and in general musicology. He began composing at 2 years, as I mentioned to you previously, and has been actively asking for a mentor experienced in this area.

He is currently studying the violin with an outstanding violinist and, in whatever setting we find ourselves, would need to continue that course of study. He is viewed as an outstandingly talented musician by this outstandingly talented musician.

There are areas in the traditional course of study for any youngster which, for Adam, should be pursued in a wider and broader frame of reference. Social Studies is the most prominent of these which springs to mind. Adam does not, I think, need to pursue a unit on the Eskimo, land and people. Rather I believe that it makes sense for him to have access to anthropologists, cross-cultural psychologists, economists, political historians, geographers, folklorists, psychiatrists, and those whose expertise and considerations take them into the realm of human experience through diverse channels so that he may inquire, explore, question, and, perhaps, finally, begin to comprehend the nature of the society of humans. This broad avenue of search is appropriate to him as a long-term study just as mathematics or music is, I feel, because his prodigious capacity to wonder, to absorb and to synthesize should be fed, ideally, by those who can help him inquire as broadly as he is able, not by those who would give him "facts" as if they were answers.

If Adam is to realize his rich promise as what Dr. David Feldman calls an omnibus genius, then he must have an omnibus education.

In line with that, those who study the abstract domains of human thought, the history of ideas, the nature of reality, the ethics of human life, the process by which decisions collectively and individually are to be made, the abstractions and theologies of humanity and its literatures, these persons are, if anything, more important to Adam's education and realization of capacities than any of the persons referred to above. Without access to philosophers and historians, etc., to continue the process I have referred to in this letter, the most vital part of a practical education for a person who can reasonably be expected to have significant impact on his society, if he can realize his talents, may well be left unattended.... Let me remind you, too, that it is important that Adam feel that although he may be divergent from the norm, he is appropriate and normal for himself and that he learn to secure and return the affection, trust, and positive regard of his peers. For that he needs an environment in which he can be with age-mates, non-age-mates and supportive adults in appropriate activities. His congenial nature and amiable personality make this easier than it might be, for which I am deeply grateful! My contention is that to enclose him in the preconceived limits of a customary educational experience is to deprive him of what he needs and can profitably employ in the flowering of his enormous gifts and, perhaps, ultimately to deprive ourselves of what he might have otherwise have been able to return to us as members of his culture when he is able to make those contributions which he is now only potentially capable of.

This letter is typical of Nathaniel and Fiona's articulate, yet insistent, inquiries regarding assistance in Adam's education. Despite the fact that Adam has a playful, easygoing side, there is an intensity to his studies that few instructors can accommodate. As a result, Fiona and Nathaniel's overtures to teachers have often been met with less than satisfactory responses. It may even be that the form and extent of their request is such that it would be impossible to comply except to adopt the same degree of commitment given by the Konantoviches. This has rarely happened. Still, many have recognized Adam's talents as genuinely worthy of special efforts and have tried to accommodate to his seemingly boundless enthusiasm for exploring fields that interest him. In retrospect, this was exactly the problem with the Boston experiment. Although a number of people were interested in giving Adam some of their time, nobody but the Konantoviches themselves were willing to spend the amount of time and energy needed to monitor Adam's needs, secure appropriate mentors and tutors, and coordinate the variety of lessons and activities that filled his days.

For these, and perhaps other reasons, Adam's Boston commute was terminated: Fiona wrote to us in the fall of 1980 expressing their deep sense of disappointment about the failure of the experiment, and particularly about the loss of The Learning Place.

Adam was, unfortunately, unable to continue at The Learning Place. .... The school may well not survive as an institution consonant with or recognizable in its former shape. His sadness at this loss was profound and pervasive. We are all struggling to cope with it and with the void which it leaves in his life.

AFTER BOSTON

Adam has spent the last four years, up to and including the present time, in search of programs near and far as the struggle to find an adequate school environment continues. The search has led them to an open school in a nearby suburb (three months), a special program almost two hours away in a different state (four months), a tutoring arrangement with a gifted education specialist of yet another school system (six months), and forays to a nearby city to see if something could be done by the people at one of the major universities there. All their efforts have met with little or only temporary success or satisfaction. The Konantoviches have also pushed their home school district almost continuously to be more responsible and responsive to Adam's special needs, and they have scoured the region for other school districts that might do a better job of providing him with the necessary stimulation.

The process of finding resources for his more specific interests and needs continues. By the time Adam was seven or eight he had begun to focus more and more on music, and the need for composition and instrumental teachers has been a pressing one. As usual, Adam seems to be moving apace. In the fall of 1983 Fiona was invited to present a report to a professional meeting detailing the Konantoviches' experiences in rearing a gifted child. Adam was also invited to prepare some of his music to be played for the audience. According to Fiona, when Adam heard of his invitation he announced, "Great! I'll compose a symphony for it." And he did. Fiona and Nathaniel hired a quintet to record the symphony, and the piece was played during the session. A professional pianist also offered to participate in the session. Comparing Adam's compositions at age nine with those of Mozart and Mendelssohn at roughly the same ages, she judged Adam's work to be extraordinary and complex, more intellectual, and, while somewhat less musical when compared with the other two, "difficult to play but well worth the effort." More recently the dean of a prominent conservatory, himself a notable composer, found Adam's compositions astounding. "Works like these," he judged, "do not even come along once in a lifetime!"

This development toward serious musical study both delights and worries Fiona and Nathaniel. Fiona says she is concerned that Adam will become another "violinist psychotic" like so many others. In a phone conversation with her several years ago Fiona also announced that she'd decided that Adam finally really "needs an education." I asked what they thought they'd been doing up until that time. She replied, "That was intro." As our conversation continued, Fiona asked (not at all rhetorically) how one finds an Aristotle to tutor Adam. I replied that I didn't know, but that we could use a few. She then reported that Adam walked by and remarked, "Oh great, I'm going to die at thirty-three" (as did Alexander the Great, Aristotle's pupil).

I think it best to close this section on the Konantoviches' response to their extraordinary child by noting that I am constantly moved by their genuine, sincere, and deep feelings about their mission and by their courage and strength to persist in their convictions. Their efforts on Adam's behalf are nothing short of staggering. They inspire awe and wonder, and perhaps a little guilt too. The rest of us, parents and teachers, are rarely putting anywhere near as much into the education of our children as they are putting into theirs.

The Lemke Family

Now consider the case of Leslie Lemke (his real name), profoundly handicapped and seemingly beyond all remedial efforts of medical science or education, in order to underscore the critical role of environmental forces —and in particular the right parents—in identifying and nurturing individual ability. I have tried to make the point that even in extreme cases of talent such as those described in this book, exogenous conditions must be favorable if that talent is to emerge and flourish; in particular, the specific gift characteristic of the prodigy requires a unique response, a special environmental niche for it to express itself. But what of the child who seems to possess no gifts whatsoever?

Leslie Lemke was such a child. He is not a youngster I have followed personally but a case I have read about and seen on film.[5] He provides a stark contrast to Adam's extraordinarily facile and wide-ranging mind. Leslie is in many respects as far from Adam as one can be in terms of talent and still be considered human. In fact, there were those who had some real doubts about whether Leslie Lemke should be considered human at all. According to written accounts in the popular media, Leslie was about as hopeless a case as one could imagine. As a newborn in the early 1950s he was assessed to be severely mentally retarded and to suffer from debilitating cerebral palsy. For some unclear medical reason his eyes had been surgically removed shortly after birth. Tactile and auditory stimulation produced no discernible reaction in this tragically abnormal child. His parents, presumably advised that Leslie's condition was terminal, had relinquished him to institutional care. For some time he remained in the hospital while the medical personnel waited for him to die. After six months and many thousands of dollars, Leslie was still hanging on. To cut costs, hospital officials contacted May Lemke, a woman in her fifties who had provided occasional hospice care, and asked if she would take the hopeless Leslie home with her until he died.

According to the media accounts, May agreed to take Leslie but refused to accept the medical opinion that he was doomed. A deeply religious woman, she had already raised five children of her own. She believed strongly in the God-given integrity of each of the Lord's creatures and, with all due respect to the medical profession, preferred to trust in God's plans for Leslie rather than the doctors' prognoses.

From the day that May and her husband, Joe, took little Leslie into their home by the side of a lake in Wisconsin, they began to teach and love him. He gave them absolutely nothing in return, at least nothing that parents usually get. For more than fifteen years he remained unresponsive to any and every effort at interaction and stimulation. And yet May persisted. Her curriculum was total and continuous, covering everything from helping Leslie suck from a bottle to showing him when she was crying by touching his hand to her tears. May's faith in the possibility of Leslie's educability was unshakable in spite of his unresponsiveness; it was an expression of her own faith in God. God simply would not have placed Leslie in her care without a reason, and it was not for her to question why He might have chosen to do so.

Without any help from so-called professionals, in fact in the face of discouragement and skepticism from them, May and Joe devised their own teaching methods, their own prosthetics, their own techniques for introducing and sustaining Leslie's experience with the outside world. They had a chain-link fence installed around the property and "walked" Leslie up and down the perimeter of the yard by standing behind him, placing his hands in successive holes in the fence, and pushing him along. They religiously took this constitutional every day. Leslie finally stood on his own for the first time, supported by that fence, when he was sixteen years old. From this beginning, May tried coaxing Leslie to move away from the fence, and, months later, he could walk a few steps on his own.

May prayed for Leslie every day, asking for nothing short of a miracle. Although he had been given up for dead, he had managed to survive. After showing absolutely no response to her and Joe's efforts for so many years, at last some small progress was being made. Dare she ask for more? It is difficult to know where miracles begin and where extraordinariness takes over. Certainly what happened over the next few years is unbelievable if not miraculous. And whether or not one chooses to believe that God played a part, there is no question that May and Joe Lemke played theirs.

One day when Leslie was about eighteen years old, May noticed that he seemed to enjoy playing with a string she had tied around a package, plucking at it with his finger. Sensitive to any activity Leslie initiated on his own, May puzzled about what he might be trying to tell her about himself. She concluded—perhaps grandiosely—that plucking the string was Leslie's way of making music. From then on music was added to the Lemke household in a serious way. She played him records. She sang to him. She bought a secondhand piano and tried to show Leslie how it worked. As usual, nothing much seemed to happen.

And then there was the miracle.

It happened in the winter of 1971. May was awakened by the sound of music. It was 3 A.M. Someone was playing Tchaikovsky's Piano Concerto No. 1. She shook Joe. "Did you leave the radio on?" she asked.

"No," he said.

"Then where's the music coming from?" She swung out of bed and turned on a living room light. It dimly illuminated Leslie's room. Leslie was at the piano. May saw a smile glowing on his face.

He had never before got out of bed on his own. He had never seated himself at the piano. He had never voluntarily or deliberately struck the keys with his fingers. Now he was actually playing a concerto—and with deftness and confidence.

May fell to her knees. *Thank you, dear God, You didn't forget Leslie.* [6]

I have seen May describe this event on film. Reading popular accounts of May's dedication and faith is dramatic. Watching her recount Leslie's passage with simplicity, faith, and awe has been more than enough to bring tears to my eyes. For in her own way May is as gifted an individual as anyone else described in this book, maybe as gifted as anyone, period. She refused to be daunted by Leslie's glaring handicaps and persevered in providing a rich, stimulating, and loving home for him long after anyone else would have despaired and admitted defeat. While we are not used to recognizing and appreciating as a gift such pure and unwavering dedication or such unremitting tenacity in searching for educational experiences, it is often a crucial one to co-incidence.

May and Joe Lemke have been given what is in a way a humble gift, but it is nonetheless a rare one. Never have I heard of people giving so much and receiving so little for so long. May shows, in as dramatic and clear a fashion as any child prodigy or savant, what a pure gift is like. It operates in the absence of great general intellectual capability, of encouragement or support from authorities, organizations, or bureaucracies. And it will become evident only if other conditions coincide. For May, the opportunity to care for a child like Leslie is what allowed its expression. And for Leslie, it was May's gift of faith and Joe's support that probably kept him alive and that undoubtedly helped him to finally find a pathway into the world.

Leslie's (and May's) story does not end on that winter's night. From this beginning, Leslie developed a repertoire of gospel songs, jazz, and rock tunes, all learned from records or radio and played from memory. Unfortunately, we have no information about how Leslie learned to play the piano. But we do know that after years of virtually total unresponsiveness to people or the world he burst forth with capabilities overwhelmingly beyond those that anyone, except perhaps May and Joe (and maybe Leslie), thought possible, becoming able to express himself through music. And his breakthrough at the piano led to speech, first an occasional word, and eventually short, context-appropriate utterances. By the age of twenty-eight he still could not hold a normal conversation, but he could ask questions, answer them, and make simple statements.

Leslie Lemke is, of course, hardly a prodigy. His gifts are those of a savant. They operate in strange ways, isolated and fragmented in a fashion few human beings have to deal with. Yet over time his behavior has become more and more coherent (from our point of view). He can have something like a conversation. He can dress and eat more or less by himself. He has joined the human community to an ever greater degree. It has taken thirty years to get him this far and may take thirty more years to get him further. Unfortunately, May is herself now in her eighties, so it is likely that Leslie will spend some of his years in the care of others. On the other hand, if it is possible for Leslie to be doing what he is doing, perhaps May will live until 125 to show us, once again, that miracles do happen.

Savant and Prodigy

The message of Leslie Lemke and May's miracle is profound, and in many ways it is the same as the lessons learned from Adam and his family. Leslie's entry into the society of responsive and responding human beings was the product of unremitting dedication and unflagging attention to the most minuscule cues about the stimuli that could reach him from the outside world. The Lemke educational strategy shared many important features with the Konantovich one, although the level of intellectual activity in the two families could hardly have been more disparate. Both families provided continuous activities and information for their children, coupled with constant availability, great affection, and an enduring responsiveness to the child's needs and interests. Both families were flexible in their curricular plans, readily incorporating what they perceived to be child-initiated changes and additions into the types of activities offered. They both possessed an unusual willingness to act immediately on requests or other signs of interest, virtually regardless of time or place, and both sets of parents possessed an incredibly strong conviction—transmitted with great love, physical affection, and even vehemence—that their child was extraordinarily special and wonderful. In both cases, I think that it was the delicate interplay of these family qualities with qualities of the children themselves that allowed their abilities—which in one case were massively abundant and in the other, quite severely limited—to emerge.

One cannot help but wonder what would have happened if, by some twist of fate, May and Joe had ended up with Adam to foster, and Leslie had appeared in the Konantoviches' midst. It seems to me that much of the Konantoviches' child-rearing revolved around the delight of interacting with a very bright, inquisitive, and talented child; perhaps finding themselves with a child from the other end of the spectrum would have yielded less intensive efforts. It might also have worked in the opposite way with someone like May. My guess is that if May were asked to care for an infant like Adam, who was already conversing at six months, she would have loved him and cared for him well, but I doubt she would have nurtured his talents in the same way she tried to coax Leslie out of his dark and lonely world.

Leslie Lemke would no doubt have languished, if not perished, but for the herculean efforts of May and Joe. It is equally true that Adam Konantovich would not be doing the things he is doing today were it not for the *very different* things that Fiona and Nathaniel and the others they have brought into the process have done on Adam's behalf. Though both sets of parents seem blessed with extraordinary energy well beyond the average, and both are extreme in the proportion of their energies that go to these fortunate children, the two families are still very different from each other. Just imagine what Adam's life would be like now if May and Joe had been his parents, or Leslie in Fiona and Nathaniel's considerably more intellectualized and academic environment.

I think that with extreme situations like those of Adam and Leslie we have the opportunity to witness the most delicate coordination of complementary forces at work. One malfunction in the system may cause the whole thing to go haywire. No one can really say for sure, of course. The point is simply that one never knows the extent of an individual's biologically determined potential unelss the *maximum* and the *optimum* set of environmental conditions is provided, including the most appropriate human and cultural catalysts to bring forth the qualities that are there waiting to be developed. Rarely if ever are the conditions optimal. Furthermore, I can't imagine how one would devise reliable ways to determine just when such conditions are met. But when we see extreme cases, like the Konantoviches, or perhaps even more clearly, the Lemke family, we are able to use their example as a kind of yardstick against which to measure the distance that the rest of us have gone toward providing precisely those conditions for bringing about full expression of our children's potential.

I do not intend to suggest that parents seriously attempt to measure up to the Konantovich-Lemke yardstick. If what I have written about Adam Konantovich, Leslie, and their parents leads to the conclusion that the only adequate way to raise a child is to give it everything you've got twenty-four hours a day, then I have failed to make my point. These cases are extreme ones. They were chosen because they were extreme, thus highlighting the role of families in developing talent. They were selected because they show, beyond a doubt as far as I am concerned, that the responses of those in the environment are crucial to optimal expression of potential.

One of the central features of co-incidence, then, is the environment's response to the child's talent. Even a child with extraordinarily great potential will not develop into a prodigy unless people, institutions, and technologies are shared with him or her in just the right ways and at just the right times. Likewise, other, less intrinsically talented children will not achieve their full potential (in whatever way that may be) unless there are thoughtful, sustained efforts to provide conditions that engage and support the expression of their capabilities. Unfortunately, there are few specific, definite rules of conduct for bringing out potential in children. There are also no shortcuts, formulas, or curricula that will work without fail for everyone, even though there are certainly enough "experts" who claim otherwise. The families of prodigies show us situations where a child of truly exceptional talents has appeared and demands a response to his talents. It is not the parents but the children in the families I have studied who have initiated and, indeed, demanded sustained attention and effort. In each of the six families, responses to the child's talents were considered ones, specific and dictated by the characteristics and proclivities of the individual child. What the experts who offer recommendations for producing "superbabies" and gifted children have ignored is the delicate quality of the relationship between children's interests and proclivities and parents' efforts to develop talent. Parents can provide enriching and stimulating experiences for their children, and should be sensitive observers of their children's preferences and interests. They can respond to their indications of interest and ability, encouraging and facilitating their progress. But they should not force-feed or push their children into activities. The primary impetus must come from the children themselves. They, not their parents, must possess the motivation and drive to pursue excellence. The families of the prodigies I have studied demonstrate the importance of this point quite clearly.

The families of Einstein, Darwin, Freud, Newton, Locke, Mozart, or Wiener must have done, at the minimum, what was necessary for their offspring to be prepared to accomplish extraordinary work. Chances are that the early educations of these men were not, on the whole, as engineered and pressured as they are in a "superbaby" environment but rather were an expression of the particular tastes, styles, beliefs, traditions, and customs of their families and cultures. In few cases were the early environments hothouses for early growth, except insofar as the conditions for such growth happened to be present anyway. Mozart's father certainly pushed him hard, but this was largely in response to, not independent of, the child's talent. This is not to say that we should ignore the possibilities for enhanced early learning, only that there is no particular reason to believe that genuinely great achievement is made possible by artificially contrived techniques of stimulation that operate independently of the unique qualities of a given child and a family's response to those qualities. The prescription for successful child-rearing, in other words, must be specific to the child, the family, the culture, and the time. And there is no shortcut to factoring that complex equation. None.

Families and Co-incidence

One cannot comprehend the development of potential without understanding when and how the environment responds to it. As many different forms and qualities of human biological potential as there are, there are an equal number of ideal reciprocating environmental responses, and both must co-occur if we are to see the full expression of ability. The error of virtually every educational prescription I have seen is that it makes things too simple, as if there were a single best method of fostering talent, and we have only to guess what it is. If there were such a single best method to bring forth human potential, it is reasonable to guess that it would have been discovered.

This chapter has described the most intensive and responsive involvement in child-rearing and education that I am aware of. Adam Konantovich has had the most intense early experience of any gifted child I know of, and that experience is driven by a deep and powerful belief that Adam's gifts require such an effort. Given their expectations that Adam may well revolutionize some body (or bodies) of knowledge, they have set themselves some considerable challenges and responsibilities. But perhaps if not in this generation with this child, then maybe it will happen in the next generation, or the next. There are factors in the co-incidence equation that go beyond the fate of one particular child at one particular time in one particular culture, and there is only so much that can be done to maximize the potential for outstanding contributions. The domain itself, the cultural milieu, even the political climate exert their influences, as we shall see.

Despite this reminder that there are factors in the realization of talent that lie outside an individual's control, several critical factors can be influenced. The support of the prodigy's family is as crucial to the process of development as is any aspect of the child's talent or personality. To find a young child with prodigious talent may not be so difficult; to sustain that initial force is the burden of all who become closely involved with the child. If a family is not willing to make the commitment to respond to the demands of talent, the prodigy's gifts will probably languish or at least will fail to develop fully. A prodigy is a group enterprise, and nowhere is this need for a team approach more evident than in the coordination and organization of the child's education. Whatever else prodigies are, they are still children, and they are not able to make many of the decisions that will be crucial for their future. For better or worse, these decisions fall to parents and advisors, to teachers and patrons.

In several of the other families in my research, the tension between the demands of the child's talent and the perfectly legitimate needs of the rest of the family were worked out in a number of different ways. I believe that the chess players, for example, abandoned the game partly because the price was too high for other family members. For children who continue to develop extraordinary talent, the families have continued to orient their lives substantially around the demands of the child's education.

In the case of Nils Kirkendahl, which we will discuss next, the Kirkendahls readily admit that their decision to put their resources into Nils's musical education came at his younger brother Loki's expense, even though their younger child may have been equally talented musically. It simply was not possible to do what had to be done for two children at the same time.

When extreme talent shows itself, it demands nothing less than the willingness of one or both of the parents to give up almost everything else to make sure that the talent is developed. Sustaining an active career of one's own and bringing up a prodigy at the same time is not often feasible. On this basis, I suppose that one could predict fewer prodigies in this society in the future if trends continue toward more women working full time, unless some form of social organization picks up the slack.

Finally, the lesson of Leslie Lemke's family is that it is impossible to reckon the extent of human potential without total commitment and absolute faith. To be able to bring forth Leslie's gifts in the face of decades of discouragement is itself a gift as precious and rare as the most extreme case of a prodigy. It is well to keep this in mind as we continue our efforts to understand how co-incidence works in cases of extreme talent.

6

Choosing Teachers and Changing Directions

ONE of the myths about prodigies is that their talents are so over-whelming that they will be fulfilled regardless of what happens in their environment. My experience with prodigies makes it clear that precisely the opposite is true. The more powerful and specific the gift, the more the need for active, sustained, specialized intervention from those who are responsible for the child's development. The children I know with prodi-gious talents often have a remarkable sense of "inner confidence," which seems to reflect an internal awareness of the presence of a gift and the expectation that it will continue to flourish. Yet, while the children them-selves display a kind of noblesse oblige with respect to their abilities, this quality in no way reduces the reality of their need for massive educational support from parents, mentors, and teachers.

For virtually all fields in which prodigies perform, the most critical source of knowledge and skill is teachers. Whatever degree of confidence the child has—indeed, whatever degree of talent—it will come to fruition only under the guidance of teachers who are themselves greatly gifted in the ability to catalyze potential into durable achievement. It is rare that a single teacher can direct the entire course of development of a prodigious talent. Benjamin Bloom and his associates have found with high-level performers in several fields (who were not necessarily prodigies), that at least three teachers at different levels of expertise played significant roles in the performers' development.[1] Prodigies may study with even more teachers, since they begin the process of mastering a field at a very early age: they may be on their second or third instructor at an age when most students are just beginning their first lessons.

Prodigies and Their Teachers

The instructional histories of the children I have studied have been varied, but in one way or another teachers have been central for each child's development. In the case of Nils Kirkendahl, as we shall see in detail later in this chapter, the choice of teachers set the entire tone and direction of his musical education: the kinds of decisions the Kirkendahls made about selecting teachers had as much to do with the type of career preparation Nils would receive as it did with issues of educational philosophy, curriculum, or teachers' personalities. The career implications of teacher selection in the other five cases have not been as portentous, although teachers have certainly been central in the development of the children's talents.

FRANKLIN MONTANA AND RICKY VELAZQUEZ

Often the teachers are themselves a source of insight into the learning styles of the students they teach. In the case of my two chess prodigies, for example, the most striking thing about their teachers was the contrast in instructional technique, overall philosophy, and personal style. It is difficult to imagine that two such disparate styles could have developed such equally fine players, but the differences between Ricky's and Franklin's teachers were also reflected in the two boys' quite different personalities and approaches to learning.

Franklin began studying with George Kane (his real name) at age six, after two years of relying on his father and on chess books to improve his game. George was a former Chess Olympian and a U.S. Master player who, in his late twenties, was making a meager living as a private chess coach and teacher at several colleges and high schools in and around New York City. In spite of the lack of financial reward for his work, George was acknowledged by the chess world as one of the best teachers in the country. The fact that Franklin was taking lessons from a master teacher, however, was not in and of itself extraordinary in the chess world. Because chess as a career is such a chancy way to earn a living, master teachers in this field are far more accessible than in many others. They basically earn their living by giving lessons, and they can't always be too choosy about their students' talents. Unlike the intense competition for master-level instruction in other fields—for example, music—even relatively unskilled but dedicated chess players often have the opportunity to learn from the chess greats. There was, of course, no problem of meager talent with Franklin, who showed about as much promise as a six-year-old could.

George Kane's approach to chess play and instruction was based on discipline and organization. He had developed and written about an elaborate chess curriculum which he tailored for Franklin to suit his specific needs as a player.[2] George and his associate Bruce Pandolfini (his real name) prepared hundreds of flash cards showing various opening, midgame, and closing positions that Franklin was required to memorize and be ready to play for each week's lesson. George stressed what might be called chess fundamentals: rigorous discipline, technical mastery of the game, and outstanding preparation for tournaments, including the analysis of opponents' games and the careful preparation of both tactics and overall strategy before competition. Although George's serious, no-nonsense and no-frills approach to the game seemed well suited to Franklin's own serious and intense style, the boy was hardly a passive receptacle for George's chess insights and wisdom. Franklin had a mind of his own and constantly challenged George's instructions, analyses, tactics—indeed every aspect of the curriculum. Their lessons were like a test of two strong wills, one of which happened to reside in a small child's body.

In contrast to George's intense, serious, disciplined, and systematic approach to teaching the game of chess, John Collins (his real name), who was Ricky Velazquez's teacher, took a more folksy, historical, and organic approach to the enterprise. John is a Life Master, an ageless senior statesman of the chess world, and teacher of champions (perhaps most notably Bobby Fischer and William Lombardy).[3] He holds forth in his small Manhattan apartment, which is cluttered with chess books, memorabilia, and, often, people from the chess world. John Collins is an endless source of chess lore and history, and his enthusiasm and love for the game rubs off a little bit on everyone who enters his presence.

His teaching is as low-key and informal as George's is intense. Mr.

Collins's presentation and attitude toward chess is simply that it is a great
and enjoyable way to spend one's time—it is not simulated war, but fun
for the analytic minded. An astute and wise teacher, he is able to assess
a player's style and level of skill after five or ten minutes at the chessboard.
His lessons then build on this assessment in an effort to guide his student's
progress to higher and more elaborated levels of understanding and ability.
Unlike George Kane's orderly and logical drill and practice, John Collins's
teaching focuses almost exclusively on the game board. His lessons are
devoted to reviewing and analyzing games that his students have played,
presenting particularly instructive games from other students or competitors, or playing and analyzing historical matches that, to his mind, will be
both illustrative of specific points and fun too. Armed with an encyclope-
dic knowledge of the game and its history, Collins draws freely from his
sources to challenge and excite his students, using an instructional process
that can best be described as organic and spontaneous, yet highly prepared
and thoughtful.

His style is to make chess as much fun as possible. Lessons are frequently interrupted by laughter, chiding, joking, and chess anecdotes.
Collins's home is one of the centers of the United States chess world,
perhaps *the* center, and John himself is as close to royalty as one gets in
chess without becoming a world champion. He is known to all, loved by
most, and respected as a leader and great teacher by all who know or know
of him. He inspires loyalty not by intensity and analysis, as George Kane
does, but by simply being the warm, fun-loving, and dedicated man that
he is. He is, to use his own word, a totally "chessical" person.

Ricky Velazquez fit this environment like a glove, just as Franklin was
perfectly at home with George Kane's style. Certainly the fit between
student and teacher was no chance occurrence, since both Franklin's and
Ricky's fathers had chosen their son's teachers after extensive investigation. But the matches seemed to be strikingly good ones, almost as if the
teacher-student pairs had somehow been preplanned. I had the unmistak-
able impression that if the boys had been sent to each other's teachers,
their playing careers would have been significantly different. In fact, Bill
Velazquez had met George Kane and decided not to engage him as Ricky's
teacher. Bill felt that George was too young to offer the kind of chess
education that would benefit Ricky most. In contrast, Franklin's chess
career all but ended when Kane moved to the West Coast and left him in
the care of another highly competent and respected teacher. With George's
absence there was simply no one around who was able to challenge,
encourage, wrangle with, and earn the respect and affection of young
Franklin. While this is assuredly not the only reason Franklin began to lose

interest in chess, it may have been the most important one. The loss of a teacher can be a difficult blow.

RANDY McDANIEL

Like Franklin and Ricky, Randy McDaniel also has had a sustained relationship with a single teacher, but because that teacher is also his father, the relationship is much more complex and the issue of compatibility of personalities, instructional technique, and learning style is difficult to assess. Darren McDaniel has overseen Randy's writing (as well as many of his other studies) since Randy first rolled a piece of paper into a typewriter. Since Darren himself is a writer both by profession and inclination, he has been able to evaluate Randy's work with a sharp analytic eye and an appreciation for fluency of both style and substance. Many writers believe that it is impossible to teach the craft of writing to others, and while Darren does not subscribe to this strong position, neither has he been didactic with his son. His strategy with Randy has not been to intervene or criticize; rather he has sought to guide Randy's development by selecting readings illustrating particular genres, themes, or styles, and by discussing Randy's own writing projects. This instructional strategy was consciously selected. Both Darren and Jeanne felt that more active, critical intervention into Randy's writing would only stifle his creativity and interfere with Randy's exploration of his own literary voice. Like John Collins, Darren's teaching techniques have been largely organic and responsive. He has basically let Randy set the agenda in terms of interest and focus and has worked within this framework to explain, discuss, and indicate literary themes and writing styles.

The special quality of Darren's relationship with his son has had its drawbacks as well as benefits. Randy could not have hoped for a more ardent supporter or impassioned teacher, nor would anyone else have been so constantly available to work on Randy's writing. What may be most unusual about Darren's role as Randy's teacher is that it has continued in reasonably full force for more than ten years. While it is not at all unusual for a parent to be a prodigy's first teacher, it is uncommon for the parent to remain the only, or primary, source of instruction. This situation has persisted in Randy's case largely because formal instruction in writing is difficult to come by and because schooling in institutional settings has had sporadic success at best. Randy has attended a summer camp for the past several years where writing is a major focus, but even here sustained and systematic instruction is not available. The camp publishes a daily newspaper to which Randy contributes, and he gets to knock around at the camp with other children who like to write and who do it well, but there is little in the way of individualized or intensive instruction. Randy's relationship with his father has provided by far the bulk of his preparation as a writer. It may have been the only way to do it.

BILLY DEVLIN AND ADAM KONANTOVICH

Unlike the other children in my study, Billy Devlin and Adam Konantovich have not had sustained instruction with one teacher. Their interests and needs seem to have been better served by engaging the services of a variety of tutors and providing supplemental "enriching" experiences such as frequent forays to museums, universities, and laboratories, as well as correspondence (and occasionally meetings) with leading practitioners in different fields. I do not think it is an accident that these two children are the ones in my group whose talents seem to be the least specialized: their interests cover a fairly wide range, and their parents have sought educational experiences that address their breadth of interest.

When we met Billy Devlin, he was receiving individualized tutoring in mathematics for several hours on Saturday mornings. His instructor, Mr. Salton, was an engineer who had done some postgraduate work in mathematics. Although he was neither a professional mathematician nor a teacher, he had been recommended to the Devlins as someone who was competent mathematically, and who was patient, thorough, kind. He was also somewhat familiar with children who possessed unusual abilities and interests. Because the tutorial relationship was as new for Mr. Salton as it was for Billy, he had selected to begin working with Billy on a prepared curriculum for advanced high-school mathematics. It was as an observer of this intensive activity that, in part, had led me to think that Billy was going to be a mathematician. I had heard of Billy somewhat earlier from Professor Julian Stanley at Johns Hopkins, who runs a major program for "mathematically precocious youth." Stanley had conferred his blessing on Billy and later had claimed that he was "Nobel prize potential," a prediction he shared with Billy's family.

Observing Billy it was clear fairly early on, however, that his interests were broader than mathematics. He was doing well in the curriculum; his level of mastery at six was more like that of a high-school freshman or sophomore. But Billy's spontaneous conversation revealed that he was equally fascinated with the planets and the stars, with telescopes and computers, with physics and astronauts: in short, he was strongly attracted to a broad range of the natural sciences. And although Billy was formally tutored only in mathematics, his parents also diligently worked to provide additional contacts with physicists, chemists, astronomers, geneticists, and biologists, as well as to visit a wide variety of museums. The core of Billy's education, then, was not spent exclusively with a carefully selected master teacher in a field that it was clear he would pursue, but rather consisted of supplementary tutoring in one area where he had expressed interest and obvious talent. This pattern of providing supplementary, accelerated instruction and experiences has continued, more or less unchanged, through the years.

The same pattern has also characterized Adam Konantovich's education, only more so. Mentors and tutors have been Adam's major source of educational stimulation since his second year. The Konantoviches spend an enormous amount of time and energy arranging, organizing, implementing, changing, rearranging, evaluating, and raising the money to pay for Adam's tutors. Because his interests are so wide-ranging, Adam does not really fit my notion of the prodigy as a special-purpose organism. As time has passed, interestingly enough, he has concentrated more and more of his energy on music, and many of his most sustained relationships with teachers to date have been in this domain. But the pattern from age two onward has been for Adam to spend time with experts in each of the fields in which he has expressed an interest. He has never had fewer than three or four such relationships during the period we have known him, and in a given six-month period (about the half-life of many of his tutorial arrangements), he may see as many as six or eight tutors a week. Consider, for example, Adam's self-selected plans for his education in 1980–81, when he was five, as listed in a letter to us from Fiona.

Adam's Curriculum for 1980–81

Physics*	Latin*
Philosophy	Archaelogy and Anthropology
Karate†	History of the Middle Ages
Astronomy	Violin*
Computer Science*	Piano*
English Literature and Creative	Composition*
Writing	Ballet†

*Currently being studied
†Will be begun as time permits—mentor available

... Adam will have his first recital this coming Thursday. He will play one movement of a violin concerto by Seitz on the violin, of course, and an Ecossaise by Beethoven on the piano. He is delighted and so are we. (Letter from Fiona, fall 1980)

Of these topics, I believe that Adam in fact made at least an initial foray into all of them, but he had less success in getting tutors in literature, the Middle Ages, and ballet than in the other fields.

For each of the children I have followed, teachers have played a central role in sustaining commitment as well as providing the major force for advancement in the field. For children like Ricky Velazquez and Franklin Montana, the match of temperament and intellectual style may make the difference between continued pursuit of a field and the loss of interest and commitment. For children like Billy or Adam, the relatively casual relationships with tutors may have prolonged their exploration of different fields and perhaps delayed their settling into a specific area for serious and intensive study.

Perhaps the most difficult part of the process for parents and the children themselves is knowing who to choose as an instructor and when to change teachers. Selecting the most appropriate teacher at a critical period in the prodigy's development may spell the difference between sustaining a budding talent and curtailing that child's trajectory of achievement. This is a decision that the child is generally not capable of making alone. A teacher will sometimes volunteer that a change is needed, noting that he or she feels unable to teach the child anything more, but generally it must be someone else who decides that the time has come to move on to another instructional environment. That someone is almost always the child's parents.

The remainder of this chapter focuses on the delicate process of choosing and changing teachers for one of the prodigies, Nils Kirkendahl. Specifically, a transition that occurred between Nils's ninth and twelfth years will be described in some detail. During this period the final direction of his musical education was set, shifting from preparation for careers as both composer and performer to an emphasis on performance only. Describing this transition is revealing not only about teachers and how central they are but, as co-incidence theory indicates, how crucial it is to monitor the teaching process to ensure that it is best serving the child's development. These are problems familiar to parents of prodigies and nonprodigies alike, of course, but they are intensified when the stakes are as high as they are in the cases described in this book.

The Education of a Music Prodigy

Folklore about prodigies in music suggests that very little education is needed for the exceptionally musical child to perform dazzling feats. We read of the young Yehudi Menuhin who, when given a toy violin at age three, smashed it because it would not "sing."[4] This sort of myth about untutored brilliance also circulates in chess circles. Vladimir Nabokov's novel *The Defense,* which is loosely based on the life of chess master Samuel Reshevsky, describes how the five-year-old protagonist is mesmerized the first time he sees chess pieces on a chessboard, and it is clear almost from this first confrontation that this child was born to be a chess player.[5] K. K. Karanjan, a teenage chess prodigy, reports that at eight years of age he chose a chess set from a shelf in a toy store, not knowing anything about the game, but finding the pictures of the pieces fascinating.[6]

The origin of myths like these probably lies in the prodigy's rapid and seemingly effortless early mastery of a field. It takes others years to accomplish what the prodigious child does in months; these seemingly sudden, seemingly spontaneous achievements are common features of the child prodigy image. Yet, it is clear that early prodigious achievement (even in music and chess) does not occur without extensive, and usually formal, instruction. It is true that in certain fields a child may reach a *relatively* high level of performance with *relatively* little instruction, but past this point, if the child is not provided with expert instruction, continued development of the talent is likely to be attenuated. The role of expert instruction was and is critical in the life of Nils Kirkendahl. He could not have progressed from early talent to entrance into a select musical circle without the introduction of systematic training by master musicians.

Virtually all of my observations of Nils were in the "middle phase" of his musical education. By the time I met him he had already completed two years of Suzuki violin instruction and three years with a local teacher. His musical training had shifted from his hometown to Boston, where he studied composition with composer and performer Dr. Daniel Aaron. He also studied various aspects of musical performance with a number of other teachers associated with Dr. Aaron and, later, the Music School at Boston University. Nils, his mother, Helen, and often his brother, Loki, would drive to Boston on Saturday mornings for a full round of lessons. A typical weekend day consisted of five separate classes: solfege, piano, string quartet, a master class in violin with one of Boston's leading teachers, and a composition lesson with Dr. Aaron.

During this period my co-workers and I observed more than one hundred hours of Nils's classes, performances, and conversations with other musicians. We saw lessons in piano, violin, chamber music, solfege, and, of course, composition. We watched performances: student recitals, competitions, and professional appearances, including one with a major Boston orchestra. It was during this middle period that Nils made his decision to abandon his study of composition in order to pursue a performing career.

This was not the first time in Nils's career that a decision had been made to change the focus of his musical education, nor was it the first time that Nils himself had been consulted about the change. It is unusual that despite his tender years Nils had participated in virtually every major decision regarding his training. He had played well as a Suzuki student, and when Nils was almost five his parents sought a private teacher. Nils was delighted with the individualized instruction and advanced quickly. He remained with this teacher for about three years, until it became clear that he was in need of more sophisticated instruction. He had also begun composing, when he was six, and his parents thought he needed a more structured and comprehensive musical education. It was soon after his eighth birthday that plans were made to have Nils begin the ambitious program of study that was to catapult him into the world of the aspiring professional musician.

Ironically, Daniel Aaron was recommended to the Kirkendahls as a composition teacher by Rudolph Howard, a violinist and master teacher who eventually played a central role in precipitating the split between Nils and Dr. Aaron. Although Helen researched, interviewed, and eventually selected the instructors, Nils himself also had a great deal to say about his own education. In the crucial decision to concentrate exclusively on performance and terminate training in composition, it was in fact left to Nils to finally choose. Quite a burden to place on the shoulders of an eleven-year-old. But Nils seems to have had broad enough shoulders to carry the burdens placed on him. In fact, he was a young boy of exceptional maturity, insight, and clarity of purpose, which has helped him weather transitions with equanimity and move his career forward. Since early adolescence he has been attentive yet pragmatic about his education—both musical and general—seeking a balance between his development as a violinist and as a well-educated and thoughtful individual.

By the time Nils entered high school he was also enrolled as a special student at Juilliard under the wing of the well-known violin teacher Dorothy DeLay. His schedule of classes there made it necessary to commute to New York even more often than he had gone to Boston, and his regular school work simply had to be fit in wherever there was time. When Lynn and I visited his private secondary school in 1980, his teachers were universally generous in their praise of Nils's qualities as a student and as a member of the school community. The school staff seemed to appreciate Nils's unusual talent and allowed him to come and go during the school term as necessary. They generally reported Nils was well liked by other students, although not one of the most popular or well-known members of his class (hardly surprising, since he was often absent from campus). It probably did not hurt that Nils was gifted academically as well as musically. His school records showed his grades to be quite good, and his aptitude and achievement scores on standard tests were uniformly in the 99th percentile.

Nils left for New York to enroll full time in the collegiate program at Juilliard at the age of fifteen as a National Merit Scholar as well as a promising music talent. We talked about his move to Juilliard several months before he enrolled, and Nils's biggest concern was that his fellow students were going to be too unidimensional, too preoccupied with the world of music to see that there was a great deal more to life, particularly the life of the mind, than music. We had what was really a philosophical discussion, and I remember thinking that Nils's mind was a searching and reflective one, clearly not limited to or completely focused on music. I am convinced that he was not showing off, that he had a genuine intellectual curiosity and interest in the discussion. Nils asked whether I thought Hegelian idealism made sense, or whether philosophy as a discipline and focus of study was worthwhile, since you could never know the answers to the questions it raises. I explained that the value of philosophy for me is its discipline, its way of thinking, its tradition of analysis. As the discussion turned back to music he said that he worried that he would not be able to express anything new on the violin. It was clear that he was becoming reflective about his talent in the context of becoming reflective in general, all of this when he was fourteen years old.

The quality of the exchange between us, in contrast to earlier conversations when he was ten or eleven, was of two adults talking about matters of mutual interest. It was not a show in any sense. My earlier experiences with Nils, when he seemed precocious and affected, were perhaps instances where his musical abilities far exceeded his ability to express himself verbally. But somehow I doubt it. It seemed to me that by fourteen he had become more comfortable with his mind, more attuned to his own sensibilities. In any case, Nils was becoming an exceptional student and thoughtful young man even as he was becoming an outstanding musician. Somehow he had weathered the stresses of being a child prodigy, for he surely had been one, and seems to have made the transition into young adulthood even stronger and more committed to his musical and intellectual development than ever.

At Juilliard Nils says that his education is not at all broad, that everything revolves around music. This he mentions with some regret. The courses are heavily oriented to music. In his opinion, courses not directly related to music are not taken very seriously. In fact, students are more or less expected to slight them because the music regimen is so demanding, he says. Nils has become acclimated to both the career-oriented environment of Juilliard and the fast-paced social life of New York. He is comfortable but not the least bit overwhelmed. His decision to pursue the elusive goal of concert violinist seems to have been well made. But a few short years earlier Nils was in the throes of a wrenching, traumatic, confusing effort to achieve safe passage to the next phase of his musical education.

To get to this place, both literally and figuratively, Nils had to go through a major transition process, abandoning his composition career and throwing all of his energy into performance. How he was prepared to make this decision is the main concern of the remainder of this chapter. In the pages that follow I have tried to capture some of the flavor of Nils's experience as a composition student and to present the circumstances that precipitated his decision to change his career course. It is worth examining in detail how this change was achieved. When we see a talent like Nils performing, the tendency is to assume that his course has been smooth and true. In fact, Nils Kirkendahl's course has been the smoothest of any of the prodigies in my study. Even so, he had to deal with an extremely delicate, complex, and confusing conflict over the direction of his musical studies that might have knocked the ten-year-old Nils irretrievably from his course.

THE JOVANOVICH METHOD

Daniel Aaron, Nils's remarkable composition teacher, was one of the most extraordinary people within one of the strangest groups I have ever encountered. Dr. Aaron was then a man in his early forties, balding, slightly rotund, and with a beautiful baritone voice. His face was childlike, his manner somewhat officious and formal. Even after we became friends he never really loosened up. When he felt uncomfortable he often became combative and somewhat defensive, with colleague and student alike. This, to my mind, made Dr. Aaron a tough teacher for Nils to have at a very critical time in his development: he was not the gentle, encouraging type. I remember one conversation on Nils's tenth birthday when Dr. Aaron belabored the fact that he himself had started to play the trumpet at twenty-one months, while Nils was "an old man, carrying a cane" because he started at three years. Later that same day L. R. Harleston, a composer and mutual friend, stopped by, and Dr. Aaron went through the entire routine again, including trotting out a photo album containing a yellowing snapshot of young Daniel with trumpet in hand at the tender age of two. While perhaps not typical, this little episode revealed a great deal about how Daniel Aaron approached his youngest student.

Daniel Aaron had confided to me a few months after I began visiting his studio that Nils was ". . . too good to be true. He has no faults and that's terrible, it's frightening, marvelous, but frightening because you just can't believe that this is all going to happen, that it's going to continue." Much later, after Nils had decided to leave Dr. Aaron's tutelage, the teacher saw it as a confirmation of his earlier fears that Nils was literally "too good to be true." Dr. Aaron's assessment of Nils was an expression of many things, including his own particular personality and temperament. His underlying philosophy and orientation to life and music was unusual. This, too, must have had its impact on Nils's training as well as his sense of self and purpose. Dr. Aaron belonged to a tightly knit community of musicians presided over by a septuagenarian named Madame Jovanovich, who occupied the apartment directly above Dr. Aaron's. The first time I met Madame Jovanovich, she was not satisfied with a handshake or a simple "Hello." She immediately put her hands to my temples and announced that I was too tense. She then proceeded to tell me some personal things about myself that were pretty close to the mark. Although nonplussed, I was impressed both with her directness and her accuracy, not to mention her unorthodox style. She did say (to my relief) that she felt my project was well motivated and humane, and that it was okay with her for me to continue to visit. I had the feeling that if I had not passed the temples test I would have been out on the street in short order and looking for another music prodigy to study.

This music-centered community was held together by more than its passion for discipline and intuitive interpretation of temples: with Madame Jovanovich at the helm, they had developed a number of unusual beliefs and practices only indirectly related to music. An extremely disciplined, demanding bunch of students and fellow professionals, this group of ten or fifteen people was fiercely committed to music as a field of study and form of personal expression. Madame Jovanovich was famous for taking on students whom others had given up on in despair. She never gave up on a student and was known for producing the most remarkable results from the most unpromising of individuals. Formidable, eccentric, yet lovable, she set the emotional tone for everything that happened in Daniel Aaron's studio below.

Madame Jovanovich's circle were also firm believers in reincarnation: that every individual has lived in various forms and at various times in the past and would appear again in the future. Daniel Aaron once told me of his own ideas concerning one of his previous incarnations. He had recently seen a painting of a musician who had lived from 1400–1474 (whom he did not name), with his right hand raised, fingers extended, and one finger pointing on his left hand.

> I found a picture of myself around the age of two with this exact same pose. Now to me that's very striking. It doesn't prove anything, it may be coincidence, but if you add that up to similarities in music, this particular composer was known to have mastered all the musical styles of his time and is said to have been the most versatile of all musicians . . . , being able literally to function and create in every area. Well I happen to be this way myself. . . .

This may seem a long way from music education, but it profoundly affected the atmosphere of Nils's musical environment. Dr. Aaron attributed Nils's uncanny maturity and musical ability to his having lived before. Nils simply had the benefit of several earlier lives to perfect his musical skills. In fact, Dr. Aaron had identified several musicians from earlier times who he thought were good candidates for Nils's previous incarnations. No one was exempt from such speculations: Madame Jovanovich had told me that I had been a woman in one previous life, a judge in another. While this may be fascinating and fun for an adult to think about, it is a fairly heady message for a nine-year-old.

The notion of reincarnation also seems to have affected the music curriculum Dr. Aaron constructed. It relied largely on historical recapitulation, being very selective in the use of musical works of past composers. Dr. Aaron chose these composers at least in part because he felt them to be Nils's progenitors musically if not literally in his previous lives. His aim was to get Nils to work through the progress made by previous owners of his skills—those who had given him the precious gift of an early start— and then eventually to move beyond them to express his own unique musical identity. Thus, even though the reincarnation belief was unconventional, it led to a framework for teaching that makes a certain amount of sense. Indeed, I have found that much of the teaching done by master teachers is recapitulationist. The notion of reincarnation is simply an extreme form of a common practice.

To the extent that they were able to do so, Dr. Aaron, Madame Jovanovich, and their cohorts attempted to control Nils's musical education. One of their group was assigned to be Nils's piano teacher, another his violin teacher. The idea was to create a total musical environment to prepare Nils for a career as a composer, since this was the vision of him they had come to. The Jovanovich group's musical interpretation was sometimes idiosyncratic and subject to strong criticism by other musicians and instructors. As we shall see, their insular and possessive attitude toward Nils became the crux of the conflict concerning his musical education and future. Despite this attitude, young Nils seemed to move through it all like a self-possessed force, always respectful but very much with his own sense of who he was and where he was going. For all the strength of Dr. Aaron, Madame Jovanovich, and their colleagues, Nils Kirkendahl had more than enough of his own personal power to balance these forces when necessary. In this effort Nils was assisted by the formidable presence of his mother who, in her quiet, determined way, made sure that whatever was done was best for Nils. In the end, the team of mother and son was more than a match for the rich but ultimately confining musical environment offered by the Jovanovich clan.

In his lessons with Dr. Aaron there was always a great deal of attention to other matters besides music itself. Dr. Aaron's studio was a wonderfully chaotic environment filled with photos, records, tapes, wall hangings, posters, and books of all descriptions lying about. It had the look of a very alive, purposeful place, where important work was done. During the first year I visited Dr. Aaron's studio, Nils's lessons lasted well over an hour, sometimes more than two. Conversations often turned to philosophy, art, or ethics, always in relation to music. Dr. Aaron used the materials in his studio to supplement and explain the points he was trying to make. A poster containing an optical illusion was used to convey the notion that one can hear only one thing at a time, even though more than one might be going on at once. A great deal of discussion centered on the recordings and performances by well-known artists. They often attended concerts in the Boston area and discussed them, both before and after. Dr. Aaron was also a jazz musician, and he tried to convey a healthy respect for the less formal, less classic modes of making music.

I remember one lesson that was spent on how to select paper for a notebook, rule neat staffs on paper, arrange pages, and pick the right pens and ink for writing scores. I had the sense of a craft being passed from one generation to another, in a way that can never be done by reading a book or simply observing. This aspect of the composer's craft was treated with the same care and love as the more musical and technical aspects of the domain. Much of the lesson time, of course, was spent going over Nils's compositions. Several weeks were spent on a violin sonata, for example, that I never actually heard played all the way through. Each note was discussed, each phrase worked and reworked, at a level of detail I could only begin to appreciate as a nonmusician. This was serious business. Yet I should not give the impression that the atmosphere was somber. Quite the contrary. There was always a great deal of laughter, friendly kidding and chiding, and a good sense of the absurd. At least this was true during the period of about a year when Nils's education was relatively stable, his schedule with Dr. Aaron the same from week to week, and Dr. Aaron himself seemed to be relatively secure in his role as mentor.

THE TURNING POINT

All of this began to change when Nils enrolled in the Young Musicians program at Boston University.* As I look back on it, this probably marked the beginning of the end of Nils's career as a composer. The program at Boston University was unabashedly aimed toward the preparation of performers, which placed it in direct conflict with his composition career. According to Madame Jovanovich's theory of preparation, public performance was anathema to a proper education in music even for future performers, let alone aspiring composers. They felt that putting young children before audiences was to seduce them with the easiest part of music, the lights and the applause. The demanding life of a true musician was a far more serious and higher calling than that reflected in the glitter and pleasure of audience admiration. To prepare for that life, performances were to be given rarely and virtually never before a general audience. Perhaps one performance a year for one's teachers, fellow students, and their families was about right. To do more was to seriously compromise the high calling for which the student was being prepared. Nils's teachers

*The real name of the program.

at Boston University, while not pushing their students into frequent performances, nonetheless believed that the only way to develop musically, whether as performer or composer, was to play in front of audiences. There was precious little middle ground for Nils to tread between the two philosophies of his two groups of teachers, and the tension mounted as time passed.

Another and more immediate consequence of the change in Nils's musical regimen was that his Saturdays became more tightly scheduled. Whereas before he might have had three lessons, all given in the same building by members of the Madame Jovanovich school of music education, Nils was scheduled for as many as five different lessons, several of which were at the Boston University School of Music, located in a different part of town. Since one of these lessons was scheduled right after composition, it was no longer possible to dawdle with Dr. Aaron and meander around topics in music in both productive and unproductive ways. Even if it had been less of a threat, it would have changed the whole tone of the lessons, in part because of time constraints, and in part because, as I was soon to learn, the Kirkendahls and the Jovanovich group were moving into a clash of educational philosophies that would cause turbulence and hostility for more than a year.

The epicenter of Nils's education was subtly shifting from a combination of composition and performance to performance alone, particularly with the addition of string quartet, solfege lessons, and master classes with prominent violinist Rudolph Howard, who took Nils under his wing as only a person who sees himself in another could do. The conflict reached a climax in a way that seemed surprising at the time; it was too petty, too off the point. In retrospect, I suppose we all should have anticipated that such a crisis was inevitable, and that the particular incident which proved to be the flash point was immaterial. The Jovanovich mentality was by its nature extreme and self-contained and did not deal well with outside intrusions. The road to concert solo violinist is similarly demanding and tolerates equally few distractions. When two such worlds clash, only one can survive. But it was not to be expected that the explosion would come because of a performance before a Women's Club group in Nils's hometown.

Despite his objections to public performances, Nils's piano teacher, Girard Kinley, himself a student of Dr. Aaron, had agreed to accompany Nils's performance at the Women's Club. According to my assistant, Richard Bensusan, who was present when this agreement was made, Girard was reluctant from the outset. First of all, as a member of the Jovanovich group there was his general aversion to performance. Second, Girard seemed to resent that Nils was not really much interested in the piano. Girard's lesson with Nils was scheduled last among the five on the Saturday Boston tour. I had observed that Nils would visibly tire, and sometimes even fall asleep in these lessons. In general, they were not the high point of his musical day. All in all, it appeared to me that Girard was not particularly favorably disposed toward Nils, and certainly did not see himself as an available adjunct to Nils's performance aspirations.

Girard Kinley was later to claim that Mrs. Kirkendahl had pressured him into accepting the role of accompanist. According to Richard there was probably some truth to this charge. In any case, Girard backed out the day before the performance. As the scene was later reconstructed by Mrs. Kirkendahl, the conflict came to a head at another performance of the piece the day before the Women's Group concert. Rudolph Howard, Nils's violin teacher from Boston University, and Girard Kinley had a vehement argument about Kinley's interpretation of the piece. Howard argued that it was "incredibly wrong musically," and that it would be a travesty for Nils to perform it as rehearsed, regardless of whether it was for a Women's Club group or a major concert audience. The argument quickly escalated into more personal realms, and Girard refused to travel the next day to play with Nils.

At ten o'clock that night, Mrs. Kirkendahl made the two-hour drive with Nils from their home to Boston and directly to Dr. Aaron's studio to confront him about Kinley's defection. She knocked repeatedly on the door but no one answered, despite the fact that the lights were burning brightly in both Dr. Aaron's apartment and Madame Jovanovich's place upstairs. Furious, Mrs. Kirkendahl packed Nils back in the car and drove back home. From there, in the middle of the night, she called a friend at Boston University and asked him to come to their rescue. It was arranged that an accompanist from B.U. would drive in early the next morning and rehearse with Nils until the performance at half-past one that afternoon.

I had arranged to attend the Women's Club performance, but was totally unaware of the intrigue that was unfolding. While Helen Kirkendahl had been steaming toward Dr. Aaron's apartment, I had driven to their hometown and spent the night in a hotel. I called the Kirkendahls the morning of the performance just to check in and heard from Helen that the previous day had been "the worst day of my life." She gave me a brief description of the incident with Kinley and Dr. Aaron, and explained how she had patched things together. I decided to go to the hall a little early to observe some of Nils's eleventh-hour rehearsal with his new accompanist.

When I arrived about an hour before the performance I found Helen and Loki Kirkendahl and, of course, Nils and his new accompanist engrossed in their work. I was most surprised that Nils seemed to be only slightly nervous. Everyone else there (except Loki) was very upset, but Nils maintained a remarkable calm, which he sustained right through the performance and afterward as well. It simply did not seem to bother him that the entire equilibrium of the performance was in danger of being severely upset. And Nils's performance was extraordinary. He played with enthusiasm, gusto, and showmanship. He received thunderous applause from the audience, which clearly had not the slightest inkling of the tensions that had preceded the performance. It had simply been announced that the accompanist listed on the program had become ill with the flu and a replacement was there instead.

As usual, I had made a tape of the performance for later review, which I had promised to deliver to Dr. Aaron the next day. I had begun taping lessons and performances as a matter of course about three months after I began my observations of Nils. The tape recorder never seemed to make much difference to Nils, although for a time his teachers were self-conscious about it. While the tape recorder did not seem to affect Nils's behavior, for Dr. Aaron it was another story altogether. Our first taped conversation was extremely awkward and delicate, with several gaps when he insisted the recorder be turned off. One such instance was in response to a question about how Nils had come to study with him. Yet when we turned to the issue of what could explain Nils's awesome talent, Dr. Aaron unhesitatingly launched into a lengthy, taped account of reincarnation. I never did figure out why certain fairly tame things seemed too sensitive to tape and others were fair game.

Dr. Aaron had hoped that my tape of Nils's Women's Club performance would unquestionably demonstrate that Nils had made a big mistake by allowing himself to be cajoled into performing before such insubstantial audiences as women's clubs and synagogue congregations (besides, he wasn't even Jewish). After the difficulties of the previous day, I had decided that I would not give the tape to Dr. Aaron unless Mrs. Kirkendahl specifically agreed to let me do so. She did, but she was very worried about what he and Madame Jovanovich would think of it. To give you an idea of just how intense the interest was in Nils's performance, when my assistant Richard delivered the tape to the studio, Dr. Aaron asked him how he thought Nils had played, even though he knew full well that Richard knew little about music.

By the time the tape was in Dr. Aaron's hands none of the principals were talking to each other. The Kirkendahls were extremely upset and fearful of calling Dr. Aaron about continuing with Nils's composition lessons. Dr. Aaron was deeply offended that his prize, once-in-a-lifetime student had ignored the advice of his teachers, even Madame Jovanovich. And besides, Dr. Aaron had been hit on the head with a lead pipe while walking out of a bookstore on precisely the day when the Kirkendahls had knocked futilely on his door. He was, he said, lying in a daze when Helen Kirkendahl had stormed up to his house.

This last incident may seem even more peripheral to the matter at hand, but it too had its role to play. A week or so earlier Dr. Aaron decided to take up speed-reading and therefore told the Kirkendahls that he would not be available for lessons at his usual time on Saturdays for the next several weeks. This he explained was a totally innocent decision, not intended to inconvenience the Kirkendahls. It just so happened that the only time available in Nils's busy day for composition lessons was that very hour when the speed-reading course met. If that meant that Nils had to drop one of his Boston University courses to be able to schedule Dr. Aaron's composition lesson at a new time, surely that would not be too great a sacrifice. Richard and I were convinced, of course, that Dr. Aaron was rationalizing for having arranged to be unavailable. Our interpretation was that his competitiveness with Nils was getting out of hand, and he feared that he was in danger of losing him to the teachers at Boston University. So he forced a showdown. But what he did not anticipate was that his preemptive strike was to prove disastrous.

Perhaps Dr. Aaron had begun to realize that events were getting ahead of him when he was unceremoniously knocked off his feet at the bookstore. Or perhaps that blow, as he was later to admit, knocked some sense into him. In any case, he decided that in view of the delicate equilibrium in his upper reaches he had best not push things just now by taking a speed-reading course. And so, the day after Nils's performance, Dr. Aaron was again available in his usual time slot to pass on the craft of composition to his now somewhat reluctant student. He also allowed that Nils had played well, very well, in front of the Women's Club. Even a recording as poor as mine revealed that Nils had played with an intonation and sensitivity that Dr. Aaron was surprised he possessed. This, plus the fact that he was going to lose Nils unless he made some gesture of reconciliation, probably led the stubborn Dr. Aaron to recant at least enough to win back his student. But as it turned out, it was easier said than done. After all, no one was speaking to anyone else. Here again my role as participant-observer was complicated.

I had decided when I began the study of child prodigies that if a conflict arose between the welfare of my study's scientific purity and my subject's welfare, the former would simply have to be compromised. I recognized that by playing the role I did in Nils's case (and from time to time in the lives of the other children as well), it might mean that my research would be less "scientific" and objective. So be it. Not that I really believe that anything I did or might have done would in itself have made a crucial difference. It seems clear to me now that the outcome would have been the same, though perhaps it would have been resolved a bit later.

It was actually my assistant, Richard, who suggested our course of action. Dr. Aaron was reluctant to call Mrs. Kirkendahl, for what are now obvious reasons. Similarly Mrs. Kirkendahl was fearful of talking to Dr. Aaron. I suggested to Dr. Aaron that he call Mrs. Kirkendahl and simply let her know that, for fortuitous reasons, he was again available on Saturday mornings. I had already told Mrs. Kirkendahl that this was the case, so she would be able to respond appropriately.

This is more or less what happened. Dr. Aaron did call, Mrs. Kirkendahl did set up a lesson for the following Saturday, and they both agreed that Nils was old enough to make his own decision about the direction he would follow in his musical education. I must confess that when I heard this I thought they had abrogated their responsibilities by telling Nils to make up his own mind; the boy was barely ten years old. But on this point I said nothing. Getting involved has its limits, and this surely was one of them. I attended the lesson and it was fascinating, although I purposely (again at Richard's suggestion) was there for the last half-hour only. And I did not tape it.

Dr. Aaron made the most remarkable about-face. He may have sensed that this was his last stand, or he may have had some insight into the destructive effect of his earlier competitiveness, or both. Whatever his motivation, he was lavish in his praise of Nils's ability as a composer. Dr. Aaron reviewed with Nils a program from a conference of composers that his group was attending in Boston. He pointed out names of the program participants and their dates of birth and then made a great show of saying that Nils Kirkendahl, born in 1965, ought to be there as well. "They would say it was a misprint, there must be some mistake, all the composers were born at the earliest 1950." He even praised Nils for his performance before the Women's Club.

The event that made it clear to me how hard Daniel Aaron was working to be positive and facilitative was a brief conversation that Helen Kirkendahl, Nils, Dr. Aaron, and I had about Nils's younger brother, Loki.

Someone mentioned that Loki had shown some musical talent or interest. Without hesitating, Daniel Aaron noted how important it was that Nils not be competitive with his younger brother and that he try to support Loki's musical efforts. Mrs. Kirkendahl agreed that the two boys were a bit competitive, but Nils jumped in and argued that he was helping Loki learn fundamentals, like how to notate simple pieces. I must say that it made me feel a bit smug to have anticipated the theme that so clearly surfaced, this time in reversed form, during the pivotal meeting.

Just when it looked as though we would get through the lesson with most of the damage repaired and with a fair amount of confidence that composition lessons would continue, Madame Jovanovich arrived. She wasted no time in telling Mrs. Kirkendahl, in front of the assembled group that by then had grown to include Girard Kinley and another member of the clan, that it was entirely Mrs. Kirkendahl's fault that all of this had happened and that she hoped Helen had learned her lesson. It was partly in response to this ill-timed attack that everyone agreed Nils should make his own decisions. It did seem, at least to me, as we left the studio that morning, that Nils would continue to study composition with Daniel Aaron. It turned out that I was right in only the most trivial way. Within a few months Nils unequivocally turned toward a career in performance and had stopped studying with Dr. Aaron. In retrospect, Nils ascribed this decision to his sense that "twentieth-century music was going nowhere" and that he had little to say as a composer. I think that probably as much as anything it was Girard Kinley who was the reason for Nils's decision. Since studying piano was a nonnegotiable adjunct to studying composition, since (from Dr. Aaron's point of view) only Girard Kinley was a properly qualified teacher, and, finally, since Girard Kinley had not been inclined to give praise or reinforcement, Nils chose the more rewarding path. Despite my disappointment—it really messed up my research plan to have Nils leave composing behind—it seems clear that he had made the right decision.

That October I visited Dr. Aaron's studio. We talked some about Nils, and Daniel Aaron recalled an excerpt from our first recorded interview. He pulled the transcript out and read me his answer to the question of how good Nils really was. The gist of the answer, it will be recalled, was that Nils was "too good to be true. He had no faults, which was terrible and wonderful at the same time." Dr. Aaron took these words to have been prophetic: they predicted that there was something about the child that was going to break down. He was not human enough. Daniel Aaron was obviously deeply hurt by the Kirkendahls' decision to leave his community. Yet he remained convinced that the whole problem was an internal Kirkendahl matter and not a criticism of the Jovanovich method.

The Process of Teaching Prodigies

I said at the beginning of this chapter that teachers and teaching are central to the development of prodigies. The case of Nils Kirkendahl helps illustrate several points that give substance to this generalization. Nils's situation was unusual in certain respects, even among prodigies, but in other respects it shared many features of the experiences of the others in the study. First let us reflect on the exceptional features of the situation facing young Nils, then turn to some of the common characteristics of the relationship between teacher and prodigy student. In fact, many of the issues between prodigies and their teachers are faced by anyone who seeks highly specialized instruction in a demanding field.

First, it is unusual for a child, prodigy or not, to become enmeshed in a collective attitude toward the subject matter that is as opinionated and encompassing as that of the Jovanovich group. This is not to say that the teachers of the other children in the study were not unusual themselves. As a group, the teachers were nearly as striking in their talents and personalities as the children. This meant that the teachers tended to have strong and definite ideas about what they were doing. It also meant that their relationships with the children were sometimes complicated by their own ambitions, prejudices, or idiosyncratic views about the field they were teaching. In general, the teacher/student relationship seemed to work best when there was a complementarity between the career of the teacher and that of the student. When a teacher is still striving for recognition and is preoccupied with his or her own achievement, as I observed was the case with Dr. Aaron, there is a much greater likelihood of stress and competition between student and teacher. John Collins, on the other hand, had gone as far as he was going to go in chess, was not ambitious in that sense, and was therefore much more successful in creating an unambivalent relationship and facilitating the development of his students.

A teacher who is not necessarily a performer of the highest rank may nonetheless be very helpful during the earlier phases of a student's career. The first teacher is typically responsible for introducing the student to the fundamentals of performance on the chosen instrument. More important than being a top-level performer in his or her own right, the teacher should be kind, enthusiastic, encouraging, positive, and patient. This means that even for the education of children with extraordinary ability, there are places for teachers of varying talent who are at various stages in their own career development. However, the relationship between the teacher's talent and career, on the one hand, and the student's talent and career on the other is a delicate one. This seems to be one of the areas where the relationship between Daniel Aaron and Nils Kirkendahl came to loggerheads. Had Dr. Aaron been younger when he taught Nils, or had he achieved more of his own personal goals before becoming involved with Nils, things may have gone differently. This is not to say that Nils would be a composer now, but that the competition that arose in their relationship might have been less disruptive. These issues are especially germane when dealing with such extremes of talent and specialization, but to some degree they pertain to any relationship between teacher and student.

Nils's teachers were also unusual for prodigies and non-prodigies alike in their emphasis on reincarnation. At first glance this notion seems bizarre. Yet there is an aspect to the reincarnation belief that may translate into valid curricular practice. Nils's instruction followed a carefully constructed *recapitulation* of the field of musical composition, starting from the earliest examples of works known by "progenitor" composers, and working systematically toward the modern period. The rationale for this technique may be open to question, but I have been struck with how common this approach is in advanced teaching. In fact, I believe that an essential feature of teaching advanced students in any field or discipline is recapitulation in some important sense. I saw it with the chess players especially, where each teacher, in a unique way, tried to build in his student an understanding of the advances and turns that his field had taken as it developed. Obviously, not every single event in the history of a field can be reexperienced; the course of instruction would take nearly as long as the original events, maybe longer. But a distillation of the life span of a field into a sequence of critical events seems to characterize the best curricula at this level. The nature of the distillation and the specific topics that are highlighted in the sequence might differ. But to a remarkable degree, some form of recapitulation seems present in the instructional environment created by master teachers.

I have tried to use this insight from my research on prodigies in my own teaching, with good results. For the past few years in seminars dealing with creativity, intellectual development, and theories of development I have quite consciously tried to bring my students through a historically based sequence of experiences, emphasizing the conceptual, research, and theoretical transformations that characterized each shift in the field. In effect, I ask each of my students to reconstruct the field in relation to critical changes in its history. This is not quite the same as if I were to construct a tailored curriculum for each student based on what I know about his or her interests, proclivities, and talents, but it approximates what I have observed in the instruction of prodigies. More recently, I have begun to study the process of learning through historical and conceptual recapitulation, and the results seem promising. While I am no subscriber to the notion of reincarnation, as with most ideas that endure over time, this one may have something to it.

Nils's transformation from composer to performer was a conscious decision influenced by particular circumstances and requiring hard, self-confident decisions. This case demonstrates both the typical developmental trajectory for musicians and the subtleties of a specific process of preparation uniquely constructed for Nils Kirkendahl. The typical situation involves several teachers and extensive educational preparation, not the least of which includes an important socialization process into the circle of professional musicians. It also illustrates how delicate and confusing a process it can be, especially where there are powerful forces and counterforces at work, as in his case. Fortunately for Nils, he was blessed with a sense of inner confidence that gave him the strength and judgment to see his way through.

It is only recently in human history that the idea of the master teacher has become part of our thinking. The teacher of prodigies is perhaps the best example of teaching as a specialized form of work. Music currently seems to be the most developed field in this respect, with a hierarchy of effort that tends to bring the most promising students through a series of levels until they are taken in by one of the great master teachers of the day. This is what ultimately happened with Nils Kirkendahl. In retrospect, I think that much of the tension between Dr. Aaron and the Kirkendahls was that Dr. Aaron, a middle-level teacher, saw himself as a top-level one. He could not relinquish Nils to other mentors. Furthermore, he was committed to developing Nils's composition talent despite Nils's own preference for performance. Daniel Aaron had the personality, the ambition, the drive, to be a great teacher, or perhaps a great composer. To this date, I do not believe that he has become either. It may simply not be his time. In his own terms, this life cycle may not be the one in which he will rise to the heights of his talent and ambition.

As for Nils, he has wistful affection for Dr. Aaron and his entourage. Madame Jovanovich died a few years ago and Dr. Aaron become the new leader of their little community. Nils speaks with great respect about his experience with the Jovanovich group. He believes that some of their better qualities are still part of his approach to music. In particular, the dedication to pure form, the placing of musical perfection as a continuously held ideal, the care and attention to every phase and aspect of the craft, are values dearly held by Nils. Whatever trauma or disappointment the transition may have held for Dr. Aaron, it is clear that Nils was able to take the best from his work with his teachers and go on. Nils seems to draw on a deep inner sense of direction that most of the rest of us, perhaps including Dr. Aaron, may not have.

As a final note to this chapter about teaching, let me touch once again on the unusual events I have described here. The reader should not think that situations and events like these were typical; however, they were not altogether different from other experiences I have seen with prodigies. One must remember that prodigies and their teachers are extreme cases, delicate, specialized, focused individuals who often strike a casual observer as bizarre. One of the reasons that prodigies and their teachers arouse such strong feelings is that what may be normal for them is unusual for most of the rest us. As a result, I tend to be skeptical of journalistic or first-impression accounts of prodigies; I have heard their parents and teachers described as fanatics obsessed with their own importance. Within the context of everyday experience this may be a reasonably accurate description, but the prodigy does not live in an ordinary world. One must suspend judgment until enough time is spent with and around the prodigies, their families, and teachers to understand that extreme responses to the prodigy's educational needs are often required. The events described in this chapter, while somewhat unusual even in the case of prodigies, are not altogether atypical of the kinds of things that happen with such unusual teachers and their unusual students. Teachers of prodigies, after all, reflect the prodigy's own qualities, both of which probably evolved during a long history of reciprocal influence.

7

Social and Emotional Issues in the Lives of Prodigies

MORE THAN half a century ago Franziska Baumgarten observed that the child prodigy exhibits a curious mix of child and adult qualities.[1] In the intellectual sphere there is at least one realm in which the child prodigy performs as an adult. This is of course what defines the child as a prodigy. And yet, the child's mind is not all of a piece. Amazing precocity in a specific field may not accompany advanced reasoning in other areas. Some prodigies tend to have relatively pure talents, demonstrating extreme ability in a single area while being generally average in most others. The young artist Yani seems to be such an example in the visual arts; Mi Dori's accomplishments on the violin far outstrip her school record; and in my own group of six subjects, Randy McDaniel is an accomplished writer and sometime poet, yet has not always distinguished himself scholastically.

The prodigy's rapid mastery of a specific field of intellectual endeavor is generally not accompanied by a corresponding maturity in social or affective development. Child psychiatrist Rima Laibow (her real name),

who sees a number of extremely gifted children in her practice, has recounted a telling story about the mix of child and adult qualities that
characterize the prodigy. A four-year-old boy was being interviewed by
a professor of psychology to determine whether he would be allowed to
use the resources at the professor's university. During the interview the
psychologist asked the boy about a stuffed cat he clutched tightly under
his arm. The child replied that it was Fluffy the cat, his "transitional
object." The psychologist asked the child what he meant by that, and the
boy went on to explain the purpose and function of transitional objects
using accurate psychological terminology. Laibow reports that he concluded his discourse by noting, "I like to carry it with me. It makes me feel
good."[2]

Prodigies are by no means unique in displaying a mixture of propensities and talents; they are simply more extreme examples of what is true of
the rest of us in this respect. And the degree of disparity between their
advanced capabilities and the more unremarkable areas of their development is one of the special problems facing the prodigy.

There are actually two sides of this problem. One is primarily a personal matter having to do with becoming comfortable with their own range
of competencies. For some prodigies, progress in their special field of talent
is so natural, so easy, and so much fun that they begin to expect that
progress in other areas will follow as directly and quickly. When they then
have difficulties they are unprepared to deal with the failure and may even
be unable to find ways to persevere and advance. Several of the children
I have studied are remarkably short on persistence in areas that they find
they do not "click" with quickly. For example, when Adam was five years
old we asked him to draw a map of a model village. At the time he knew
a good deal about maps and was particularly taken with the schematic
guide of the Boston subway system, but it quickly became apparent that
he could not make an accurate rendering of our model. Rather than continuing as best he could Adam altered the task, producing an elaborate
calligraphy key rather than the map itself.

A second kind of problem that may emerge from disparities in the
prodigy's development is an interpersonal one. As the prodigy grows older
it becomes increasingly evident to him that other children do not possess
equally unusual abilities. This may lead to feelings of difference and alienation from one's peers. The child begins to discover that his age-mates are
either uninterested or unable to participate in the activity that consumes
so much of his own time and energy. Friendships must either be restricted
to a very small group of others engaged in similar activities or must be
formed around other, sometimes limited, areas of shared interest. The

prodigy who is passionately involved in the exploration of his own abilities sometimes finds it difficult to set these interests aside and behave like an "average" child. Because most other children simply cannot keep up with the prodigy in his or her special area of interest, it often falls to the prodigy to search out the common ground, to go more than halfway to establish friendships with schoolmates and neighbors.

Reflecting on his own childhood, Norbert Wiener attributed some of the alienation he felt as an adolescent to his straddling two worlds.

> As the infant prodigy comes to realize that the elders of the community are suspicious of him, he begins to fear reflections of this suspicion in the attitude of his contemporaries. . . . Every child, in gaining emotional security, believes in the values of the world around him. . . . He wishes to believe that his elders . . . are all wise and good. When he discovers that they are not, he faces the necessity of loneliness and of forming his own judgment of a world that he can no longer fully trust. The prodigy shares this experience with every child, but added to it is the suffering which grows from belonging half to the adult world and half to the world of the children about him. Hence, he goes through a stage when his mass of conflicts is greater than than that of most other children, and he is rarely a pretty picture.[3]

While Wiener had always felt that adults had viewed him as some sort of oddity it pained him to develop this status with his age-mates during an already difficult adolescence.

In these kinds of ways the prodigy assumes social and emotional burdens that differ from those of other, more typical children. This chapter considers some of the spheres of social and emotional development that may represent special challenges to such special children. In some respects the prodigy's unique talents thrust him into situations quite unlike those normally experienced by other children of the same age. Yet in other respects there is much that is familiar about the prodigy's experience, much that makes the prodigy like any another child growing up.

Relationships with Parents

The very uniqueness of the prodigy's talents leads to certain unusual aspects to the parent-child relation. Before I began this study I had expected the children and their parents to behave toward each other more like colleagues and peers than parents and children. After all, these children are as competent, if not more so, than their parents in some areas. I thought this might lead to a respectful equality among minds.

Instead I found that rather than enjoying an equal footing with their parents, if anything, the prodigies tended to be treated even more as children than other youngsters their age. Whether because of the child's special ability, or in spite of it, the parents of prodigies seem to maintain a period of dependence for their children that is often longer and more intense than in families with more typical children. This is most extreme in the cases of prodigies who are only children. If this prolonged dependence is due to the child's special ability, the parents' behavior may derive from the same kind of source that engenders close relationships in families with children who have disabilities. In both cases, parents may recognize that their child is different in ways that will make life more complicated and more difficult than for other children. This understanding in turn fosters a tendency to protect the child from the knocks and jolts that no doubt will come from the outside world. The childlike quality often reported as characteristic of prodigies may originate in part from parents who infantilize their offspring longer than average. Extending this period of childlike dependence may not always serve the best interests of the child.

An extreme case of this sort of extended infancy and childhood must have occurred in the case of the Hungarian piano prodigy Erwin Nyiregyhazi. It was said that as an eighteen-year-old he was still unable to tie his own shoes, feed or dress himself, let alone make career decisions on his own. Such extreme dependence upon parents and caretakers is a real liability and may have contributed to the early end to Nyiregyhazi's public musical career. Other famous prodigies also seem to have depended on others' attentions past childhood. Mozart found cutting his own meat too laborious a chore, depending on his wife for assistance at the dinner table. Yehudi Menuhin and Norbert Wiener were also objects of prolonged family caretaking, although their cases are not among the most extreme on record. Nonetheless, their parents were still managing many of their daily routines well beyond the age when other children are looking after themselves.[4]

In the families of my own subjects the tendency to treat prodigies as young children is also present, although not in extreme form. The boys' activities were carefully monitored and often included the presence of a parent. In two of the families—the McDaniels and the Konantoviches—the boys were almost continually in the presence of one parent or the other. Neither couple, for example, socialized much unless they included their son in the activity, nor did the boys often play with other children without a parent present. However, in all six families there seems to be an awareness that their children will have to begin making their own way in the world sooner or later and that they must be assisted in the process of growing up by assuming some level of independence and responsibility.

In fact, what I have observed in terms of parent-child relationships in the families in my study is probably fairly typical for single-child families, where parental attention, energy, and resources can be focused exclusively on the one child. In no case is it likely that the children I have followed will find themselves unable to care for themselves when they reach adulthood. Their transitions to adult life and independence will probably be successful and without extensive trauma.

Although I cannot comment about the experiences of adolescence from direct observation of my own subjects, as all but one are still too young, others have noted that the process of separating from parents seems to be more prolonged and difficult in prodigies' families. Psychiatrist Rima Laibow attributes separation difficulties in part to the disparity between the children's advanced abstract, intellectual understanding of situations and their age-appropriate emotional capabilities for dealing with them. Like the four-year-old who was intellectually cognizant of the theoretical function of transition objects, but whose need for their comforting quality was strictly age-appropriate, the *Sturm und Drang* of a prodigy's adolescence may include the additional tension between knowing and feeling. While he may comprehend some of the reasons and causes for his adolescent Angst, he is unable to respond or remediate at the level of emotions or actions. Impatience and feelings of impotence are more generously peppered into the usual mix of adolescent turmoil.

I am sure that the difficulties with individuation and separation from the family are also due to the closeness and intensity of the parent-child relationship during the earlier years. By and large, parents and prodigies are more involved with each other than are many other parents and their children. Parents of prodigies play an extremely active role in their children's lives. They arrange and monitor educational experiences, advise and guide them in career decisions, and try at the same time to provide a stable emotional atmosphere and normal social life. The process of disengaging from this intense and highly invested relationship can be slow and painful. Norbert Wiener recounted that his own assertion of independence from the parental bosom took many years, during which he was intensely depressed and relatively unsuccessful in his studies. He recalled that his father's unwillingness to surrender control over major postgraduate schooling decisions (among others) left Wiener with a sense of dependence and insecurity well into his adult years. His mother's tactic was somewhat different.

> It may be asked why [as an adult in my twenties] I did not leave the family
> to take lodging somewhere for myself. . . . It was made clear, particularly by
> my mother, that the separation would be held against me for all eternity, as
> a sign of my ultimate failure, and would mean the complete and final collapse
> of family relations.[5]

And yet, this predicted course of unusually intense adolescent turmoil
does not seem to characterize my subjects. Nils Kirkendahl, the one subject
who has reached late adolescence, seems to have made the transition
toward adulthood with the same aplomb that he has managed every other
developmental milestone. Furthermore, I do not find this particularly surprising. Nils seems to be exceptionally mature and sensitive to issues of
growing (and growing up). He is also extremely responsible and independent, levelheaded and trustworthy—qualities which have stood him in good
stead. To a significant extent he and his parents have always enjoyed a
relationship of mutual respect and admiration that has assisted in smooth-
ing his separation from their direct care and supervision.

Fourteen-year-old Billy Devlin has also begun to separate from his
family. As a college freshman he lives on campus, returning home for
weekends. While his parents still play a significant and active role in the
major decisions and activities in Billy's life, he manages daily routines and
school activities on his own. Ricky Velazquez and Franklin Montana are
nearing college age. Although we have not followed them carefully
through their high-school years, I am in touch with their families. As far
as I can tell, Ricky has continued along a smooth and trouble-free path,
both socially and academically. I know less about how Franklin has fared
during this period. Since he had all but given up playing chess by age
eleven or twelve, in all likelihood the issues he is confronting in adolescence involve dealing with being an ex-prodigy rather than finding ways
to integrate his prodigiousness with the normal demands of the teen years.

Adam and Randy, too, are beginning to test their independence in
asserting their talents and interests, but they are still quite young and by
and large have not entered the full-blown period of adolescence. Over the
past two years or so I have begun to see occasional rebellion—an unwillingness to continue with a particular topic of study, some disagreements
with parents about the meaning or value of certain works, an occasional
free-floating recalcitrance. But it is no surprise that I am most sensitive to
these themes and issues with these two children in particular, for they are
both closely tied to their parents and are also the children I have seen most
and know best.

All in all, the six boys appear to have warm and affectionate relationships with their parents. There is occasional evidence of rivalry with fathers, but I don't think that it is more intense than in families where children's gifts are more modest. Some of the parents occasionally seem to show a particularly strong investment in the uniqueness of their child, but not in a way that would seriously threaten the child's being able to develop a strong and separate sense of self. Nor do any of the parents I have observed seem to overemphasize the value of their prodigious child's gifts relative to the special qualities of his siblings. It would be amazing if the prodigies' parents were not very proud of their children's unusual accomplishments, and, of course, they are. But they are, by and large, sensitive to and appreciative of the individual strengths of each member of the family: I think this in turn helps these unusually gifted children to put their talents in some perspective and to develop an appreciation for being one member of a larger enterprise—the functioning of the family unit—where sometimes prodigious talent is an asset and sometimes it is not.

The parents in this study are generally traditional and firm in their handling of their childrearing duties. They are not indulgent, responding slavishly to every whim and wish of their tyrannical children. There is no question in these six families about who are the parents and who are the children: limits are generally clearly set and the children have, for the most part, accepted parental authority with graciousness. The children seem to sense that their parents are doing the best they can to provide the resources and support necessary to develop their gifts, understand how much the rest of the family is called upon to give (and sometimes give up) for this purpose, and recognize that their situation requires the best of the whole family if they are to continue along a prodigy's path.

Neither have the children I followed been tyrannized by their parents. Unlike the popular stories (apocryphal or not) of talented children being pushed mercilessly by their extremely ambitious parents, this is not what I have seen. No child was forced to study or to practice, nor was he denied other activities: no one was chained to a piano, or prevented from playing with his friends. Rather, the parents I know have made great efforts to facilitate their children's interest and progress, working hard to make it possible for them to fulfill their potential both as prodigies and as growing boys. Possibly this quality of responsiveness rather than control accounts for the easy, affectionate relationships between children and parents that have been characteristic of my subjects.

I am not suggesting that the ways my subjects' parents have chosen to guide and respond to their children are necessarily the best ones for ensuring that they will develop into the great scientists, writers, or musicians of the upcoming generation. It is certainly possible (and in certain historical cases it seems to have been true) that strongly controlling parents who take an active, even driving, role in the management of their children can make the difference between competence and greatness. Mozart is often cited as an example of a prodigy whose father's efforts pushed his son toward the pinnacle. It is also possible that Mozart's greatness would have emerged regardless of his father's interventions, or perhaps that in Mozart's particular circumstances of time and place such parental intervention was necessary, although it would not be now. It is too early in my subjects' development to know if true greatness will emerge in any of them. If it does not, who knows if a different style of parenting might have yielded a different outcome? All I can say at this time is that I have observed dedicated and ambitious parents, but not parents who drive their children into activities that the children themselves do not seem inclined to attempt or pursue. I find this reassuring from a childrearing standpoint, for it suggests that it is the children who provide the primary source of energy and determination for developing their talents. The parents' role seems to be to respond, support, and encourage these efforts. Only time and more study will tell if there is a strong relationship between certain styles of parenting prodigies and their achievements and fulfillment as adults. In fact, I believe that we are unlikely to uncover any clear-cut relationships between parenting and prodigies' outcomes, since the optimization of talent involves the complex interaction of a number of factors rather than the simple relation between parenting style and children's abilities.

Relationships with Friends and Siblings

For the most part the prodigies I have studied have grown up in positions of privilege within their families. These positions are, in part, related to their birth order. In all but two of the families the boys are either the only child or the oldest one. In both of the exceptions, the older sibling is quite a bit older than my subject. The eight-year differential between Billy Devlin and his older brother, Nelson Kevin, has meant that in some significant ways the two boys have each effectively grown up as only children. While they do share some interests and activities, by and large there is little overlap in their daily lives. Franklin Montana also has an older sibling, but his sister, too, is enough his senior that they have never been serious playmates or rivals. And although Franklin is the second child in his family, he is the first-born son, making his position in the family somewhat different than if his older sibling had been another boy.

Since the six families tend to be traditional in their role definitions and expectations, it is difficult to know whether the prodigies' special place in their families is primarily a function of their special talents or whether that position was guaranteed regardless, simply by virtue of being the first-born son. It may even be that the opportunity to express some special talents was accorded these children because of their status within the family structure. First-born children have the benefit, at least for a time, of exclusive parental attention. Until other siblings appear on the scene parents are free, if so inclined, to devote their childrearing efforts exclusively to the identification and encouragement of their child's proclivities. Our two exceptions to the first-born or only-child status indicate that parents certainly can recognize and respond to extreme talent in subsequent children. These exceptions do not tell us, however, whether it is common for parents to have the interest, time, and energy to devote themselves to the intensive training and nurturing of prodigious talent in a second or third child.

It is interesting to speculate on what the dynamics might have been in my subjects' families if the sorting out of special abilities had been slightly different. For instance, what if there were another child close in age who also expressed extraordinary talents? We know from several historical cases that in families with several highly gifted siblings, one child nonetheless often emerged as the premier talent. Mozart toured Europe with his sister, Nannerl, until he was about fifteen, at which point her career as a piano prodigy declined and Wolfgang's continued. Yehudi Menuhin had two younger sisters, Hephzibah and Yalta, who were also highly accomplished musicians but whose careers were never as stellar, nor as seriously nurtured, as their brother's. In my study, Loki Kirkendahl apparently showed many of the signs of strong musical talent as a preschooler. I remember attending one of Nils's rehearsals early on in my research when I heard someone begin a piano piece while Nils and his accompanist were taking a break. I looked toward the piano, expecting to see Nils at the keyboard, or maybe even his pianist. But I saw no one. Walking around to the front of the instrument I was greeted by little five-year-old Loki, feet dangling off the bench and chin barely clearing the keyboard. He was having a grand old time. Several months later his mother somewhat sadly confided that while she suspected Loki was potentially as talented as his big brother she had neither the time, resources, nor the energy to try to develop and encourage his talent as well. For his own part, Loki seemed to lack the singlemindedness and drive to insist that he be given the opportunity to live and breathe music. And so he has not.

There are also families that do seem to be able to nurture more than one extraordinary talent. Michael Deakin has described one such family in his book *The Children on the Hill*. [6] The four children in this Welsh family each demonstrated unusual precocity in one of several different domains —piano performance, mathematics, art, and, seemingly, moral philosophy or judgment. The fact that each child was involved in a separate field may require a different juggling of parental attention, and sibling competition may be somewhat different when the talents and educational needs of the individual children do not directly conflict. I do not know whether this kind of situation is more likely to yield more than one child who achieves the "premier" status of a Menuhin or a Mozart, but I imagine that the family dynamics differ in some substantial ways.

There are yet other family-based situations that may have a profound effect on the prodigy's identification and development. In my sample of predominantly eldest sons one wonders what their fates would have been were they the second or third boy born into their families, or if the family resources were so limited that the parents were unable to respond to their son's special talent. We can imagine that such situations are likely to make a difference in the family dynamics, although it is impossible to speculate on the specific kinds of effects that might result.

Given that the prodigies were accorded special status in their families, how did the children handle it? For the most part it seemed to me that there was a gentle, generous quality about the way that the prodigies and their siblings treated each other. It was as if the prodigies' particular talents were so obvious and indisputable that they generally did not lord it over the rest of the family: they did not require buttressing of self-esteem or family status through bullying or condescension. Nor were the boys treated as prima donnas. They were expected to participate in family activities and responsibilities just as their brothers and sisters did. We have also had little sense that the other children felt slighted by the attention their talented brothers received, either from their parents or from the outside. The special talents were admired as the thing that their brothers enjoyed and did well, but they themselves had other interests and friends that were their own special ken. The other children seemed to accept with good grace that it was sometimes necessary to make accommodations to their brother's special needs (usually in the form of sacrificing activities or having parents unavailable to them). Parents also indicated that they tried hard to provide individual attention and activities for the others so that there was as little imbalance as possible between children.

I am sure, nonetheless, that the boys' siblings had moments of resentment and jealousy, but this was not the general impression I had of the families. It was unlikely that the children were simply on their best behavior when Lynn and I were around, for the general goodwill and affection we observed took place in too many instances over too long a period of time with too many different families to have been put on for the occasion. My overwhelming impression was that the siblings possessed a mixture of pride and indulgent good humor toward their unusual brothers. For the prodigies' part I saw children secure in their position, who accepted matter-of-factly their own specialness as well as the particular qualities of the other family members.

Not surprisingly, the picture of the prodigies' development with respect to friends is a bit more complicated. Where it is reasonable to generalize that the relations between my subjects and their siblings are on the whole healthy and without excessive conflict, it is not possible to summarize the nature of the boys' friendships so succinctly. Having friends is important and desirable to the boys, but how they find friends, build friendships and maintain them, and integrate them into their pursuit of excellence in their special fields are complex and subtle issues.

For the McDaniel and Konantovich families the issues of school and friends were intertwined; in both cases it was hoped that finding a school environment would lead to the opportunity to establish friendships. Although the circumstances differ for these two boys, there has been a continuing preoccupation in both families with finding peers with whom each boy could find companionship. Indeed, when it transpired that Adam and Randy would be classmates there was even some hope that the two boys would find such possibilities in each other. For six months at The Learning Place they had the opportunity to test their affinity for one another, and the result was clear: the fact that each child possessed unusual abilities did not particularly lead to their liking each other. In fact, they were by and large attracted to different children in their class. Randy began to seek a set of friends who appreciated and responded to his theatrical flair. He could most often be found with the boys in the class who delighted in his word play, energetic dramatic recitals, and tall tales. Adam, on the other hand, seemed attracted to more intellectually oriented peers. His best friend during his stay at The Learning Place was a boy who loved some of the same unusual activities as Adam. They delighted in translating hieroglyphics and doing calligraphy exercises together. For Adam, then and now, however, friendships have come mostly with adults.

The other children, especially Billy and Ricky, gave friends an increasingly central role in their lives as they grew older. Whereas friends during their earlier years were often other children who shared their special interests, by age ten or eleven they had broadened their social affiliations to include a range of friends from their diverse suburban communities. For Ricky in particular the attractions of the larger peer group were powerful enough to jeopardize his commitment to continuing the intensive study of chess.

It is not necessarily good or bad for prodigies to respond to the social pressure for belonging, but there may be important implications of such a tendency. The increase in sociability may be a signal of a decrease in the singleminded dedication to prodigious achievement. For the families I have followed this change was generally welcome from the point of view of the children themselves as well as their parents: better to be less committed to prodigious mastery and have some friends than to be a chess champion or writer of note and feel isolated and out of step with one's peers. The children made these decisions consciously for the most part, with an understanding of the possible implications of such actions for the future trajectory of prodigious achievement. Perhaps some of the parents encouraged their children's excursions into sociability because they suspected that the boys' talents would not survive the test of time: it would not be worth the cost of subordinating the more normal array of friendships and activities to continue singleminded pursuit of a talent that might not continue to develop. Perhaps parents have encouraged their boys to develop friendships in spite of their belief that their children's exceptional talents might well take them to the pinnacle of success. As an outside observer, it is difficult to tell.

While friendships have been important to all of the children I have studied, when the presence of friends became a major preoccupation, the pursuit of mastery became correspondingly less central. In those families that have maintained as their central goal mastery and development of the prodigy's talent, friends have been less evident and apparently less diverse, coming almost exclusively from the restricted pool of children studying and working in the same fields of interest. Those subjects whose intense concentration on narrowly specialized fields is waning have begun to select friends from more varied backgrounds, developing and extending their own range of interests along the way. In summary, it is fair to say that all of the families I have observed are committed to the importance of a social life for their children, but in some it has become a central issue, whereas in others it has had to play a supporting role. It is the latter situation that is most likely to maintain the child on target in developing his talent.

Effects of Success

One of the most obvious differences between prodigies' experiences and those of the rest of us is the prodigy's dramatic success at a very early age. Contending with the effects of such success adds an extra dimension to the demands on these children's social and emotional development. The burdens of success are sometimes too great for an adult to carry: what happens when success, fame, and adulation are conferred upon a child? Those who work with music prodigies in particular seem to have become sensitized to these issues in recent years, perhaps because this group of talented children is currently receiving the greatest public attention and acclaim. In fact, intensive media interest has even led some of the more prominent music teachers to deny that music prodigies exist anymore. Some view this denial as an effort to protect the child's still developing talent from the assaults of public expectation and adoration. At the very least it signals that those who prepare children for performing careers are aware and concerned about the possible negative effects of too much attention and praise coming too early in the prodigy's career. Parents' efforts to shield their children from extensive attention often originate from a concern about their personal rather than professional health and development.

Concern with the detrimental effects of exposing the prodigy's still formative talent to public scrutiny may mean protecting the child from the attentions of eager teachers, entrepreneurs, curious media representatives, and a range of individuals who seek the reflected glory of others. Families differ in the degree to which they sidestep the limelight and also in the ways by which they seek to instill a sense of normality and regularity in their unusual children. Norbert Wiener reported that his father, who designed and supervised his studies from infancy through his first postgraduate year, was both relentless and merciless in his criticism of his son's extraordinary knowledge and progress. Furthermore, he took credit whenever he could (both in press and in private, according to Wiener) for having carried off an extraordinary pedogogical experiment with a basically average child. In retrospect, Wiener saw his father's behavior as an attempt to shield him from the undue egocentrism that would come from realizing his true status in the intellectual world. This was an extreme strategy, and by

Wiener's account an excessively destructive one, despite the fact that he felt his father acted mostly in good faith.

Several of the boys in my study had been subjects of public attention while still in elementary school. Magazines and newspapers contained feature articles on both Franklin and Ricky, touting them as eight-year-old chess wonders. When Ricky's family visited Spain a year later, he was feted and treated as a celebrity. Spain is a country with a longstanding passion for chess, and Ricky was as good a young player as they had seen in some time. Although Franklin was a bit less comfortable in the limelight, he still seemed to enjoy the attention he received from an all-too-eager press. From my observations, both boys' fathers were invested in the public rewards of chess prowess, and to some extent sought out opportunities for showcasing their children. While they certainly were not guilty of extreme tactics that exploited the boys' talents or privacy, they did promote the boys some through public attention and exposure.

In general, the children I observed took their success and all the attendant attention with equanimity and good grace. Though they tend to be confident, there is little arrogance about them. While they are certainly proud of their achievements and ability, there is also a matter-of-fact acceptance of their talents that may be one of the hallmarks of such highly pretuned minds. They are doing what they love and need to be doing. Of course they are doing it well: it's what they're meant to do. But they also make mistakes, experience failure, and recognize they still have much to learn. In fact, they may suffer from these failures more acutely than the rest of us because they are so strongly moved to master their fields.

The importance of external recognition and the trappings of success seem to vary from child to child and family to family. Ricky Velazquez was rather guarded about his chess prowess with his junior high school mates, preferring to emphasize their shared interests rather than his more unique talents. Franklin Montana was much more casual about his chess interests; although he did not advertise his chess life and fame to classmates and friends, neither did he attempt to hide or lessen his accomplishments. The Konantovich family has been extremely protective and guarded in sharing news of Adam's talents with the media, while the McDaniels are nearly always ready and willing to grant interviews. In part, the degree to which the children attend to their success and outside attention is probably a function of their own confidence in their abilities and investment in expressing their particular talents. In part, it is probably due to the range of other activities, friendships, and opportunities for praise available to them. But no matter how important or trivial the external acclaim becomes for these children, they must deal with a degree of outside attention and interest that the rest of us do not know as children and most of us do not know as adults. The children I have observed have managed to do so in a healthy and positive way.

Motivation

What is it that motivates the prodigy to spend so much time and energy mastering a field? Why do child prodigies seem almost driven to perform at ever higher levels? How do they sustain the intensity of their commitment year after year? Are they pushed by ambitious families and teachers who distort their childhood and turn them into precocious professionals? As with other aspects of the prodigy phenomenon, it is not easy to provide complete answers to questions such as these, but it is possible to provide some perspective on what motivates mere children to do an adult's work.

In my experience it is rare for parents of prodigies to be so obsessed with their child's ability and success that their perception of his natural proclivities is severely distorted and exaggerated. Some of the families we have followed have dealt with the special educational requirements of their children in somewhat unconventional ways, but the children themselves are unusual and often so extreme in their demands and responses to educational opportunities that conventional approaches do not seem reasonable. It is impossible to speculate on the extent to which family eccentricity is a function of parental response to a child of extreme promise and the extent to which the promise is elicited by the family's own unusual qualities. Nathaniel and Fiona Konantovich tell us that they had planned on parenting a bright child before Adam was conceived, establishing the broad framework of their childrearing strategy even before there was an exceedingly talented child to respond to. Helen Kirkendahl was determined to provide a rich musical environment for her infant son without a clear sense of why this was so important to her and certainly without any indication from five-day-old Nils that such experiences were to become central to his very being.

Whatever prior tendency the families may have had toward producing, stimulating, and developing a prodigy, these tendencies would have quickly come to naught were the child in question to lack talent and drive. In fact, it is reasonable to guess that many such situations exist where family tradition or pedagogical zeal lead parents to decide to make a "genius" of a child. Such was the case, for example, with Aaron Stern (his real name), a Holocaust survivor who decided that he would mold his first-born child into a genius using what he called the "Total Educational Submersion Method." He announced his intention soon after his daughter Edith's birth, reflecting in an ironic way the very Superman myth that the Nazis had employed barely fifteen years earlier to relegate him and millions of others to subjugation and death. The result of Mr. Stern's mission was a young woman, highly gifted intellectually, who accelerated her schooling to complete college at twelve and earn a Ph.D. in mathematics before the age of twenty-one. While Edith has subsequently become a cyberneticist at IBM, working on classified projects, Aaron Stern's hopes for creating a genius were not fulfilled. He himself seems to concur with this assessment, although he takes little responsibility for Edith's deficiencies. Stern told a reporter in 1977: " 'I'm not very impressed with Edith. She could have been much more, given what the input has been. . . . I don't believe that she is a genius.' He paused . . . 'She will be a genius when she makes a contribution.' "[7]

It is not surprising that extraordinary performance cannot be guaranteed by intensive instruction, no matter how rigorous, sensitive, and dedicated it is. Co-incidence predicts that parents' intentions be closely matched to the child's particular talents and proclivities—when child and parent are closely tuned, prodigious achievement may be possible. The motivation for great achievement can be enhanced and directed by dedicated parents, but it cannot be created by them from whole cloth, as Aaron Stern tried to do. The child must have the domain-specific talent and the will to pursue the path toward excellence.

Prodigies are characterized by an intense personal desire to pursue a particular field passionately, relentlessly, and for the sheer joy and pleasure of doing it well. If the child begins to find the pursuit tedious or burdensome, he may well abandon it to become a more typical child. The child's motivation to sustain his effort day in and day out must be primarily intrinsic. Something is not right if the source of the motivation lies outside, either with the parents or with others. In fact, with bona fide prodigies it is much more typical to see parents encouraging their children to ease off a little, often coaxing them to put away the chessboard or to spend a bit less time at the piano. Rarely do such children require a stiffer practice schedule or the reminder to work harder on their studies. With a prodigy it is rarely necessary to push.

In fact, prodigies seem largely immune to those lapses in motivation that seem to accompany normal growing up, perhaps because the desire to master a field comes so strongly from within. Were it to be sustained primarily by praise or encouragement from the outside, the prodigy's motivation for mastery and understanding would be much more vulnerable to withdrawal or failure. For those children whose motivation does begin to wane the effect can be devastating, much worse than the common disappointments and reversals most children experience. The prodigy is not used to having to deal with the exigencies of motivation, not used to disruptions in the desire to achieve. When it does happen it is so unusual, so unexpected, that many promising talents never recover. This is the situation that Jeanne Bamberger has discovered during the teenage years among music prodigies.[8]

How a child could be so committed to a single field and have relatively little interest in anything else is one of the central questions for this book. It is in fact less of a mystery why a child might *lose* his or her motivation to work eight or ten hours a day than why this motivation would continue unabated. The probability of being able to keep up the pace, to put in the necessary hours of study day in day out, year in year out, is very low. Why some children are moved to pursue a field relentlessly, yet in a healthy and productive way, may have more to do with the long-term, evolutionary purposes of such activities than with any other level of explanation.

The line between obsession and commitment is very subtle, and unless the conditions are just right a dysfunctional or even pathological personality may be the result. Again, the importance of balance, of coordination of a totally appropriate set of conditions necessary for the development of such special-purpose talent cannot be overemphasized. One of the most delicate of these is the motivational force that comes from the child. When it is on the mark it is a force to reckon with; when it goes awry it can be baffling and destructive.

PRODIGIES AND FREUD

The strong internal drive toward mastery characteristic of the prodigy provides a challenge to the psychodynamic view of motivation first advanced by Sigmund Freud. From the Freudian perspective, virtually all behavior is motivated by the same basic desires—those having to do with the satisfaction of erotic instincts. When a child is unable to satisfy these desires immediately and directly he turns to other, secondary sources of satisfaction. Although there is a fair amount of theory and research indicating that things are more complicated than this barebones account would have it, the idea persists in Freudian circles that the child only chooses to engage in an activity when the activity stands to serve as a socially acceptable substitute for what he or she really wants.

It is difficult to reconcile the behavior of prodigies with any notion of

motivation that places a central emphasis on the satisfaction of predominantly biological (and, specifically, erotic) desires. This is especially the
case for those highly cognitive fields in which prodigiousness shows itself
very early and very strongly. It is not plausible that prodigies' primary
motivation for pursuing their chosen fields stems from a discovery that
they can possess a desired parent through exceptional performance in a
particular domain that the parent wishes the child to master (or that the
parent has already mastered). In the case of Franklin and Ricky, for example, their parents initially had no interest or investment in their boys
learning chess: both children specifically requested that they be taught the
game. Furthermore, in both of these families there were other children who
could have been encouraged to follow the same path, but were not. Could
it be that for one child in a family psychodynamic factors would direct him
toward the pursuit of chess, but for another it would be gymnastics or
mathematics which would guarantee parental approval and affection? It is
simply not plausible that parents alone would provide the motivation for
prodigious achievement by targeting the domain or activity through which
the child will be able to please them most.

More true to the mark is that parents find themselves living with a
child who seems possessed with the desire to master a particular field, and
that in order for the *parents* to maintain some relationship with the child
they find themselves compelled to respond. Rather than functioning as a
vehicle for a child to satisfy desires for parental attention and affection, the
parents feel that they must go to exceptional lengths to serve their child's
growing passion. In this sense, the motivation driving the prodigy is actually quite the opposite from that hypothesized by Freudian theory. While
my account is simplified, it should be clear that the notion of sublimation
as the basic explanation for why writers write and singers sing is largely
without support as far as prodigies are concerned. Writers write and singers sing because that is how their talents and proclivities express themselves best.

Prodigies are not the only people who manage to find a very specific
form of activity that is sufficiently compelling to keep them occupied for
many hours each day for years, and perhaps for a lifetime. In his ninety-
sixth year Pablo Casals spoke of his cello in a television interview as if it
were his closest friend, a beloved companion. That there was an intense
and emotional relationship between master and music cannot be denied,
but whether it can be explained adequately in terms of Freudian principles
is doubtful to me.

Why Mr. Casals found his deepest expression through the cello and
not the oboe or the trombone is undoubtedly partly a sensual matter.

Something about the feel and sound and touch of one instrument seems to appeal to some individuals and leave others cold. There is probably a sensual element to most every discipline. I have heard chess players describe the kinds of pieces they prefer to play with: ivory or wood, ceramic or metal. Different kinds of boards also move different players and help to bring out their most spirited emotions. Without doubt there are important expressions of the sensuous side of one's craft or domain, but I do not think they are necessarily sexual; the satisfactions derived from this side of a discipline are cultural creations that help complete the desires and aesthetic aspirations of individuals already highly tuned to the broader discipline itself.

Although I think the Freudian formulation of motivational factors is incomplete, there is much about the basic tenets of the psychodynamic approach that is useful. Perhaps the more important message of Freud's approach to motivation is that there is very little a person does that is done without a reason. Freud's reduction of motivational factors to basic instinctual drives has not stood the test of time. Still, we are compelled to find some explanation for what motivates people to diligently pursue their chosen work, even if it is not quite so simple as the psychoanalysts propose. Prodigies provide a fresh perspective on the motivation issue. They seem impelled toward mastery for the sheer joy of doing something well: perhaps motivation is as uncomplicated as that, at least for some fortunate children.

Energy and Its Uses

It would be distorting the reality of early prodigious achievement and a disservice to the main purpose of this book to claim that the prodigy is just an average kid who works hard to become an outstanding talent. Prodigies are *not* like everyone else. The ways they are different from other children can be found in the social-emotional realm as well as in aspects of their intellectual functioning. Early prodigious achievement is as much a matter of temperament as it is of intellect. One without the other would yield an unbalanced situation hardly conducive to the optimal expression of ability. The lack of harmony within the overall personality of the child could manifest itself in a number of ways, and I have seen a variety of forms of unfortunate imbalance in children and also adults as I have studied intellectual development.

I have seen children who are obsessive about playing an instrument or becoming a great chess master but who simply do not have the talent for doing so. They persist as if life itself depended upon their achievements. While they perform well beyond the level one might have guessed was possible given their natural talent, their accomplishments are nonetheless more modest than their aspirations. I have also seen individuals who, though blessed with amazing intellectual capability and talent, somehow lack either the focus or the resolve to harness the power to a coherent course of preparation. These people never manage to reach their natural potential. Indeed, some of the saddest and most frustrating cases I have encountered are adults who have abundant ability but lack the resolve, confidence, healthy sense of self, or dedication that is utterly crucial to the process of developing talent. They flit from field to field, dabbling here and poking around there like a honeybee searching for the right flower. While it is certainly possible to achieve without possessing a harmonious and balanced personality—there are too many documented instances of tormented or extreme personalities who have made significant contributions in spite of their imbalance—it is simply a lot more difficult.

What often happens with individuals lacking balance is that they devise a kind of compensatory strategy: in response to the extreme demands on their energy and concentration (which are critical to becoming a powerful producer or performer), these people develop peculiar or extreme personal eccentricities. The need to focus energy and discipline on their work may bring a corresponding lack of discipline to other areas of their lives. The image of the musician or actor as stormy and temperamental is at least partly due to this tendency to focus and distill energy toward the performance. There are performers who are known as emotional wrecks, almost childishly needing support from others, except for those moments in front of an audience. The social and emotional make-up of such individuals is as much a consequence as a cause of how they apportion their energy for their work and the other demands on their lives. Certain tendencies, perhaps fairly eccentric ones, that were initially present in the personality may become exaggerated and inflated as a result of the individual's efforts to direct and control energy in the service of talent.

A recent popular film, *My Favorite Year*, was a parody of this phenomenon. The film is set in the 1950s during the heyday of live television comedy. The story revolves around the relationship between an aspiring young comedy writer and a dashing film idol scheduled to appear on one of these nightly shows. The star is entrusted to the writer's care until showtime, and although he is cool and debonair on film, he is a drunken, irresponsible, frightened man in person. The disparity between his stage and secular personas and his efforts to reintegrate them provide the grist for the film.

In fact, the importance of energy has been underestimated in virtually all studies of giftedness. To emerge as a prodigy a child must marshal an extraordinary amount of energy to create and then sustain the momentum necessary to render talent into real achievement. My overwhelming impression is that the children in my study and, indeed, virtually all individuals who have made major contributions to their fields, seem to be blessed with a great reservoir of productive energy. They may need less sleep than others, or they may work at more intense and sustained levels; one way or another these individuals are able to call upon vast sources of energy that most of us just do not seem to be able to mobilize.

There is a large and lucrative industry in this country that aims to make the average person feel happier, healthier, and more productive through various self-help methods which range from aerobic exercise to sundry dietary regimens to employing strategies for positive thinking. Prodigies don't seem to need these kinds of kick-starts to productive engagement. They have the energy to put their ambitions into motion and the reserve to draw upon when it is necessary to mobilize still greater energy to get the job done. Without that energy, which seems to be as natural a gift as talent or confidence, the likelihood of the prodigy fulfilling the potential of raw talent is vastly reduced.

Conclusion

In many respects the prodigies I have studied are healthy and happy children who enjoy good relationships with parents, peers, siblings, and teachers. To a significant extent the social relationships of the children have been limited to those whose lives were also involved in the pursuit of the prodigy's field. This was particularly true during the boys' early years. Regardless, the children are outgoing and engaging, poised and interesting companions for their peers. Relationships with parents and teachers can become complicated by the special demands created by having this "team" of adults share the child's goal of achieving success within the chosen field. There is greater pressure for parents to modify their own lives to accommodate the needs and demands of educating their children than is the case with the parents of most children, and this can lead to difficulties within the family constellation. At the least it can give an observer the impression that the balance of things has tipped rather strongly toward the child. While early prodigious achievers may be the focus of more—and more intense—parental energy than other children, there doesn't seem to be any other way for parents to respond to the extraordinary demands imposed by extreme talent. This fact seems well accepted in the families I have followed, although it leads to a somewhat different set of family dynamics than most theories of personality development, including Freud's, would have predicted.

The general sense I have of the social and emotional lives of the prodigies is that they are in several respects quite similar to those of other children and their families. To see their families interacting around the dinner table, one would most often be hard pressed to detect anything out of the ordinary. Where the major differences emerge is in how the pattern of family activity is set, how priorities are established, how the resources of the family are allocated, and what proportion of the energies of family members is channeled into a single child's education and preparation.

When all of these qualities and features are combined in a family, and when the child is confident, ambitious, and willing to subordinate other goals to that of the highest level of mastery of a specific field, then the emotional scene is set for a prodigy in the making. And when it is set, two other emotions may be satisfied, the expression of which may in fact have more to do with productive motivation than anything else: satisfaction and fulfillment. This may mean that, along the way, interpersonal skills are developed more slowly. Social maturity may be sacrificed for a time to the pursuit of the prodigy's special talent. The prodigy and his family seem to have decided, implicitly or explicitly, that they must work together to satisfy the child's extremely strong desire for excellence and mastery, and that it is necessary for them all (not just the prodigious child) to fulfill their destinies in this unusual and often exceedingly taxing manner. Clearly it is not everyone's cup of tea.

8

The Cultural Context

Up to this point I have looked in some detail at processes of co-incidence in those areas closest to the child. I have considered the extreme talent that must exist if a prodigy is to perform at a very high level in a demanding field at an early age, and the importance of a field or domain that is itself sufficiently developed to engage the child's talents. Families and teachers, schools and organizations are all of vital importance in the process of prodigy making; these factors shape, direct, and organize the world around the child of promise. I have also looked at the prodigy as a social and emotional being.

The focus up to now has been narrow, on the world that directly affects the child prodigy. This is where we spent our time as observers, and this is where our curiosity has lead us. The idea of co-incidence, though, is intended to encompass broader forces as well. We must widen the focus to include these broader, more contextual conditions to get a picture of the full scope of the co-incidence process.

One way of approaching the broader forces is to do a thought experiment with Albert Einstein as the "subject." Consider what the effect on Einstein's work would have been if he had been born at a different point in history, in a different culture, or perhaps if he had been born a girl. Think about just how precise the fit had to be between the set of possibilities that was the biological Albert Einstein and the set of experiences and opportunities presented to him. Try to imagine little Albert born five thousand years ago in his home town of Ulm, Germany, or five hundred years ago—but in Nepal. Try to think what his life would have been like if he had been a woman. Attempt to sort out how much of Einstein's contributions were due to his own "genius" and how much to the genius of history, evolution, and culture working through each other.

The point of the co-incidence concept is that it is an extremely delicate and precise set of processes that leads a child, a field, a stretch of time, a receptive culture, and a set of intellectual catalysts and organizing forces to create the conditions under which extraordinary achievement will flourish. I believe that Albert Einstein would have made far less amazing contributions of less significance for the world had any of the major forces of co-incidence been out of synch in his lifetime. To reiterate a point made earlier, this is not in any way to detract from the unique set of gifts naturally bestowed on Einstein. It is rather to claim that ability is never so robust that it will manifest itself fully and powerfully under all, or even under a wide variety, of environmental conditions. If little Albert had been a girl, I think we would never have heard of her. Were the same kind of situation to occur today with the conditions right for another great transformation in a field like physics, we would be less likely to miss the opportunity for greatness if it were to come in a female form. The history of knowledge has no doubt passed over many such opportunities for great contributions simply because the center of the co-incidence forces happened to be a girl. The work of developmental psychologist Carol Gilligan and others aims to show us just how much we have missed by ignoring so large a segment of human potential.[1]

There are several other major dimensions along which broader forces of co-incidence array themselves. There are the people around the potential prodigy in addition to family members: peers, mentors, clans, guilds, patrons. There are also technologies, artifacts, and cultural institutions. The possibilities for individual expression are always being balanced against the needs of society and the requirements for maintaining and extending various fields, technologies, and institutions. During any one lifetime there are also historical events and themes playing themselves out; for example, if there is a change in the structure of the class system within a society, this may profoundly affect how (or if) art forms will be nurtured and received. There is an institutional subculture and structure in which resources are allocated, rewards given, and privileges granted, and this framework changes at different times in history. A patronage system controlled the arts in much of Europe during the Renaissance, while in the Soviet bloc countries today there is a collectivist ideal that, at least in principle, governs what and how individual talent is to be channeled and how it is to be expressed.

There are also evolutionary forces, physical or cultural or both, that may be only subtly felt, but nonetheless have their influence. Selection pressures favoring one quality or set of qualities over another, it now seems clear, are not necessarily constant nor do they occur at a steady pace, but rather have fits and starts, periods of less intense and more intense pressures.[2] Natural events also intrude in major and minor ways. One currently popular hypothesis for explaining dinosaur extinction is that meteors showered the earth's surface, changing the climatic conditions of the globe in a way that was unfavorable to these creatures.[3] A nuclear holocaust might put the most extreme selection pressure on qualities that we can only hope might exist somewhere among our human brothers and sisters. Less apocalyptic changes in the physical environment may similarly alter essential qualities of evolutionary selection. All such conditions affect the kinds of capabilities that will emerge as valued or cultivated. Perhaps most important is the fact that, as Plato said, cultures only find and develop talent where they understand and value it.

There are also well-known associations of remarkable achievements with specific places. Florence during the Renaissance, with a coterie of artists the likes of which the world has rarely seen since; Vienna in the early part of this century with Freud, Wittgenstein, Mach, Schoenberg, Schopenhauer, and others who ushered in the current period of existential and individualistic thought,[4] the Silicon Valley in California and Route 128 in Massachusetts where microchip technology has flourished during the past twenty years. All suggest that at certain times and in certain places a flowering of productivity and creativity occurs.

The fact that during the past twenty years more than fifty percent of the top chess players have come from either the New York metropolitan area or Los Angeles and San Francisco no doubt influenced the psychological climate within which my two chess players were introduced to and played the game. Concentrations like these are probably maintained by those who, hearing of a focusing of energy in a field at a given moment, congregate in that place. Students come from all over the world to study music at Juilliard; poets, writers, artists, and philosophers flocked to Paris around the turn of the century; "flower children" descended upon San Francisco during the 1960s. As usual, there are interactive relationships that complicate matters, and increased mobility only increases the complications. Still, place and time seem to be powerful contributors to the appearance of remarkable performance within many fields, including remarkable performance by children.

In his book *Excellence,* John Gardner also observed that, at any point in time, only a finite number of fields will prove welcome for the expression of talent:

> At any given time in a particular society, the idea of what constitutes excellence tends to be limited—but the conception changes as we move from one society to another or one century to another. . . . the list is long and the variety is great. Taken collectively, human societies have gone a long way toward exploring the full range of human excellence. But a particular society at a given moment in history is apt to honor only a portion of the full range.[5]

We do not have to agree completely with Gardner's point that human societies have explored most of the ways to be excellent to see that he is on the mark when he recognizes that a society (and, more broadly, a culture) is an entity in which decisions have been made and are being made all the time about what forms of talent to value, what fields to encourage, where to invest resources, and how to reward extraordinary performance.

The Rockefeller Report on Education, published in 1958, not long after the Russians sent up the first space satellite, expresses well this sense of context.

> With rare exceptions, it is probably true that a society only produces great men in those fields in which it understands greatness. Spain in the sixteenth century produced Cortez and Pizarro and a dozen more who rank with the most extraordinary explorer-conquerers who ever strode the pages of history. It is unthinkable that the same society at the same time would have produced a Jefferson. [And it is equally unthinkable that] . . . the society that produced Franklin, Monroe, Benjamin Rush, John Adams and other philosopher statesmen of breadth and brilliance . . . could have produced a Mozart.[6]

Finding prodigies and producing greatness are, of course, not the same thing, but the point remains that a receptive, attentive, supportive context must be available if early promise is to be fulfilled. What is clear is that no society can encourage all forms of excellence simultaneously and equally. This is true for many reasons, but two particularly stand out. One is that resources are limited and the development of human potential is often an expensive proposition. The other is that doing anything well requires concentrated and sustained effort on the part of the individual seeking high-level mastery and those who assist in the process. Suzuki violin training, for example, requires many hours a week on the part of both youngster and parent.[7] It should be acknowledged that not much is known about how a society goes about setting its priorities, making decisions about fields to cultivate, fields to ignore, fields to discourage. Clearly, this is a vital set of issues for sorting out co-incidence processes.

Factors That Affect Prodigy Development

GEOGRAPHIC LOCATION

The six families in my study all live in or near major metropolitan areas on the Eastern seaboard, close to or right along the AMTRAK Boston/Washington train corridor. Thus they live near the epicenter of East Coast culture, with large cities and their resources near at hand. All of the families save one are well enough off to be called upper middle class and are comfortable in their lifestyles. All but one live in suburbia, in single-family homes, in stable communities. The fathers are the breadwinners in all families but the Konantoviches and McDaniels, where both partners share responsibility for work and finances. In the other families the mothers generally do not work, or have worked sporadically and less than full time. This has been critical, since the amount of time committed to assisting the children in their pursuits has been substantial from both parents, especially the mothers. Good public or private schools were available in their communities, and the children all lived at home throughout. (Adam and Randy, of course, have not attended school regularly.)

To what extent their locations in suburban communities influenced the course of the children's development in their respective fields is unclear, but it was quite important at least for the chess players. Both have now given up competitive chess and have not played seriously for a number of years. The chances of their continuing would have been greater had they been urbanites rather than suburbanites, especially if they had lived in New York City. Getting to the chess clubs and arranging lessons were logistically difficult, and more importantly, there were so many other attractive things to do right at home, particularly in the well-organized suburban sports leagues that put children into serious competition in soccer, baseball, football, and swimming as early as four or five. Both of my chess-playing subjects were involved in sports almost as early as they were involved in chess, and the rewards were much greater. They began playing when chess was in the public eye, in 1972, but interest in chess in this country, even around New York, quickly waned with Bobby Fischer's self-imposed exile soon after he won the World Championship. So, at both the local and more national levels, the context for supporting chess was not optimal. This, plus the fact that parental commitment was mixed at best, led to the quite understandable tendency for Ricky and Franklin to put their energies into other pursuits. And given that both boys were talented in sports and lived in towns with active sports programs, energy went largely in that direction.

TECHNOLOGY

Both Ricky and Franklin were also assisted in finding their fields by a technology unavailable only thirty years earlier—television. It is unlikely that either child would have picked up chess so early had he not seen coverage of the Fischer–Spassky world championship match on television. Shelby Lyman, a good player of some standing and a TV commentator, helped bring the match alive, and the general impact of chess on the U.S. public as a result of this match was probably unprecedented. Since neither child lived in a household where there were other serious chess players nor where chess was particularly valued, the role of the technology was critical in introducing the boys to the game. Sustaining a passion for chess could not, of course, be done by television alone, even if Fischer had continued to play and interest in chess had continued, but at least television brought the possibility of playing chess to a larger number of children, some of whom went on to develop unusual talent of their own.

Randy McDaniel was also aided by technology, although a different one. His parents had an IBM Selectric typewriter in the house and Randy was able to teach himself to use it when he was three. Would he have begun to write if this technology had not been available? Possibly, but not likely, since he found writing longhand so tortuous unless, someone else wrote down his stories. Even then, the feeling of producing words on paper may be sensually distinct from dictating, and the experience of setting down one's own thoughts may be critical to becoming committed to writing. In the future, children may not be required to learn handwriting because word processers will be so widespread and easy to use that they will eclipse the more traditional technology of written expression. This might mean that more children will be writing earlier, or that at least a different set of skills will be requisite, a set that more children should be able to master at a younger age. Will this change in technology lead to more prodigies in literature? Perhaps it will, although there are skeptics who question whether children have anything worth saying, despite technological solutions to problems of actually producing the written word.

TRADITION

Although it seems likely that tradition, both within families and in societies, plays a role in directing and cultivating talent, I have seen relatively little clear reference to it in my own subjects. Other than in the Kirkendahl family, which sported an Olympic skater on Johann's side a generation ago, there is no evidence of family traditions of high-level performance in family history. There is a clear sense that in the McDaniels' and the Konantoviches' past there are powerful family traditions that, in diffuse ways, seem to influence their behavior, but the specifics of these influences are not obvious. The importance of England for Randy, and of the seafaring and farming traditions in Darren's Scottish heritage, were powerful themes especially during the early years; and Adam's grandfather on his mother's side is something of a mystic, although there is little made of this fact in the family mythology.

Finally, where there are other children in the family, none has taken a path very similar to the one taken by my subjects. That is, no one else tried chess seriously in Franklin's or Ricky's family; Nelson Kevin Devlin has shown little or no interest in scientific studies; and Nils Kirkendahl's brother, however talented he might be, has not gone into music. The same is true for other relatives. While on the basis of my own study I can make no well-substantiated claim that tradition has played a large role, the impression of the influence of tradition nonetheless persists.

It is known that certain families have produced more than one major figure in various fields. Although there is no way to judge just how strong the effect of family tradition is, the instances are compelling and suggest that this issue should be studied more systematically. Francis Galton, the distinguished English scientist, who was himself from a family of great renown (first cousin of Charles Darwin and grandson of a prominent physician), conducted the earliest careful work attempting to document the relationship between eminence and family membership.[8] Galton showed that in English life great men of letters, science, athletics, and politics tended to come from the same families, generation after generation. He concluded that the capacity for eminence is primarily inherited. While this conclusion was unjustified, it is still a powerful belief to this day. The problem, of course, is that families are social as well as biological entities, and they function within established social and cultural organizations. That heredity has something to do with attaining eminence is likely, but its effects are so tied up with other variables that it is impossible to sort out how much is due to biology and how much is due to social, cultural, or family factors. Anyone who reflects on the structure of British society, historically and today, cannot but acknowledge that entry into the elite is carefully controlled and directed through interlocking social institutions and traditions, beginning for boys with access to the right nannies and continuing through the right school, club, social register, military regiment, wife, and job.

Yet there are enough examples of remarkable achievement within families that the contribution of heredity should not be discounted. There is the famous example of the Bach family in music, producing several first-rank composers before and after Johann Sebastian. A number of Renaissance families were noted for their painters of renown across several generations. The Darwins of England, and even the Kennedy family in this country in twentieth-century U.S. politics, serve to remind us of the possibility that propensity for achievement may run in families.

CULTURE AND HISTORY

The more removed from the direct, day-to-day experience of the child a potential influence is, the more difficult it is to gauge its impact. Yet it is important to acknowledge and specify these more indirect influences, which may take the form of general historical trends, contextual realities, events, and decisions of others. Any study of the process of development of human potential should consider such matters. Fortunately, someone has begun to do this work.

The effects of contextual factors on the achievement of eminence has been the concern of Dean Keith Simonton. In a recent book, Simonton presents a dizzying array of data bearing on the extent to which a range of factors influence the fields in which great works are done.[9] His research methods are very different from mine, but there is a surprising degree of agreement regarding the relevance of historical and cultural variations for understanding creativity. Simonton's approach is systematic, quantitative, and based on large-scale data gleaned from historical sources. His techniques contrast with my tendency to deal with small numbers of individual cases, to do primarily qualitative interpretation, and to forgo statistical analyses. Perhaps because he has chosen to work quantitatively on a large canvas, his work is better suited to sort out some of the relationships among factors such as the cultural zeitgeist, family patterns, political climate, and specific fields of achievement. I should note that Simonton's work analyzes eminence and creativity in Western cultures, and therefore deals with domains valued by these cultures: philosophy, literature, military and political leadership, and science. It is, then, in certain respects more restricted in range than my efforts here, but its scope is broader when it comes to trying to weigh the contributions of various aspects of society and history.

How do these broader contextual forces affect the development and expression of potential? As we have noted, the prodigy exists within sociocultural, historical, and evolutionary contexts that each affect the expression of potential. By virtue of the point in time and the place at which the prodigy is born, he lives within a context of a certain zeitgeist, or spirit of the times, a political atmosphere of stability or unrest, war or peace, and a cultural milieu in which role models either do or do not exist in various fields. Certain philosophies, myths, and belief systems characterize the ideological atmosphere in which the child is raised.

Defining his research method as "historiometry," Simonton, in the tradition of Sir Francis Galton, applies quantitative techniques to data abstracted from historical populations. The result is a grand overview of historical patterns of genius—reminiscent in range of the work of Arnold Toynbee—and a statistically grounded, yet richly speculative rendering of the interplay of social-historical forces impinging upon the expression of human potential. Whether or not one chooses to accept the whole of his findings, it is worthwhile to consider his work as one plausible interpretation of how this particular subset of the forces of co-incidence may affect the development of potential.

The course of Western civilization reveals clusterings of creative endeavors that suggest that a zeitgeist may influence the particular types of achievement that occur. For example, Simonton points out that the most eminent thinkers in the sciences have tended to be contemporaries of the greatest creators in philosophy, literature, and music. On the other hand, he suggests that illustrious painters, sculptors, and architects form a second cluster of achievement that does not necessarily co-occur with the first. Such concurrences, notes Simonton, make it seem that at certain times the world (or at least a culture) is ready for scientific advances, while at other times some novel development in the visual arts might be favored. A zeitgeist interpretation suggests that an individual's success may be measured partly by the concordance between his contributions and the cultural value ascribed to them. Simonton suggests that some sociocultural environments may simply favor certain forms of talent and achievement over others.

Scientific genius, notes Simonton, is more likely to appear when ideas like empiricism, materialism, and determinism are on the rise. On the other hand, a rise in spiritual and expressive ideas increases the probability that religious leaders will appear. Furthermore, it seems that social forces—for example, the political milieu—can either encourage or inhibit one or the other philosophical orientation. Simonton's studies indicate that periods of political fragmentation and cultural diversity often precede a shift away from determinism toward a view of perception and experience as the basis for understanding. Political fragmentation also seems to be associated with creative development in all varieties of endeavor.

Political fragmentation is itself related to civil disturbance (political violence that involves the masses). Simonton points out that the amount of civil disturbance in one generation is causally related to the amount of political fragmentation in the succeeding generation, and, therefore, popular revolt may be said to exert an indirect effect upon the emergence of creative achievements after a two-generation delay. Furthermore, some twenty years after the major outbreak of popular revolt, philosophical orientations appear to become polarized. Thus, potential philosophical thinkers exposed to civil strife during their own development will, in their productive phase, tend to take extreme stands on various philosophical questions. In this way, the political conflicts of one generation are transformed into philosophical ones. The ideological tendencies expressed, for example, in the writings of Machiavelli or Marx may be natural outgrowths of the particular zeitgeist of their formative years. This does not tell us why it was Marx specifically who emerged in the nineteenth century, but it does help us understand when someone like Marx is more likely to appear.

Simonton's data suggest that while political events influence the zeitgeist, the process may sometimes work in reverse. For example, international war tends to erupt about a generation after materialistic and skeptical beliefs have dominated the zeitgeist. Growing up in such a milieu, notes Simonton, may nurture a mind that will turn more readily to military solutions. Conversely, roughly twenty years after a major war, there are decreasing numbers of philosophers advocating positions emphasizing the individual or the ethics of happiness. Perhaps, suggests Simonton, this is the result of growing up in an environment permeated by wartime propaganda that attempts to reinforce patriotism and faith in national leaders.

Given these diverse sociocultural factors, it might indeed seem that the prodigy is one instrument through which such forces manifest themselves. The spirit of the times sets the parameters of both the quantity and the character of creative activity, and the individual must find a place within these parameters to express his or her talents. Evidence for the impact of the zeitgeist also comes from the occurrence of simultaneous and independent discoveries. Elisha Gray's and Alexander Graham Bell's simultaneous invention of the telephone is one example; Newton's and Leibniz's individual development of the calculus is another. It would appear from these and other such instances that when a domain is ready for a particular discovery or invention, it is bound to be developed by one investigator or another.

Moving toward an interpretation somewhat like co-incidence, however, Simonton suggests that the interaction of several factors best accounts for the data on creativity and leadership. He notes that there is an "impressive uncertainty in the operation of both zeitgeist and genius. Zeitgeist and genius both have parts to play, but they are members of the supporting cast in a creative drama in which chance has the lead role."[10] Zeitgeist, he suggests, influences achievement through linear or cyclical trends, and as the generator of economic or political conditions. These serve as a backdrop, determining to some extent the sociocultural receptiveness to an individual with a particular set of abilities. At the same time, however, other individual characteristics such as intelligence, morality, leadership qualities, productivity, aggressiveness, age, and belief can temper the general orientation set by the zeitgeist, depending on the specific area of endeavor.

All in all, it is not so much a matter of whether one is simply in the right place at the right time. It may, instead, be a matter of being the right person at the right place at the right time. A certain type of talent may have a higher probability of accomplishment when the spirit of the times favors that particular form, whereas another may have an advantage when the zeitgeist shifts to another emphasis.

CHANCE

In spite of our natural aversion to the idea, things do happen that are neither planned nor predicted. Events interact with more directed, organized, and goal-oriented activities in ways that may make a real difference or may not. It is not so much the *fact* of chance occurrences that makes it relevant; it is not even that, under certain conditions, laws of chance can be established. What is interesting is how the occurrence of chance events influences the process of co-incidence. Do they serve as catalytic events that are necessary for the rest of the system to work? Are they like litmus tests that help determine how powerfully the process is moving in a certain direction? How many obstacles have come into play that might discourage a less robust process?

We know that there are random events, laws of probability, games of chance that we can understand in terms of general principles, although we cannot make specific predictions about a particular event occurring at a given time. Weather fluctuates from day to day and year to year, earthquakes occur, the electric power goes out for a week, meteorites hit the earth, the stock market crashes, new oil reserves are found, a leader is assassinated, the next-door neighbor wins the Irish Sweepstakes. Life is suffused with events that are simply not under direct control. In certain cases it is reasonable to assume that such events have powerful effects, but it is difficult to sort out myth from reality, reconstruction from reflection, sense from nonsense. Over time, fewer and fewer events seem to be truly predictable, more events seem subject to laws of chance and variability.

Probabilistic prediction, while not powerful in the same sense of specific, or "point," prediction, nonetheless gives us a sense of not being subject to the buffeting effect of the totally unexpected. The reality of occasional deadly typhoons no doubt contributed to the Oriental notion of karma; the knowledge of weather patterns and the ability to predict the likelihood of a typhoon also probably influenced the ancient concept of fate. Yet it is safe to assume that unpredictable events will continue to occur.

In at least one instance with my own subjects, chance played a key role in engaging the early phases of a co-incidence process. Ricky Velazquez broke his collarbone the summer he was five, and was restricted to sedentary activities. He was a little boy with great energy, and when his physical activities were so limited, he redirected that energy toward mental exercise. With little else to do, Ricky turned to chess for fun and diversion. He had already learned some elementary points of the game from his father, and had watched the Fischer-Spassky matches with great interest: the spark had already been struck. But it was this extended period of enforced physical inactivity that fanned the spark into the flames of real passion for the game.

Had Ricky been able to participate fully in his usual range of summer swimming, diving, baseball, and running around the neighborhood, I doubt that he would have found chess such an interesting and challenging pastime. How much later would Ricky have become seriously interested in chess, if he would have become interested in it at all, is a question we cannot answer with certainty. Perhaps there is a critical period for engagement that might have been passed if these particular events had not occurred. One can say with absolute assurance only that the chance event of breaking his clavicle was a significant factor in Ricky's introduction to chess.

How many children of great potential have simply found themselves in the wrong sort of early atmosphere for developing their talents? Particularly in families where general organizational abilities and pragmatic strategies are in short supply, the fate of even the most promising talents may be frustration, confusion, disturbance. Fortunately for the children in my study, all six sets of parents were not themselves so preoccupied with their own careers or lives that they were unable to respond to their children's inclinations. Also, fortunately, they had neither religious prohibitions nor cultural restrictions preventing them from cultivating the talents they saw emerging in their young. But it need not have been so.

At a cocktail party a few years ago I was introduced to the wife of a former professor of mine at Stanford. She asked about my work, and when I told her I studied child prodigies, she began to tell me about her experiences as an eager young pianist. She lived in a small town in northern Wisconsin and came from a family with very strong religious beliefs. One of these beliefs was that, while there was no harm in learning to tinker at the piano, it was a sin for a little girl to have such a passion for mastering the instrument. For several years this woman fought a titanic battle with her parents over her music. She was forbidden to practice and was kept inside to prevent her from finding a piano elsewhere. When her parents were asleep she would sneak out a window, go down the street to a local church, and practice on the church organ. After several years of this, her endurance waned and she finally gave up trying to pursue a career in music. Her parents had won the war of attrition. Now in her fifties, the pain and sadness of her story were still evident. She could barely keep back the tears. She believed she may have had the talent and determination to became a successful performer on the concert stage, but was prevented from finding out by an equally determined, deeply felt set of prohibitions. How many such unfulfilled possibilities exist, and have existed over the centuries?

In the six cases in this book, co-incidence forces that could have easily distorted or even prevented potential from developing into performance did not do so. That helps explain how the children were of sufficient distinctiveness to reach public awareness, and indeed, how they found their way into my study. There may be hundreds, perhaps thousands of children with equally strong proclivities, but with slightly less optimal home or cultural situations. Given the heavy odds against them, it is, in a way, remarkable that prodigies appear at all. Since many of the forces of co-incidence cannot be controlled or altered significantly, there is without question a certain random or chance quality to the appearance of a prodigy. Of much greater interest, however, is the possibility that better understanding of these forces could increase the number of children who might be provided the resources that more closely match their propensities.

If we can predict an eclipse, if we can measure the strength of an earth-
quake, if we can stamp out smallpox, then we ought to be able to improve
the balance of co-incidence forces in our children's lives.

Prodigious achievement is the result of the forces of co-incidence
interacting in such a way that an individual with unique proclivities connects with a domain of knowledge that uniquely provides for the expression of those proclivities, under historical, cultural, social, and family
circumstances which support that expression. Individual qualities enter
complex transactions with the forces around them, toward the end of
trying to achieve a pleasing organization and balance.[11] When such deli-
cately orchestrated and beautifully coordinated co-incidences occur in the
wider cultural and historical arena as well as in the immediate, personal
one, we may witness the emergence of a prodigy.

PART III

Known and

Unknown Forces

9

Beyond Co-incidence

TRADITION and a sense of being connected to generations and times past run deep with prodigies. While little is known about such links, they must be acknowledged as part of the prodigy phenomenon. During the years I have conducted my study several of my subjects have reported incidents that have made me reflect on a possible connection between prodigies and unknown forces or influences. This chapter presents some examples of occurrences that suggest that there does remain an element of mystery and uncanniness to the prodigy. Perhaps this element helps account for why prodigies and prophecy have been linked through history. These examples are the most extreme to have been reported to me during the ten years of our research and certainly should not be taken as typical. They do not occur frequently, nor did reports surface in every family. Yet I think it would deny one of the significant aspects of the experience of studying prodigies if these incidents were not mentioned.

It is interesting that the two families to have reported episodes of mystical, inexplicable behavior are also the ones to which we have become closest over the years—the McDaniels and the Konantoviches. It might be that they shared these unusual experiences with us because we had demonstrated an openness to the nonrational, or it might be that becoming closer simply led to their trusting us enough to reveal an aspect of their experience unavailable to us with the other families. Both these families recounted the incidents with some hesitation and concern for privacy and confidentiality: they are puzzling and possibly distressing, and neither family has taken them lightly. I discuss them here not to embarrass the families but because I believe that the reports cannot be dismissed out of hand. Although I have no "hard" evidence to prove it, my intuition tells me that this whole mystical realm of experience is a significant part of the prodigy phenomenon.

I have few guesses about why we heard of such occurrences from only these two families. Perhaps the McDaniels and Konantoviches were the only families where such incidents transpired. Perhaps the other families also had stories to tell us but didn't share them because they seemed too fantastic or weird. Even the Jovanovich reincarnation explanation for Nils Kirkendahl's musical talent (chapter 6) seems somewhat tame in comparison. Nils himself never had any personal indication that he had lived an earlier life, let alone one dedicated to musical study.

There may be one sense in which notions like reincarnation may be borrowed to help explain the prodigy phenomenon. The role of transgenerational tradition in preparing the context for early prodigious achievement seems to be a dimension that is ripe for study. If the transmission of knowledge and tradition across several generations does indeed play an important role, then it makes sense to look to previous generations for evidence of experiences, abilities, and interests that might influence this process of transmission. As with some of the other myths surrounding prodigies, the notion of reincarnation has surfaced more than once as an explanation for the astounding achievements of children: the prodigious child had simply been born with the knowledge and skills of an earlier life already fully developed and ready to be activated. And as with other controversial ideas there may be something about the notion that is on the mark. It could be that certain proclivities, potentials, dispositions, physical and personal characteristics tend to reappear in different generations, particularly among members of the same family. There are anecdotes, for example, about a person being told that his gait, bearing, habits, tastes, talents, or maladies bear a striking resemblance to those of a relative two or three generations back. The reinforcement and further development of such characteristics or proclivities may underscore the appearance that the individual actually possesses uncanny foreknowledge or ability.

Consider, for example, Israeli piano prodigy Elisha Abas's reported affinity for music written in minor keys. His teacher attributed this strong preference to his "Russian soul," inherited from his mother's ancestors. His father apparently takes an even more extreme line: "My wife is the great-granddaughter of the nineteenth-century composer-pianist Alexander Scriabin. . . . After I discovered that he [Elisha] was going to be a musician, I started to read about Scriabin. I'm not a man who believes in reincarnation, but after learning what I did, it's difficult not to believe."[1] Mr. Abas reports that Elisha not only resembles photographs of the young Scriabin, but that they are quite similar temperamentally.

We need not embrace a strong version of reincarnation, however, to recognize a strong similarity between Scriabin's talent and temperament and the apparent re-emergence of these characteristics in his great-great grandson, or to appreciate that Nils Kirkendahl's teachers felt his musical sensitivities and responses were amazingly mature. Nor is it necessary for us to embrace, as Carl Jung did, notions of archetypes or prototypes running deep in the lower regions of the human psyche. Cognitive structurings and emotional tunings tend to recur in development. Given that families share a communality of genetic, situational, cultural, and personal experiences, it should not be surprising that certain types and patterns of behavior would recur, particularly when there is some family tradition or mythology preserving the value of these characteristics. This seems to have been the case among the Bach and Menuhin families and, to a lesser extent, the family of Norbert Wiener.[2] On a more mundane level, and as a matter of family pride, we all tend to look for resemblances, at least among children, parents, and grandparents. It only remains to extend the search for themes and recurrences to include more generations, more distant family members, and more kinds of family similarities.

The study of inherited family characteristics is hardly new. Francis Galton, a proponent of general intellectual giftedness as the source of genius, tried to trace just this sort of thing more than a century ago.[3] More recently Norman Geschwind has proposed that extraordinary talent may be found more frequently in children with atypical patterns of hormonal and immunological development, which may in turn represent familial characteristics.[4] Nonbiological factors may also contribute to the transgenerational transmission of talent: more careful cataloguing and study of these should yield a more complete picture of the origins and development of prodigies' talents. It may also help to explain some of the aspects of their talent that currently seem tinged with the unnatural and mystical.

I believe that there is a great deal to be learned about prodigies and co-incidence from a study of the patterns of recurrence of traits, propensities, traditions, or customs in families or groups over time. The Menuhin family has apparently been producing individuals of unusual talent for centuries. How many more such stories like theirs are there which haven't been documented? What fields seem conducive to this kind of transmission? Do families with strong traditions of excellence concentrate on developing a "chosen one" in every generation, or do families sometimes let the process of talent selection and development lie fallow for a generation or two, waiting for the right child and the right field to appear together?

As I reflect on the more mystical interpretations of prodigiousness, it occurs to me that in developing the concept of co-incidence, I was influenced in some general way by a notion of causation that is at least as ancient as reincarnation: astrology. The keystone of co-incidence is that there are many more forces influencing the development of prodigies than simply the child's own exceptional talent. Rather than resorting to a cosmic level of interpretation, however, I have viewed the forces contributing to co-incidence as encompassing matters that can be analyzed, studied, described, theorized about, and otherwise dealt with in ways that most of us would call rational if not scientific. Perhaps astrology holds some lessons or insights about ways to study the intercoordination of forces, their conflicts, and the kinds of conditions that might lead to more or less pleasing concordances of individual and environment.

Although one must remain skeptical of the explanatory power behind astrological accounts, it does not seem implausible that the tradition might hold some useful insights about development in the broad sense. Like co-incidence, astrology maintains that certain phenomena (events, situations, personalities, achievements) are the result of a delicate interplay of forces. By studying and understanding something of these forces and their patterns of interaction, further insights and, perhaps, greater control can be gained over the phenomenon.

Astrological notions have not played any significant role in my theorizing about co-incidence. My interest, knowledge, and investment in astrology is, to say the least, casual, but I must admit that I have been struck with its longevity and importance for cultures long gone. The status of astrological forecasting during the time of the Greeks is well known, but its influence was felt in other cultures as well. When touring Israel, I found that ruins of sixth- and seventh-century synagogues contained mosaic zodiacs. I am not sure what role the zodiac played in earlier forms of Jewish worship, but suffice it to say that astrological emphases in the religion have since dropped out of fashion.

I have also found myself considering these more mystical traditions because of some of the stories we have heard from Randy's and Adam's parents. These vary in the degree to which they seem removed from rational experience or the possibility of reasoned explanation, but they all are out of the ordinary; they are certainly reports that no self-respecting psychologist would embrace without comment or skepticism. For a long time, I simply filed them away without thinking about them much one way or the other. In fact, the idea of writing about them made me (and the families) a little uneasy. But over time I came to see the reports as valuable regardless of the veracity of the actual stories, because they reflected issues that were important to the boys and their parents.

I began to consider the reports themselves more carefully after coming across accounts of two very different phenomena that seemed to transcend the rational. The first, though quite removed from the prodigy experience, nonetheless served to remind me that one should not necessarily dismiss a phenomenon as untrue simply because it cannot easily be explained.

The first phenomenon concerns zombies. Their association with the otherworldly realm has long made the zombie a favorite of horror films, but the possibility of such creatures actually existing has always been dismissed as superstitious nonsense. Recently, however, ethnobotanist Wade Davis has studied Haitian voodoo culture and has found both a real phenomenon and an explanation for it. Voodoo priests "create" zombies by giving their victims drugs containing powerful neurotoxins. These drugs cause temporary paralysis and suppress metabolic functioning, making the individual appear to have died. When the effects of the drug subside, the victim returns from this near-death state and is kept under the priests' thrall by subsequent administration of psychotropic drugs. To those who do not know the priests' pharmacological secrets, the "dead" victim appears to have magically come back to life to do the priests' bidding.[5]

The second account was an attempt by Lionel Menuhin Rolfe to understand the family tradition that yielded the great violin prodigy Yehudi Menuhin, Rolfe's uncle. For largely personal reasons, Rolfe felt compelled to examine the Menuhin history and tradition, seeking the roots he shared with his distinguished uncle.[6] What he found was a family tree ripe with prodigiousness and suffused with mystical themes. These themes have been played out largely in the context of Hasidic Judaism, an ecstatic religious movement spearheaded by the Menuhins' Schneerson ancestors. Rolfe traced the Menuhin family back to the early sixteenth century and found that many of these earlier generations included religious prodigies, or *illuy*. Although Yehudi Menuhin was the first secular prodigy in the family, the Menuhin-Schneerson line seems to have produced, with uncanny regularity, individuals of transcendent talent, learning, and spiritual sensibility. Themes of extraordinary early mastery and mystical preoccupations have been part of the unspoken Menuhin legacy for generations.

If phenomena like the zombies or traditions like the prodigy-producing Menuhins have a grounding and explanation in reality, then might not other strange and seemingly inexplicable experiences be comprehensible as well? And might not the prodigy be particularly sensitive to such experiences? History and evolution seem to have given the prodigy privileged access to some of our more demanding symbol systems and allowed them to master some of our most complex domains. Is it not possible that other extraordinary capabilities and sensibilities might be part of the package as well?

The prodigy has been associated with otherworldly phenomena for centuries; I had no idea when I began this work that I would be confronted so directly with manifestations of these traditions with my own subjects. It is also interesting that neither family reporting such occurrences felt that they were of much use in explaining their child's prodigiousness. It is almost as if the strange happenings were accepted as another part of the boys' unusual abilities, but not as something to be dwelled upon. In Adam's family there is some history of interest in the nonrational (Fiona's father developed into something of a mystic in his later years), but attention to such matters is mostly dismissed as illogical and unworthy of attention. Yet the events these families have themselves experienced are reported with the same mix of disbelief and wonder as are the extraordinary achievements of their children in their various worldly projects. Like the children's talents themselves, these experiences seemed to their parents to be inexplicable, puzzling, and awesome.

I include some of the reports here because, true or not, plausible or not, they have, at the very least, become part of how these two families think about themselves and their sons. My intent in raising these matters is neither to persuade nor explain away but rather simply to raise a possibility without prejudice. For the deeper secrets of individual potential to be revealed it will take a willingness to consider seriously a broad range of cognitive activity, including the less logical aspects of human experience. Below are descriptions of several of the most unusual incidents reported about Randy and Adam. These are not all of the incidents that were reported, but they are some of the most vivid and difficult to comprehend or explain.

Randy McDaniel

Three episodes concerning Randy's experiences with the unknown have been reported by his parents. According to the McDaniels there have been numerous instances of what might be called mystical or strange situations ever since Randy was a baby. These ranged from delivering soliloquies seemingly far beyond his current level of verbal skill to demonstrating heightened sensitivity to others' emotional states. The documentation for many of these, however, is not good. In a few cases, Jeanne recorded the vignette immediately afterward more or less verbatim, and from these I have selected three examples.

Two episodes occurred when Randy was about seven. One took place after a long and pleasant day that held no hint of anything unusual brewing. After a warm bath and a discussion about the family's financial situation Randy abruptly announced:

> Truth is the word of being. People who are questioned by the being word must be answered. People who do not answer by the being word are afraid of their death. People who do say the being word open a new life. Truth is the word of being.

Jeanne asked Randy if he had remembered this passage from some book he'd been reading. Randy said that he had not read it anywhere. Puzzled and astonished, Jeanne wrote down the passage word for word.

The second episode occurred during the family's summer vacation. They had rented a trailer at the beach, not far from the legendary farm. This was their first extended visit back to their special spot after a long hiatus. According to Jeanne's account this episode of unusual behavior took place on the first night of their stay.

> I was concerned that Randy had no appetite. It was very unusual for him not to . . . eat fish and chips at a favorite place. After a long walk on the beach, where we talked about writing, he said "There's a certain stillness in the heart of things, Dad, that cannot be described. You can only write about the things that you see, and maybe you can begin the work with a poem and continue from there." The conversation continued along similar lines for about an hour. Randy went to the trailer, typed out the beginning of a new story, and announced that he was starving.

Here, finally, are some excerpts Jeanne reported from a discussion that took place in November 1980, when Randy was eight-and-a-half, and was grappling with some theological issues after having read a chapter in Hendrik Willem Van Loon's *The Story of Mankind*.

RANDY: What I mean is that God, God the Father, seems real to me . . . not in the long white robes like Carl Sagan talks about it. I think of God as space. I have thought about space for a long time. I know that there are three things, not to be argued: interior, exterior, and that other (A wave of his hand in a horizontal line).

JEANNE: Perhaps it is just that third part which is unable to be expressed.

RANDY: Yes, I know that. And I know that people are only able to discuss it who understand what it is to be free. If I look out the window now, there is nothing there. I mean, nothing. And what you said before about the difference between good and evil. I don't see any difference at all. That's what it means to be free. Things flow in your mind, and nothing interrupts those things.

These episodes are reported exactly as Jeanne reported them to me in 1980. They seem most unusual in their preoccupation with issues that can be described as metaphysical. The language and sensibilities Randy is reported to have expressed are not typical of an average seven- or eight-year-old. On the other hand, the passages are not exactly sensible either, and one cannot but wonder what they (and Randy) meant.

Jeanne has also said that until he was about five, Randy reported details of his own birth and neoteny as well as impressions and feelings that she can interpret only as prenatal ones. These memories have apparently faded over the years, and he now says that he remembers nothing at all of those times. Adam, too, has reported on similar matters.

Adam's "Other Side"

While Darren and Jeanne are on the whole comfortable with the idea of Randy's disposition toward the mystical, Fiona and Nathaniel Konantovich have been more reluctant to conclude that Adam's unique sensitivities may transcend the purely logical and rational. Aside from occasional remarks in passing about Adam's alleged prenatal recollections, only once have the Konantoviches mentioned Adam's more fantastic side. During a long and intimate conversation between Lynn and Fiona in the summer of 1982, Fiona recounted several of Adam's most extraordinary and bizarre experiences. Lynn described her conversation to me the next day; we have had occasion to mull over its contents many times over the past several years.

Their conversation began that evening with some discussion of the sabbatical year Lynn and I had spent in Israel. Lynn observed that, aside from becoming parents, one of our most significant experiences was confronting directly issues of identity, fear, and anti-Semitism; for the first time in our lives we had met people who had survived the Holocaust. Fiona and Lynn speculated, as thousands of others have undoubtedly done, on whether they themselves would have had the courage and foresight to leave their professions and possessions as Hitler's grip tightened on Europe. It wasn't the first time that Lynn or I had discussed this issue since we had returned to the States, yet Lynn reported that this conversation with Fiona took a decidedly unusual and unique turn—one that still causes her to shiver several years later.

Fiona agreed with Lynn that it was absolutely imperative to instill strategies for survival in one's children. She and Nathaniel have consciously worked to impart to Adam skills for negotiating a world that is not always safe or benign. They have been extremely attentive, for example, to environmental health hazards, carefully monitoring food preservatives and additives, and the chemical and biological status of drinking water. Fiona and Lynn agreed that it was far easier to teach a child to avoid nitrites or cans soldered with lead than it was to read a cultural climate: how did some German Jews in the 1930s recognize that their culture was becoming lethal? Fiona mused that the issue of the Holocaust was a particularly charged one for their family, not because of personal family losses, but because of Adam's odd experiences as a young child. . . .

Fiona recalled that the experiences began, as many unusual circumstances seem to, in a perfectly normal setting. Adam was about eighteen months old, lounging in his bath after dinner as he did every night. He loved the warm tub where he could splash in the water or just lean back on his big, spongy baby raft and have a relaxing visit with his parents. It was during just one of these visits that Adam suddenly sat bolt upright in the tub, screaming and shouting, "The men! The men! They're coming! They're coming!" Wavering somewhere between petrified parent and concerned clinician, Fiona stared at her son, trying to understand what was happening to him. A shadow had seemed to pass over him. His eyes were focused on some distant object and he appeared unaware of where—or even who—he was. Her own anxieties under tight reign, Fiona tried to probe gently around the edges of Adam's fear.

She asked him who "they" were; he could only reply, "The men! The men!" Again Fiona asked him to explain who he meant: she didn't know what he was talking about. Adam told her with mounting hysteria in his voice that they were the men in uniforms and high boots with guns and they were coming to get him. With a calm she did not feel, Fiona tried to assure Adam that he was safe in his own bathtub with his mother and father as his only real companions. Then, as suddenly as the episode had begun, it was over. Adam seemed unaware of its occurrence. As he finished his bath Fiona tried to find some reasonable explanation for the incident she had just witnessed.

Unable to easily find such an explanation, Fiona and Nathaniel tried to dismiss the inexplicable transformation as an anomaly. But other such episodes followed. Perhaps there was even a certain inevitability to them —might not Adam's powerful mental abilities and sensitivities also some-how increase his ability to resonate with the darker (or at least inexplica-ble) side of life?

The "trance" states occurred most often in the tub, when Adam was comfortable and relaxed. Fiona told Lynn that he came to understand that he occasionally behaved in a way that was unusual and very distressing to his parents. But, still a preschooler, he could not reflect on what was happening to him, nor did his descriptions of the experiences help Fiona and Nathaniel understand what was troubling Adam while in the trance state.

The trances continued on and off for about a year and a half. During that time Fiona and Nathaniel pieced together that the men with the boots and guns seemed to be Nazi storm troopers who rounded up and massacred an entire village of Jewish families. Nathaniel and Fiona set about in their thorough and systematic way—this time tinged with fear and anxiety— to determine how Adam had learned about the Holocaust. They wanted to know what had frightened him so deeply and thoroughly that his subconscious was triggering these trance episodes. They found no expla-nation.

Adam spent virtually all of his time with either Fiona or Nathaniel. They carefully monitored and directed the amount and type of informa-tion he encountered. They had never presented material about the Second World War to him, nor had the two of them discussed Hitler or the Nazis in his presence. Although Jewish, they had not been directly affected by the Holocaust; both Fiona and Nathaniel's extended families lived in the United States during the war. In any event, Nathaniel and Fiona were quite sure that Adam had not heard war stories from grandparents, aunts, or uncles. The only remaining potential source was a babysitter who had occasionally watched him for an hour or two during this period. As one might expect, the woman had been very carefully interviewed and ob-served before Adam was ever entrusted to her care, and Nathaniel and Fiona were reasonably comfortable that she was as caring, responsible, and responsive to Adam as an outsider could be. Not surprisingly, after the trance episodes began she was very thoroughly questioned about how Adam had spent his time while in her care. Finally, she was asked directly whether she had ever talked to Adam about the Nazis. She replied indignantly that she certainly had not, adding that such a horror was no kind of thing to talk about with any child, and certainly not with Adam.

With great reluctance and even greater concern, Fiona and Nathaniel were forced to conclude that no one had introduced him to any sort of information about the Nazis and the plight of the Jews. Scientist and clinician, rationalists to the core, they had no logical explanation for Adam's behavior. Other incidents continued to intrude, though, making them even more uneasy about this aspect of Adam's "specialness."

Fiona related to Lynn how Adam loved to play in her office when she wasn't seeing clients. Like other clinicians with young patients, her office is filled with an engaging assortment of toys for play therapy. (And while Adam did not lack for toys, the ones from his mother's office had a special allure.) One of his favorites was a puppet theater with a stylized backdrop of a medieval European city. Fiona reported that one afternoon, when Adam was about two-and-a-half, he was playing in the office, keeping her company while she caught up on paperwork. Suddenly he looked up and began screaming hysterically and pointing to the theater. Fiona asked him what was the matter, and Adam pointed again to the backdrop of the theater. She asked him why her puppet theater was suddenly frightening to him—he'd played with it hundreds of times before. Adam replied, "I've been there." "Where?," his mother asked. With mounting terror in his voice, he told her that he'd been to school there. His screams became louder and more terrified, and Fiona took Adam out of her office. After he had been soothed and quieted, Adam managed a more coherent account of the source of his fear. He explained to his stunned mother that the theater city was Göttingen, where he had studied medicine "before the war." Fiona tried to probe Adam gently about his fantasy, and learned that the character he spoke of was a French Jew who had been a medical student in Göttingen. Adam related this tale lucidly, in relative calm, and with no reference to the trance episodes involving men with guns who were rounding up Jewish families.

Later that day, Fiona and Nathaniel went to the library. They found that the town of Göttingen, nestled in the Rhine valley, dates back to the Middle Ages. The town square is distinguished by a statue not dissimilar to the one depicted on the backdrop of Fiona's toy theater. The University of Göttingen, established in the eighteenth century, has boasted among its students and teachers the mathematicians Gauss, Hilbert, Wiener, and the physicist Heisenberg.

How had Adam learned of this place? Fiona or Nathaniel may have had occasion to mention Wiener or Gauss to him; had he then read somewhere that as young men these mathematicians had attended university there? Had he found "Göttingen" to be an interesting place name one day while perusing an atlas, subsequently using the city as the basis for a fantasy of power and aggression? Fiona and Nathaniel almost began to hope so. Their best efforts at reflection and query of Adam led them nowhere.

When Lynn told me of her conversation, she mused about how difficult it was to fully comprehend Fiona's narrative, let alone to decide if it was credible or not. Had Fiona's and Nathaniel's acceptance of Adam as an exceptional child gone too far, giving credence and value to Adam's most bizarre fantasies instead of encouraging him to enter the present world of the American child? We had known the Konantovich family for four years at the time of Fiona's narrative, knew them well enough to appreciate Adam's uniqueness. We also knew them well enough to know that Adam's activities were assiduously monitored and that Fiona had not been coy in asserting that they had no idea how Adam knew about Nazi persecution or German universities. She really did *not* know. Furthermore, she was not speaking for publication; she was telling a friend—somewhat reluctantly—of experiences that both confounded and frightened her.

Lynn asked Fiona what sense she made of all of it. She shrugged her shoulders and opened her eyes wide, in a characteristic expression of astonishment. "It *doesn't* make any sense! This kind of thing doesn't happen to regular, rational people. We kept hoping that these were just a few weird episodes that we could push in the corner and forget." But, she went on, until Adam was about five years old, one thing or another kept intruding, making the whole of it very difficult to ignore.

The Nazi theme—and, indeed, Adam's "adoption" of another persona—waned both in frequency and intensity as he grew older. Fiona recalled a later episode that had been a very matter-of-fact conversation among the three of them, quite different from the paralyzing fear of the trance states of some two years earlier. Fiona and Nathaniel were enjoying an evening's reminiscences about a vacation they had taken together in England when Adam interjected that he had also enjoyed England, particularly the countryside.

Fiona corrected Adam, reminding him that although they had traveled extensively with him in Scandinavia and on the Continent, their trip to England had been before he was born. Adam became impatient with them, announcing firmly that he had indeed been to England. Furthermore, he added that he had actually lived there, and that he especially enjoyed the countryside during the springtime when the stickle bushes were in bloom. Nathaniel told Adam that he had never heard of stickle bushes, and asked him where he'd read about them. Adam replied irritably, "I didn't read about them. I *distinctly* remember enjoying them."

Fiona and Nathaniel headed for their library. They consulted tour books, biology texts, horticultural guides. No stickle bushes. The next day Fiona called the New York Horticultural Society. She explained that she had come across a passing reference to an English plant whose common name was the "stickle bush," but had not been able to find an identification of it herself: could they help? The next day a researcher called with a proper Latin identification and the additional information that the bushes grow in southern England, where they are popularly used as hedges. They bloom in the springtime with a rather distinctive flower.

Lynn confided to me that when Fiona finished, she had goosebumps. She asked Fiona if she thought Adam had some sort of prebirth memories of an earlier life. And why had the incidents ceased? Fiona could offer little insight or explanation, and her very inability to find logical answers had added to her unease. She and Nathaniel found it unsettling and even frightening to have their fundamental beliefs in logical causality challenged. As difficult as it was to entertain the possibility that Adam has some extraconscious knowledge of another life, Fiona and Nathaniel felt as if they had eliminated all possible logical explanations for the episodes they had witnessed. Fiona only had guesses about why the incidents had ended. She suspected that the episodes had stopped because, as Adam grew older, he (like all children) had become more conscious, deliberate, and in control of his own mental processes and hence less susceptible to these unconscious intrusions.

Lynn and Fiona talked about other aspects of Adam's early experiences that were also quite unusual, though somehow less threatening. Fiona and Nathaniel had always suspected that Adam had heightened sensitivity to the physical world. He also seemed to have had perinatal (and possibly prenatal) memories. Although Fiona had mentioned such memories in passing before, she had never been very specific about Adam's recollections. That evening Lynn asked her exactly what Adam had described. Fiona replied that he remembered certain experiences of being in the delivery room. She related that when Adam was about twelve months old, again while taking a bath, he turned to her and said: "There are some things I don't understand from when I was new." Both puzzled and taken aback by what Adam might mean by "new," Fiona asked him what kinds of things were unclear to him. He proceeded to list a number of questions. He told her, for example, that he didn't understand why there were such bright lights, or why "they" put something into his nose which hurt. As if to demonstrate, he made a suctioning sound. Fiona could only conclude from his demonstration that he was describing the suctioning of mucus from his nose and mouth at birth. Though Fiona and Nathaniel had told Adam about Fiona's pregnancy (which was fraught with complications) and about the general process of labor and delivery, they had not told him the incidentals of his own birth. They concluded that the description of an intrusive suctioning bulb and the stark, bright environment must have come from his own memory of the delivery room.

On other occasions, Adam related sensations from the womb. He told his parents that he remembered seeing pink lights and his hands in front of his eyes. He also remembered that periodically the "walls were closing in on me—they hurt." This, Fiona and Nathaniel hypothesized, must have been Adam experiencing the uterine contractions that threatened to terminate Fiona's pregnancy from the fourth month onward. And there were other sensations, too.

Fiona is a serious folk singer with, by her own account, "a big voice." She often sang to her unborn baby, and noticed that it seemed particularly responsive to sea chanties, with their resonant bottom notes. These low tones were guaranteed to initiate a great deal of fetal movement, so Fiona, feeling a sense of connectedness and harmony with her growing baby, would sing them often and delight in the movement she would feel. Imagine how she felt when, as an infant, Adam reminisced that occasionally his prenatal world had been filled with a most horrible, painful sound that he could not escape—no matter how he tried to twist or turn away from the noise, it was always there!

Somehow, the idea of Adam's having memories from these earliest moments did not seem as startling or unusual to Fiona and Nathaniel, or to Lynn and me, as did the reports of Adam's other experiences. Similar kinds of pre- and perinatal recollection have been reported by others, from Salvador Dali to Randy McDaniel. The difference between reports of this nature and Fiona's other revelations of that summer's night is the difference between skepticism about the accessibility of experience to an individual who is arguably not yet a fully conscious being and incredulity at the idea of an individual possessing knowledge and information that (if it is to be believed) he had not acquired by any known means.

While it might be possible to come to terms with the idea of perinatal recollections, and possibly even prenatal ones, it seemed that the variety and frequency of extraordinary events involving Adam might actually defy logical explanation. Perhaps he was just geared to perceive and receive from the world differently from most of the rest of us. Fiona described two more examples of Adam's experiences to Lynn, one from the same period as the others, one much more recent.

When Adam was about four, Nathaniel's Aunt Bessie died. Fiona and Nathaniel attended her funeral out of family obligation rather than a strong feeling of attachment or affection for the woman. She had not played an active role in their lives—indeed, she had never even met their son. Unable to find a babysitter for Adam, they brought him along to the chapel but let him decide whether he wanted to attend the service itself. Adam declined. It seemed like a sensible decision; funeral services aren't the best of places for four-year-old boys, even ones with the mentation and sensibilities of Adam.

Fiona and Adam sat alone in the anteroom, talking about this and that, while Nathaniel attended the funeral service. After a while, Adam interrupted their conversation. Looking across the room, he asked his mother who the two ladies were who had just joined them in the room. Fiona looked up, but saw no one. She asked him which ladies he meant, and he replied, "The ones standing by the clock." Puzzled, Fiona told Adam that there weren't any ladies standing by the clock; no one was in this room except the two of them. Adam demurred, insisting that he saw two old ladies standing and talking by the clock. He thought they might be waiting for the lady who had just walked into the room. Adam asked whether the newcomer mightn't be Aunt Bessie. Flustered, puzzled, and concerned, Fiona replied that she didn't see any old ladies in the room, unless he wanted to include her.

Undaunted, Adam described the three women's dress and what appeared to be a brief conversation among them. He observed that the first two ladies seemed to escort "Aunt Bessie" up a flight of stairs at the end of the room, stairs which were also visible only to Adam. Once they had ascended he matter-of-factly resumed his earlier conversation with an astonished Fiona.

As the service ended Fiona and Adam were joined in the anteroom by mourners perceptible to both mother and son. Eventually Nathaniel also returned to collect his family. As a dutiful nephew and son, he had remained after the service for the family viewing of the coffin. Somewhat hesitantly Fiona asked Nathaniel to tell them how Aunt Bessie had been laid out. Not surprisingly, Nathaniel was taken aback at Fiona's unusual request, but when he realized she was serious he described Aunt Bessie's general appearance as best he could recall. It matched Adam's description of the invisible old lady escorted up the phantom stairs by her two equally imperceptible friends.

But this event, like the others Fiona had related to Lynn, was past history. No activity of this sort had transpired for about four years. Nathaniel and Fiona had basically come to think of these phenomena as a part of Adam's early development, which they didn't understand, but which no longer demanded careful analysis or explanation—they were over. Fiona observed that their tentative "truce" with this side of Adam had been somewhat shaken quite recently—by another great-aunt, as it happened.

Fiona explained to Lynn that one afternoon, not long ago, she had received a call from one of her aunts. Fiona noted that this aunt was not close to her, and the phone call was the first communication she could recall in at least fifteen years. The woman had very nearly died several weeks earlier and was recovering slowly in a hospital about an hour's drive from the Konantoviches. She had called Fiona to ask her to come to the hospital for a visit; she felt she had something very important to say to her niece. Fiona told Lynn that she remembered her aunt as an irascible, judgmental, humorless, and thoroughly unpleasant woman. She could only guess that her aunt had somehow struck in her a chord of family responsibility, for Fiona felt obligated to heed the summons. She arranged to make a perfunctory visit to the hospital.

The woman Fiona found convalescing, however, was nothing like the aunt she recalled from her childhood. This woman exuded a warmth and gentleness Fiona described as radiant. Her calm and knowing air created an impression of beatitude absolutely unlike anything Fiona had experienced before. That it was emanating from a woman Fiona remembered disliking intensely made the experience even more unsettling.

They had a pleasant and engaging hour's conversation. Fiona couldn't help but remark on the change to her aunt, who, for her part, agreed wholeheartedly and joyfully about the transformation. No, the change was not the result of a long effort in therapy; it was, regretfully, of a much more recent vintage, due to an ironical serendipity. It had followed an episode of near fatal cardiac arrest. She described to Fiona her experience of dying, with images of light and darkness, tunnels and open spaces. Fiona noted that her description sounded much like others reported in a growing popular and scientific literature on "out of body" experiences; she asked her aunt whether she was familiar with any of these writings. Her aunt replied that she was not, but added that when she had described her experiences to the doctors shortly after the trauma they had responded to her much as Fiona just had. Though skeptical, Fiona could not help but hear the conviction in her aunt's voice. And the personality change was quite apparent for all to see.

But Fiona's aunt told her that she had not called her niece to her bedside simply to apprise Fiona of the transformation, but to speak to her about Adam. The Konantoviches are an insular family and have relatively little contact with others outside of their own nucleus. Like Aunt Bessie, Fiona's aunt had not met Adam. She only knew in the most general way that Adam was an unusual child. Nonetheless, she told Fiona that she had felt an urgency about the boy, an urgency that she was impelled to communicate to Fiona. She did not understand how or why she knew it, but she was certain that Adam was some kind of beacon and that somewhere, somehow, there was something very powerful and special about him to be known. She herself did not know what—she could only express an unarticulated certainty that Adam bore careful watching and nurturing. She was frustrated with the lack of clarity of her feelings, but their sheer strength had moved her to contact Fiona despite her inability to provide a clear message about Adam.

Fiona's recounting of this meeting probably preserved some of the puzzled urgency that her aunt must have communicated to her. When Lynn asked Fiona what sense she made of her aunt's message, she replied that she didn't really know. Three things seemed important to her. The first was the startling change in her aunt. She had been so struck by the transformation that she had described the woman's appearance and behavior to a colleague, who noted a similarity to descriptions from Eastern mystical beliefs and practices. Had her aunt perchance read *The Tibetan Book of the Dead?* Fiona said that she couldn't know for sure, having been entirely out of touch with the woman for fifteen years and never close enough to her before that to have traded literary recommendations. She guessed, however, that her aunt was as likely to have read *The Tibetan Book of the Dead* as *On Relativity*.

The second salient aspect of the conversation was that her aunt felt compelled to try to articulate to Fiona how important Adam was, despite the fact that she knew practically nothing about him. The third was that after a substantial amount of reflection on their conversation, Fiona still had no idea what her aunt meant about why Adam might be so important. It seemed to Lynn as a listener that, although nothing was said explicitly, Fiona felt the visit with her aunt had once again verified Adam's unusualness and specialness, although in a very intangible way.

I am not sure whether Fiona's narrative should be taken literally. When talking with Lynn, Fiona admitted that it was possible that she and Nathaniel had overlooked some logical explanation for the incidents she had recounted. Adam might have learned of the Holocaust, of Göttingen, and of the English countryside from sources of which they were unaware. He might have seen a picture of Aunt Bessie in her favorite dress—the one that was subsequently chosen for her burial. Fiona's aunt might have known something about Adam's unusual abilities through channels of which Fiona herself was unaware, perhaps through correspondence with her parents. These were all possible, but improbable, to her mind.

As for Lynn, she says that she, too, does not know. She certainly believed Fiona's earnestness, her confusion, her awe, her fear. They shared goosebumps and shivers on that sultry July night. What we both believe is that whether actually true or not, Fiona's story needed to be listened to seriously. If nothing else, Fiona and Nathaniel's experiences with Adam's seemingly extrasensory side have helped to shape and color their life with him.

Perhaps Adam does live at the center of a strong psychic aura: some who have known him seem to resonate to a special part of him that goes beyond his exceptional ability to learn and understand a startling variety of intellectual domains. Adam's first karate teacher reluctantly resigned his position after several months. He explained to Fiona that he was "darkness" and Adam "light," and that he feared they would become locked together in a conflict of psychic forces that Adam was still too young to manage. Adam's Hebrew tutor once fervently declared him to be the Messiah. His great-aunt transcended fifteen years of indifference to advise Fiona that she had an unusual and important son. Perhaps all were tuned to a part of Adam that is imperceptible to the rest of us. Perhaps sometime in the future we will have the opportunity to find out.

Postscript

I have presented the episodes from the families of Adam and Randy because they have been important to the families themselves. They may also help explain why prodigies have historically been linked with prophecy. I can only report as faithfully as possible what Lynn and I have been told and leave you, the reader, to make of the material what you will. It is sufficient to acknowledge that there are aspects to the prodigy phenomenon that remain mysterious. Some of these aspects will undoubtedly be clarified and better understood as the phenomenon receives more serious attention and scrutiny. But perhaps others will not. Even as we make headway in revealing some of the important qualities of how the prodigy comes to express his potential and why, new and puzzling qualities are being uncovered that have yet to be comprehended.

10

The Game: To Create Conditions That Express Potential

> One way that's kind of a fun analogy in trying to get some idea of what we're doing in trying to understand nature is to imagine that the gods are playing some great game and you don't know the rules of the game, but you're allowed to look at the board at least from time to time. And in a little corner perhaps and from these observations, you try to figure out what the rules are of the game, . . . the rules of the pieces moving. (Richard Feynman, "The Pleasure of Finding Things Out," "Nova," January 25, 1983)

WITH THESE WORDS physicist Richard Feynman tries to express the scientist's quest for knowledge about nature and how it feels when some secret is revealed. In the somewhat awkward language of the interview, Feynman draws an analogy to some great, complex game that we mortals get to peek at from time to time. The physicist labors for years to be able to take just one good look at the game board, to move a playing piece or two, to come an inch or two closer to understanding what is really going on. What are the situations that are most likely to provide that long-awaited opportunity?

"The thing that doesn't fit is the thing that's the most interesting, the part that doesn't go according to what you expected," continues Feynman. The exceptions, the anomalies, are the phenomena to be watched—but this means that there must be a solid base of established fact from which the anomaly can be perceived as departing. An anomaly can only be seen as such if the more typical situation is well established and understood. One of the reasons that science is so hard, says Feynman, is that the effort required to establish a base of knowledge is enormous. This is one of the reasons Feynman believes that social science has not produced any knowledge that can be called scientific. There is simply not enough known as a base from which interesting anomalies and exceptions can be observed and interpreted.

With due respect for Feynman's sobering and discouraging words, the purpose of this chapter is to treat the prodigy as just the sort of anomaly that the physicist finds so interesting. Recognizing full well that psychological theorizing is still quite shaky and that the kinds of "laws" that a natural scientist requires are well into the future, we will, nonetheless, consider what the prodigy might reveal about the "game" that nature is playing with human cognition and evolution. Without pushing the analogy too far, I would say that my feelings about studying prodigies are strikingly similar to those Feynman has expressed for his physics. I would never claim that the knowledge gleaned from watching prodigies is of the same sort as the knowledge gained from systematic physical experiment, but the quest and search is motivated by similar goals. By paying attention to the behavior of the prodigy, we may learn something about the overall pattern of human evolution in the largest sense. The premise of this chapter is that the prodigy is a source of knowledge about the long-term prospects for humanity. In contrast to physics, perhaps, the game of human evolution—including cultural evolution—is one that can possibly be played better, as we shall see.

Evolution and Prodigies

Recall that in the early chapters I introduced four time frames that have to be in near perfect coordination for a prodigy to appear and develop: the lifetime of the individual; the history of the field which he or she will pursue; the history and present status of the culture within which both individual and field co-exist; and, finally, the longer-term historical and evolutionary forces that give rise to and constrain the features of cultures and their populations. What is being referred to in these time frames is a large-scale evolutionary framework that operates as a kind of overlay to the biological processes of mutation, genetic recombination, and natural selection. While these biological processes seem adequate to account for how species survive, adapt, or die out, they seem inadequate to explain some more distinctly human tendencies like reflection, ambition, mastery, recognition, fulfillment, and, most of all, creativity. As scientifically risky as it may be to propose broader forces than those of the Darwinian or neo-Darwinian sort, it seems necessary to do so if the prodigy is to be comprehended.

If we accept that any such proposals of broader forces must be, at best, highly speculative and, at worst, simply whistling in the dark, it remains true that the prodigy cries out for explanation. More than this, if my intuition is at all on the mark, then the necessity that I feel about understanding the prodigy is not simply a function of my own curiosity, although that would be justification enough. Yet it strikes me that there is a greater urgency about understanding the present problem, one that led me to the kind of explanation for prodigies that I present in this chapter. What I have done up to now is to describe several dimensions that must be taken into account for a prodigy to develop. The deeper question of *why* such extreme cases appear in the first place can only be presented now that the complexity and delicacy of the prodigy phenomenon has been described.

Just as physicists like Feynman see their goal as understanding nature's physical game, I see the purpose of my work with prodigies as understanding the psychological and cultural levels of the game. Ultimately, perhaps, the two games are one, and the physical game is the only game in town. Perhaps the one I am interested in will be fully accounted for by the physicists' game. Perhaps, but I do not think so. As soon as it became clear that the physical universe was in continuous transformation, that the phenomena of the physical world were affected by the nature of the observations being made upon them, the physicists' game and the game I am thinking of became more reciprocal, but not identical.[1] It becomes critical to understand the observer in order to be able to understand the observed. Once this leap is made, then the psychological qualities of human observers enter the physicists' realm. And vice versa, of course, but this has already been accepted.

I believe that the prodigy has something special to tell us about the psychological purposes of human development. By being an anomaly, something that does not fit our usual assumptions about how development works, the prodigy presents a challenge to those assumptions and at the same time forces us to consider certain broader issues that seem to have, for the most part, escaped our attention until now. The prodigy has the effect of forcing a reconsideration of the reasons a person chooses particular domains to master, toward what end, and for what purpose. Without assuming that individuals are necessarily aware of their motives, the prodigy has taught us that a powerful human motive driving a great deal of behavior is to use the talents and capabilities that are one's special set of gifts. To put it more strongly, one of the qualities of human beings that may operate powerfully when conditions permit is the desire to express the uniqueness of their personal abilities, experiences, and understanding of the world. For a prodigy these issues are keenly focused.

Now, enlarging the level of our discussion of the individual to include the group, we can see that the consequence of this desire could be ruthless competition, or worse; indeed, there is plenty of evidence of such things in human behavior. Certainly among highly talented children, competitiveness and raw ambition can be extreme. But other qualities also surface, and the more extreme the talent, the more likely they are to do so. In the face of truly awesome talent, however, competitiveness often gives way to appreciation for the depth of another's gift, and the establishment of a sense of community supporting and encouraging the individual's further development. Extraordinary talent, like that of Mozart or perhaps Mi Dori, seems to be recognized as such by others, as if it transcends the efforts and abilities of most of the rest of us. Even from the individuals themselves, and often from those around them, there is a kind of acceptance and admiration for the purity of the gift and the quality of its expression. Just what is it that is being recognized? What does it mean to those who witness the performance of the prodigy when there is absolutely no doubt that the performance is sublime? An answer to this question would also help us unravel the mystery of the game that nature has been playing. Let me try to put forth as straightforwardly and clearly as possible a first effort at describing what the game seems to be about. This is not done with the idea that it will be adequate, but rather to give force to the proposition that some explanation must be sought. It is no longer safe to assume that physical science alone will give us the answers even to questions about the physical universe. For the psychological universe especially, questions will have to be formed at the psychological level. This is what I am trying to do in this chapter.

The Game: Fulfillment of Human Potential

The object of the game is to create conditions that will use as much as possible of the human potential evolved across human history; in particular, to provide conditions that will allow those who are able, to do something unique and significant. The name of the game is more than survival in the biological sense, since it may well be that survival could be achieved with a simpler set of conditions. Instead, it is possible that survival might be enhanced in some more subtle way through a psychological mechanism that allows people to experience fulfillment and satisfaction. Part of the game is to continue to survive as a species; another part is to increase the degree of expression of varied forms of human potential. It is reasonable to assume that anything that contributes to productive diversity is likely to contribute to survival of individuals and, ultimately, of our species.

The possibility of expressing unique potential could serve the purposes of overall survival by increasing the range and variety of available skills and specialties among the population. Since it is impossible to know in advance what the crucial skills for continued survival will be, it behooves us to have as many of these skills as possible in our collective repertoire. One thing is for sure; this game of expressing potential is one of very large numbers, with low probability that any single person will manage to make optimal use of his or her talent. The strategy seems to allow for enormous sacrifice of potential over time for the opportunity to hit it big with a single individual at a single moment. A wide range of capabilities have evolved over human history, with the bet that the conditions necessary for utilizing that range of potential are going to be made sufficiently available and accessible to continue the game for at least another round. Not everyone's potential will be expressed to the fullest, but the more people who find some opportunity to exercise their special talents, the more likely the game is to continue.

While it may be true, as Stephen Jay Gould asserts in his book *The Mismeasure of Man,* that the current gene pool of homo sapiens is remarkably uniform,[2] variations in human *behavior* are astoundingly large and often culture-dependent. The issue of diversity and variation is somehow key to the questions that interest me in this book. Prodigies represent nothing if they do not represent extreme variations in ability. Indeed, this is one of the main reasons that we are so amazed by them. They violate our expectations about what falls within the expected range of behavior. Diversity is one of the keystones of biological evolution; it also seems to be part of nature's game plan to catalyze development of potential into personal fulfillment. Nature has done its part through genetic mechanisms in biological evolution and in evolving cultures within which extreme variations in talent can be expressed. Why things might have worked this way is, of course, one of our preoccupations in this chapter. One answer is that it permits even greater variety and therefore greater possible adaptability for our species. And not incidentally, the greater the variability, the greater the possibility that individuals will find a match between their own specific proclivities and a set of specific opportunities made available by the culture.

For the past few years I have been keeping an eye out for examples of unusual preoccupations pursued by otherwise ordinary individuals. I have found newspaper and magazine accounts describing people who spend their time bird watching or wine tasting or playing backgammon or weaving or building stone fences or collecting everything from matchbook covers to nuts. For example, a local newspaper carried an article about a self-styled "thimbecile" named Ruth Mann who has six display cabinets in her dining room containing more than 2,000 thimbles. Her collection includes "hand-painted thimbles, gold thimbles, cloth thimbles, bog oak thimbles, ivory thimbles and more. She's got exotic thimbles inlaid with mother-of-pearl, diamonds, sapphires and opals."[3] According to the newspaper article, Mann is also a founding member and former president of an organization called Thimble Collectors International, a group that holds a four-day convention each year to talk shop. Mann's passion for thimbles is purely frivolous, for she does not even use them in her own sewing, although she does expert needlework. She just happens to find thimbles an endless source of fascination. There may be no particular importance to this kind of interest, but it makes no difference to Ruth Mann. It does no harm either. And more to the point, there is no way to know what kind of knowledge and what sorts of interests will turn out to be of value in some future impossible-to-predict situation.

There is something to learn about the importance of encouraging a diversity of interests other than the fantastic notion that some time in the far-flung future an expertise in thimbles will save the world from impending disaster. In fact, this rather absurd scenario may express the lesson to be learned best of all, and that lesson is that the overwhelming majority of the time that we spend studying, thinking, and working has very little to do with "survival" in any direct sense. Our very intelligence has allowed us to create and develop domains of knowledge which are probably only peripherally related to staying alive and fecund. And because of this, the need to find activities which yield a sense of playfulness, productivity, fulfillment, satisfaction, and pride may be as important to humans as the need to produce offspring. This is the goal of the game: to achieve a psychological, as well as a biological, flourishing of the human race.

The prodigy represents one type of powerful match between the individual and a domain of knowledge, where the passion for developing one's ability and rapid mastery of a field indicate that one move in the game of expressing potential has been won. But, though sizable, payoff for this strategy is too infrequent—other ways of playing the game must be sought to increase the odds of more people winning. Few of us will possess the extreme ability or enjoy the optimal environmental conditions that characterize the prodigy. And among prodigies these conditions are themselves very fragile.

The key, I think, lies in the stimulation and encouragement of diversity in interests and activities. The deep intuition shared by many is that humanity's strength lies in its variety. As much as we might like those around us to be soul mates, and as much as we want to be comfortable with them, there is also the belief that as a species we have come this far by cultivating variability. Since the critical sort of variability is not likely to be caused directly by genetic variation, the variability must be carried along by cultural provisions for encouraging it. The evidence for humanity as a variety-producing animal is so overwhelming that it hardly needs comment. The prodigy phenomenon demonstrates that there is a process by which cultures create the conditions that allow diverse potential to be expressed as actual achievement. When a prodigy appears, the precise conditions for optimal expression of potential have been provided, and this is reason to celebrate—and reflect.

If the game indeed works through matching an individual and a field, then it operates primarily at the level of culture, since the underlying genetic material of our species has remained substantially unchanged over the centuries.[4] It is how the biological substrate interacts with the environment that is most changeable and changing. Taking this point of view would suggest, for example, that prodigies have always been with us, at least in terms of their genetic or intellectual potential. Whoever or whatever is playing the game has been sending potential prodigies into the fray throughout history. Occasionally there is a moment in time when the other forces coincide, which allow these highly pretuned individuals to use their potential to best advantage. This is not to say, for example, that each potential chess or music prodigy is genetically similar to every other chess or music prodigy, but only that the talent for playing chess or music well was probably part of the genetic pool of abilities for a long time before there was a game of chess to play, and probably will exist for a long time after anyone will be interested in playing chess or music as we know it.

To push the metaphor of the game a bit further, it is not the nature of the individual playing pieces that has changed over the broad evolutionary time span, but rather the board on which the pieces move. In fact, one of the things that makes understanding the game so challenging is that it is in constant flux; not only do the playing pieces move about, but the board on which individual moves develop is itself constantly changing. This dynamic quality actually makes it more like the game of go than chess, except that in go the board remains unchanged even as the pieces themselves change their function. This game has a changing board and changing pieces too. Only a master strategist or a player of brute force could keep the game going, which in this case might be tantamount to winning.

What do prodigies have to do with this game? I think that they help us understand the game's deep underlying structure. The prodigy is the expression of one way that nature has enhanced its ability to provide enough variability to guarantee a sublime match between individual and domain of knowledge. By producing highly specialized individuals pre-tuned for certain very specific functions, nature sets the conditions for an occasional extraordinary coordination of talent, time, culture, and field. The whole game depends on the creation of external catalysts for the maximum realization of potential: in the case of the prodigy, the potential belongs to children powerfully pretuned to a specific domain. Nonetheless, a symbol system must be available through which their highly specific potentials can be expressed, and there must also be specific domains of knowledge and skill through which these symbol systems can be utilized for real world activities.[5]

Winning the game by finding a way to give voice to one's unique potential depends then at least as much on cultures that gather and store knowledge in organized, externalized, recognizable, and usable domains as on talented individuals. Individuals who have the capability to express their psychological and intellectual potentials uniquely, perhaps through rarefied and subtle domains, are continuously being produced as part of our biological legacy of variability. The difficult part of the game is finding which conditions will do the trick for bringing forth the potential of a given individual, and providing those conditions at the proper moment. Timing is everything. Prodigies are masterpieces of timing, individuals who manage to find a fully resonant domain very early in their individual life games. One can only imagine how many times similarly organized and pretuned minds have searched in vain for the match that would seem to have been made in heaven.[6]

NATURE'S GAMBIT: AN OPTIMAL MATCH

This book has proposed that a number of forces must successfully co-incide if specialized potential is to express itself in dramatic form. Only a very long-term game plan would use a strategy with probabilities weighted so heavily against the optimum expression of potential for any given individual. Nature's gambit, then, has at least two manifestations. One we have already discussed: in order to improve the chances of an occasional perfect match of person and field, many people will fall short of finding the optimal match of their proclivities and a culturally available domain. It is for the opportunity of a fortuitous, extremely rare, but also extremely intense instance of such a match that the gambit is taken. The gambit, as in chess, accepts sacrifice (in this case frequent sacrifice of optimal use of potential) in order to set the conditions for critical advantage over the course of the game.

The second manifestation of nature's gambit is more subtle. The long-term prospects of the game may depend on the individual pieces beginning to take over some of the game strategy themselves. This feature sets the human aspect of the game apart from the aspects studied by physicists. To control the game we must know more of what it is about and, in particular, how to play it to advantage. I think that perhaps the deeper message of the prodigy may be to remind humanity that, at some point, we must understand how to enhance the process of human development in order to remain in the game at all, let alone to have a chance at winning in any meaningful sense. Survival itself seems tenuous in these apocalyptic times. The prodigy may have something to tell us that might help tip the balance toward our continued existence on this earth.

We, of course, are the pieces in the game, the pawns and rooks being moved about the board by forces that are little understood. In this respect —and probably only this respect—I find B. F. Skinner's view of behavior to be of real relevance. Skinner has demonstrated the power of one set of forces influencing co-incidence, the rewards and punishments in environments that shape individual behavior. While this is only one among several sets of crucial forces, we must begin to understand how these mechanisms influence choice and judgment so that they can be used for positive purposes.[7] Because Skinner saw but one relatively narrow dimension of human behavior he could only recommend as a goal that more people be positively reinforced more of the time. In the context of co-incidence, we can broaden the interpretation of the forces that are crucial to the realization of potential, thereby also broadening the view of what might constitute an "optimized" environment.

The prodigy provides a clear and articulated source of information about how the processes of co-incidence work when the level of coordination and organization among person, culture, and field is extremely high. As we have seen from some of my own cases, even such rare and extreme cases of match of talent to domain do not necessarily sustain themselves for very long. For both of my chess players, six years was about the span of time when the interplay of forces co-incided. This leads me to yet another side of nature's gambit, a side I have downplayed for the most part.

If it really is true that each person has one and only one way of using the potential that evolution has bestowed upon her or him, then the sacrifice of talent would be so immense as to be intolerable. Except for rare and for the most part happy co-incidences like the prodigy, the rest of us would never come close to finding engaging and challenging work or play and perforce would be destined to live unfulfilled and unsatisfying lives. Since this is manifestly not the case, it seems that nature has another way to hedge its bets.

As I proposed in earlier chapters, it seems more plausible to assume that we each come equipped with two sets of potentials, a special-purpose set and a general-purpose set. Some people seem to have more specialized and less generalized capabilities, whereas the proportions in others are reversed. The tendency that we have evolved toward generalized talent is what helps us settle on some compromise between the exquisite concordance represented by the prodigy and the frustrated lack of engagement of the single-purpose specialist who is deprived of an appropriate field. The odds are so heavily against optimal use of specialized mental abilities that most people must rely on more generalized talent to help them find something worthwhile and interesting to do. The result may not be a beautiful tuning of mind to field as in the case of a prodigy, but nature seems to have provided us with more than one road to a reasonably satisfying life. If we do not manage to find that special match, we still have a set of generalized mental abilities that can be used in the widest variety of ways in the widest variety of cultural settings.

At least three of my subjects (and in truth, probably the other three as well) were blessed with a healthy and robust general intellectual acuity as well as a specific, preorganized affinity for a particular domain. For Franklin and Ricky in particular, given the prospects of a career in chess versus other more valued possibilities, it is no real surprise that they chose to pursue other things. Billy Devlin's trajectory, in retrospect, also seems to indicate that his gifts were more general than we had thought when we first met him at age six, making his apparent shift in interest from mathematics to a broader spectrum of scientific subjects a sensible one. Mathematics, at least in its more esoteric forms, may well require what Roger Brown has dubbed a "kinky gene."[8] Having both general and specific sets of intellectual capabilities gives one the option of selecting from several possibilities. Having only an idiosyncratic, "kinky gene" for music or chess, mathematics, art, or linguistics massively constrains one's choices. In the most extreme cases of specialized talent, a prodigy appears with relatively little in the way of general intellectual capability and enormous specific talent preorganized to express itself only through a very narrow set of channels. There is some evidence that Mozart was such a case.[9] It appears that the more generalized intellectual abilities often also include a healthy dose of pragmatism that helps people manage the mundane particulars of everyday life.[10] When the "pure" or single-purpose prodigy lacks even a modicum of this more generalized capability, the task of negotiating and managing relatively simple daily activities can become overwhelming and near impossible to manage. Mozart's wife cut his meat for him.

The value of general intellectual talent for individuals destined to pursue highly specialized forms of expression is that it can assist in the coordination and organizing functions so crucial for sustained prodigious achievement. If these qualities are lacking or inadequate it puts that much more of a burden on those around the prodigy to make sure that everything is kept in proper balance. Nils Kirkendahl, for example, is highly gifted in general intellectual and interpersonal capabilities as well as in music, and from a relatively young age he was an active and energetic participant in the decisions that affected his career. The choice to pursue violin performance seriously, with the concomitant decision to give up serious composition, was made at a mere eleven years of age. Fortunately he was up to the task, and his family understood that his own sense of self was sufficiently well developed and robust to permit him to carry that heavy responsibility.

The literature is rife with examples, however, of prodigies who were so dependent on their families, mentors, and teachers that they were utterly helpless and incompetent without constant supervision and maintenance. This lack of general ability may, for example, have led to Erwin Nyiregyhazi's retirement as a concert pianist in his early twenties and his peculiar reclusive style as a composer. In short, if the prodigy does not have the general intellectual skills to monitor and control his own development, he had better have someone else around who is committed to his talent and who can keep the many aspects of a prodigy's preparation in proper coordination. The young Mozart appears to have been one prodigy who was

216

unable to manage his special talent and the exigencies of eighteenth-century Viennese life, nor was anyone around to help him secure and organize the resources necessary for a more sustained career. These conditions almost certainly contributed to his early death.

The way the game works, then, is that a tiny number of individuals in each generation are super-specialized for expression through a single, narrowly defined domain. Some people who are gifted in these domains are recognized by the culture as having valuable qualities, and some are not. An even smaller number of individuals are also gifted with sufficient general adaptiveness to recognize the need for a specific outlet for their unique potential, to organize the resources necessary to develop their talent, and to function within whatever cultural context is available to sustain the delicate coordination of forces essential to the expression of their gifts. For individuals lacking these more general skills (and for *all* individuals during the early years), there must be substantial assistance from others in the culture.

It appears that a process very much like the gambit I have been describing has been at work in one family, the Menuhins, for many generations.[11] It was intuitively but very consciously a decision of the Menuhins, for example, to direct the family's resources toward son Yehudi's preparation for a musical career; the talents of his two younger sisters were substantially sacrificed in order to fulfill the family's primary mission of developing Yehudi's talent. Yehudi's nephew, Lionel Menuhin Rolfe, has suggested that the Menuhin family has been doing something like this for centuries: picking out one child in a family and orienting their resources toward his education and preparation for greatness. Rolfe traces this pattern through generation after generation. In more modern times, the Menuhin family apparently lost track of this thread in its history. But even without having an explicit model, the pattern repeated itself, although with variations: previous generations had focused primarily on rabbinical and scholarly fields, not specifically musical ones.

But in order not to invest the prodigy with more long-term importance than is appropriate, it is necessary to put the status of the prodigy into proper perspective. To return to the game metaphor, the prodigy is an individual designed to make maximum use of some aspect of the game board during some specific period of time. Since the game board constantly changes, we are always talking about a *relative* match of person to situation. Given an appropriate set of conditions for a given field at a given moment in time, some individuals will be optimally organized to take advantage of the particular demands and opportunities for expression currently offered by that domain. When a prodigy appears, it offers us the opportunity to assess the state of a domain. Prodigies only appear, it seems, when fields have themselves evolved in certain specific ways, when the fields are "ready" in ways that we have only begun to understand.

A prodigy probably tells us more about the current state of a field or domain than about the direction or the ways that it will become transformed in the future. The appearance of a prodigy signals that nature and culture have managed to move into a state of reciprocal coordination; it should give us some hint about what succeeds in evolving our modes of cultural transmission and cultural preservation. The prodigy who takes to a technology, a symbol system, a set of ideas and concepts as if they were tailor-made can do so largely because, without our knowing exactly how or why, that is precisely what we have intended and striven toward.

The efforts of countless individuals over countless generations are distilled into the culturally defined and organized structure that is a field or domain as it exists at one moment in time. We seem to make this effort, at least in part, to improve the possibility that a true reciprocity between person and domain will come about, either for ourselves or for others. When a prodigy emerges we see a hint that such dramatic matches are in the offing, and those around the child and in the field do what they can to keep the process going, to keep things in pleasing and powerful coordination.

What the prodigy tells us about the game, then, is that there has been progress in making the board and at least some of the pieces work together better, thus raising the likelihood that the game will continue. This is not to say that the absence of prodigies fails to tell us anything about how other fields or individuals function. It is just that in those fields where prodigies appear, we are given the opportunity to see in somewhat more simplified form what the game is about. Nor should the message be that the only way to win the game is by having more prodigies, or more fields that produce prodigies. The prodigy phenomenon is there, I believe, to give us a more intimate look at the importance of developing the resources to fully utilize capabilities, whether these capabilities happen to manifest themselves in the breathtaking match of child to field or in the more frequent, subtle, and gradual evolution of an individual's craft over a lifetime.

The prodigy helps lay bare the co-incidence process for all to see. To expect everyone to become a prodigy by virtue of this glimpse into the nature of things would be to miss the point totally. Even trying to use this knowledge to increase the number of prodigies would be failing to comprehend their message. I think that what is important is to understand better how individual potential is expressed through the ministrations of a caring and attentive culture, with the ultimate goal that a wider range of potentials in a larger number of people may be expressed.

There is, of course, a question about how important it is to any individual that full potential be expressed. In fact, the whole idea could be considered to have a romantic quality that smacks of bad John Dewey, the 1960s, and West Coast Never-Never Land. Many people in many parts of the world are grateful to make it through another day, to survive the rigors of a ruthless and unrewarding struggle for food and shelter and safety. One only need conjure up an image of Nicaraguan death squads, a boatload of Southeast Asian refugees, or starving Ethiopians scratching their way to the Sudan as a reminder of how utopian a vision I have portrayed in these pages. I accept this sobering reminder of how far from a pleasing co-incidence of self and culture most members of our species still are.

Yet I cannot help but want to raise the probability that even a few more individuals will have a slightly greater chance of using the capabilities that evolution has bestowed upon them. For me this means trying to penetrate the mysteries of human potential and trying to show how it can be better understood. Armed with this knowledge and given the opportunity to use it, I believe the effort in these pages to make sense of extreme expressions of ability has broader significance. It is absolutely true that problems of a scope and scale much more immediate than these must be addressed before my idealistic proposals could have any relevance for much of the world's population. One does what one can, or at least what one wants to believe one can.

When I ask my students whether they believe that they have some unique contribution to make to the world, virtually everyone answers in the affirmative. Of the hundreds of young people I have asked, each one believes that he or she has something important to say or do uniquely well. If asked whether or not they will actually be able to carry out their "mission" or have their unique say, there is more diversity in response. Still, it is both significant and deeply moving that there is such unanimity in the perception of one's own valuable, unique potential. I do believe that the human condition includes the desire for full and complete use of individual talent. There is something deep and meaningful about the possibility of a perfect co-incidence of forces that allows for individual expression, and not just in the prodigy.

We know that genetically, physically, and experientially each human being represents a unique and unprecedented set of events. To go from this recognition of physical uniqueness to a belief about psychological and expressive uniqueness is a sizable step. Yet it does suggest that each of us, given the opportunity to reflect on the matter in a secure environment, would have some sense of her or his own uniqueness, of unprecedented opportunity. I think this is why we are moved when we witness the extraordinary achievements of the prodigy or the uniquely gifted artist, scientist, or humanist. The prodigy comes as close to the ideal of full and powerful use of potential as we currently understand. The prodigy, in other words, gives us a hint about why we are here and what we are trying to make of ourselves; if we pay attention, this hint might help keep the game going awhile longer.

11

Harnessing the Forces of Co-incidence

I F WE ACCEPT that we are pieces in an evolutionary board game and that it is our task to learn how to play it better, then how should we go about doing so? To the extent possible we will need to learn how to understand and work with the processes of co-incidence to maximize both the chances that our species will survive and the probability that individuals will enjoy rich and satisfying lives; these are perhaps two sides of the same coin. The prodigy provides several hints about how the co-incidence process might be working; it is important to reflect on these, to see if they can provide the basis for more general understanding of the development of human ability. A fuller understanding of this process should allow for more conscious and deliberate efforts to harness the forces of co-incidence to better go about our business of raising children, developing cultures, providing opportunities for diversity and expression, and preparing for the future.

It should be clear that there is no way to harness totally the co-incidence process, for several of the forces contributing to the emergence and development of talent are beyond any individual's power to manipulate. One has little control, for example, over the biological predispositions toward talent one inherits from one's forebears. Even if the genetic research community could identify specific markers for the expression of a particular ability and had perfected techniques to provide that "ability gene" to those who might want it, there are a number of other factors (both intra- and extragenetic) that might mitigate against the realization of such preprogrammed potential. Likewise, we have little to do or say about the particular period of history into which we are born, or even the culture in which we are raised and trained. Therefore, when we speak of harnessing the forces of co-incidence it should be clear that the goal is not to regulate every facet of the process. Even if it were desirable, this would not be possible. Knowing how the process of co-incidence works leads to more informed decisions about development of potential, but it will not altogether control it.

The fact that we are generally limited in our degree of influence over critical forces is, in part, why the prodigy is such a revealing phenomenon. The precise and delicate balance among the co-incidence forces that allows prodigious talent to be expressed is uncanny, almost as if someone had written a computer program to oversee and control the process. The sequence and timing of events, the match of child to domain, the reciprocity of mind and culture, the responsiveness and organization of family and teachers, and the precise moment in history in which it all happens seem beyond the ability of any one person to plan and direct. And yet, even when so much seems to have been programmed to perfection, it still takes the sustained, dedicated, and unflagging efforts of committed supporters to keep the process on target, maintaining the course and steering the child through the hazards and pitfalls that inevitably arise. Perhaps *because* the match of child and field is so delicate, the effort needed to maintain, balance, and nurture the process is monumental.

For the prodigy, two of the goals most of us find difficult to achieve seem to occur almost effortlessly. Connecting with a challenging field happens rapidly and powerfully. Sometimes it is already obvious as early as the preschool years that the child has a fix on a domain that will be that individual's passionate pursuit for a lifetime. The geometrician H. S. H. Coxeter reported that he was a numerophile from the age of two or three, and his mother claimed he followed stock market reports as a child simply because the numbers were so fascinating.[1] Pianist Lorin Hollander also recalled having been smitten—by classical music—long before he entered kindergarten. His parents added sheet music to his other toys when their son was three.[2] This early, rapid, and fierce attachment to a field of endeavor, so characteristic of a prodigy, is a part of the co-incidence equation that seems to fall into place effortlessly. For the rest of us, it usually takes more time and a great deal more searching.

Prodigies also begin to develop a sense of real mastery and control over their field at an early age and with relative ease unknown to the nonprodigious achiever. The natural gifts that are part and parcel of the extreme specialist make his or her initial mastery trajectory very steep. For the prodigy there are few start-up problems and few delays between first forays and real achievements. It takes most of us several years before that exhilarating feeling of true mastery is experienced. Prodigies do not have to delay their sense of full participation in a domain in this way. It is often true that prodigies continue to pursue the more difficult and complex reaches of their fields, where continued mastery and rewards are not achieved as easily, but getting over the initial hurdles of understanding and feeling comfortable in a domain is relatively less difficult for the prodigy.

It is a tremendous advantage to have these goals achieved early and with such relative ease; it is, however, equally a danger to committed, sustained effort, and must be matched with another gift—persistence in the face of slowed progress or even reversals. When such obstacles come, and they always do, the prodigy must be prepared to transcend them.

We have learned from the prodigy how early attachment to a field and early mastery can occur. We cannot, of course, expect that such knowledge will materially change the prospects for the rest of us. But we can, perhaps, better understand what it is like when child and field are beautifully matched; this will help us to know when good matches occur and possibly also how to facilitate them. We can even learn a little more about what must be done to hold such matches together—how to keep children on their trajectory for learning a field and directed toward their goals. We can learn, in other words, why some techniques for directing, organizing, and controlling a process of development and mastery seem to work and others do not.

Thus the prodigy experience will be of some use in figuring out how to deal with developing talent and assisting children to express their full potential. At the level of microanalysis, we may be able to learn what interventions benefit the prodigy and what kinds of instruction and support would benefit others. Learning how to develop the prodigy's talent is likely to benefit the rest of us primarily as a model of what happens when major co-incidence forces prepare the situation to go well. So long as the natural tendency to overgeneralize from one situation to another does not get too far out of hand, there should be lessons to learn from studying the development of the child prodigy.

Assessing Individual Proclivities

If nothing else, the study of prodigies has taught us that children differ widely in capability, and beyond that, they differ in the realms in which their capabilities can be expressed. If we are to harbor any expectations about helping children fulfill their individual potentials, then we must develop strategies and techniques for identifying talent in children whose gifts are less assertively displayed. It is critical, therefore, to establish some sense of the variety of a child's strengths and weaknesses in order to be able to respond appropriately and well. Unfortunately, there are few reliable guides for sorting these matters out. Most assessment techniques are either so broad that they ignore the whole area of specific proclivity, or else they focus on one or a few very specific skills that do not necessarily relate directly to performance in a particular domain. A comprehensive, varied, and integrated assessment technique simply does not exist, leaving parents and teachers to sort out specific talents by their own intuitions, as has been true for centuries.

My colleague Howard Gardner and I have begun a project, dubbed Spectrum, which is intended to help remedy this situation. We are in the process of constructing a set of techniques for naturalistic early assessment of individual proclivities that are to be conducted as part of the ongoing activity of the preschool classroom. The intention is to put a set of tools into the hands of teachers to enable them, over the course of the school year, to develop a sensitive portrait of each child with respect to a large number of areas of potential capability. We are currently working with about twenty different specific proclivities including music, logic, science, language, leadership, mathematics, drama, dance, athletics, and art. We also intend to provide techniques for detecting social sensitivities, temperamental qualities like perseverance (so critical with the prodigies), and humor. It is our hope that, armed with such assessment tools, parents, teachers, and the children themselves will be able to make more informed decisions about choosing schools, lessons, activities, and the allocation of resources to encourage promising areas of talent. Although it is still some distance away, we believe that a systematic effort to sample the numerous potentialities in young children will yield useful information and help guide parents and teachers in the development of their children's talent.

The techniques we are developing are generally unnecessary for extreme cases like prodigies, where talent and interest are asserted with strength and conviction. Yet with more sensitive devices for detecting specific inclinations in young children, we believe that distinctive abilities and interests will be found in virtually all children: not in the same isolated and singular form that they often appear in prodigies, nor necessarily extreme to the same degree, but we expect to be able to detect a significant pool of previously unrecognized talents in quite young children.

Even when Project Spectrum is completed, which will be years into the future, and better information is available on the talents and proclivities of children, we will still be left with the problem of how to develop these talents once we know what they are. As I have tried to stress throughout this book, there is no easy answer to the question of how to optimize the nurturance and development of talent. Each situation requires deep and thorough analysis, continuous monitoring and correcting of the child's activity in the field, and some deep faith, intuition, tradition, or philosophy upon which the child-rearing process is based. The development of individual talent is more like sailing or exploring an unknown continent than it is like engineering or accounting: there are few set procedures or formulas. Obviously, the more adequate the information available about both children and their development, the better will be the chances of providing optimal conditions for any given child.

Optimizing the conditions for the expression of talent involves attention to at least three sets of co-incidence forces: the family, the particular domain, and psychological factors. Once an assessment of a child's proclivities has been made, the family, particularly the parents, must decide whether and how they will try to facilitate the development of the child's ability. These decisions may not always be simple or straightforward. How do parents respond to a child with a number of different strengths, for example? Do the parents select a particular area to encourage, or do they provide a variety of lessons and "enrichments" and hope that the child will take the lead and show a preference? Although this latter strategy is the most responsive, resources are often limited and it may not be possible to do so. Furthermore, parents may hold strong opinions about the relative merits of different domains and may have strong preferences themselves about the paths their children follow. These opinions may be strongly tied to prevailing cultural values and opportunities, or they may have more personal or idiosyncratic origins. For example, one family might recoil from the idea that their son showed keen interest and promise in kinesthetic and dramatic activities if the direction of the child's interest was toward ballet rather than a more stereotypically masculine sport. Other families might find the idea of encouraging the development of a potential Villella, Nureyev, or Baryshnikov most exhilarating. In some cases, parents may not know what to make of a particular ability and may, therefore, have difficulty finding ways to channel the talent into what they perceive as productive and meaningful activities.

A striking example of this kind of parental dilemma was offered several years ago by journalist Roderick MacLeish. Mr. MacLeish had a businessman friend who found himself in charge of his six-year-old son one Saturday afternoon. Since the man had some work to finish up, he decided to bring his boy to the office for a few hours. The boy soon tired of drawing, typing, and poking around, and the father soon ran short of sufficiently distracting activities. Finally, he suggested that the boy amuse himself with the office wall safe: within ten minutes the man was looking at the inside of his safe. They went into another office and the boy proceeded to make short work of the safe in there as well. The father began a semisystematic investigation of his son's unusual "talent." Not only was the boy able to open virtually every safe in his father's office, but he was skilled at cracking a variety of complicated combination safes his father uncovered for him to try. Such an ability obviously poses a dilemma: certainly most parents would not want to encourage their children to become master (or even child prodigy) safecrackers. The problem becomes one of determining what such an ability means and how to rechannel and develop it in a socially acceptable manner. Perhaps this child has extraordinarily sensitive tactile perceptions that might be directed toward musical performance or, perhaps later, toward surgery. Perhaps his parents will decide that they do not wish to explore further the nature of this talent and will consciously direct their energies toward encouraging their son's other interests and strengths.

The second factor that can be monitored and influenced in the development of any talent, prodigious or not, relates to the domain of interest itself. Some domains seem to be more teachable than others, with more systematic curricula and criteria for progress. All domains can be mastered by some individuals, if not by the precociously tuned mind of the prodigy, then by the sustained effort of talented persons over years of study. It is primarily in the area of instruction that domain-related forces can be harnessed. The selection of teachers can be critical to a child's progress through a field, for without instructors who are sensitive to both the structure and nuances of the field and the level of development of the child, progress will be less than optimal. In highly structured and "curricularized" fields, the individual talents and sensitivities of teachers may be less critical to continued mastery than in domains where there is less consensus about the nature of progress or the methods for achieving it. For all domains, the quality of exchange between student and teacher is crucial, and can influence greatly the kind and degree of progress made. In monitoring a child's progress and continued interest in learning, those responsible for the child must be able to make judgments about the type of teacher and teaching that best suits the child and must also be prepared to discuss or make changes that would seem to better facilitate progress.

Finally, there are psychological forces in the development of talent that can be harnessed to some extent. In particular, motivational factors undoubtedly play a central role in the development of ability. One characteristic of the prodigy is a strong desire—some have even described it as a drive—to actively exercise his or her talent. Parents of prodigies often report having to pry their children away from the piano, chessboard, easel, or typewriter. Most of us are probably more familiar with parental coaxing and exhortation to practice. The prodigy undoubtedly represents an extreme both in terms of the intensity of motivation and the extent to which it is internally generated.

Prodigies have taught us that the motivation to do something well can be very specific. It may only express itself fully when a particular domain of knowledge is itself sufficiently developed to offer the optimal challenge to the youngster. In the case of the prodigy this match of child to field happens more or less dramatically (although not automatically). The effort to engage the energies of other children in satisfying and self-directed efforts at mastery must be more subtle and sustained. We know little about the kind of energizing effect the prodigy experiences, but one could imagine trying to catalyze this passion by providing a more organized series of opportunities for children than now exists. However it is stimulated, the importance of strong internal motivation cannot be overemphasized.[3]

There is also a more subtle psychological aspect to the development of talent, having to do with maintaining a balance between pursuing a specific domain and developing in other important realms. Parents in our society bear the brunt of the early responsibility for organizing and coordinating a child's learning experiences, both in terms of providing opportunities for detecting and directing specific talents and in helping the child to function overall as a healthy and productive individual. In other countries, for example, behind the Iron Curtain, the state performs many of these functions, but apparently much more instrumentally and without the benefit of family traditions and philosophies. This tends to separate the process of talent development from the rest of the child's overall experience and growth. As successful as some of these programs have appeared, especially in sports, they may be destined to leave children and their families feeling incomplete and unfulfilled. Perhaps this explains why individuals who seem to have so much to gain professionally by staying in their country nonetheless choose to live in a less controlling environment. When co-incidence processes are distorted too greatly in one direction people will try to find ways to restore the missing dimensions, almost as a gyroscope maintains its balance.

Perhaps in this one subtle respect it is the less precociously talented individuals who have the co-incidence advantage over prodigies. It is less tempting to sacrifice other aspects of "normal" development to the shrine of a particular talent when the individual's proclivities and potentials are less strongly expressed. It may be that children of more modest ability, or those who do not develop a particular expertise until later in life, stand a better chance of developing a fuller and more integrated personal orientation toward work, friends, and play.

Prodigies, Prophecy, Co-incidence, and Human Potential

One of the purposes of this book has been to revive some of the ancient meaning of the prodigy tradition, to recharge the notion with some of its original power and mystery. Without claiming that the irrational, mystical, and spiritual dimensions of the prodigy should become central again, I have sought to convince the reader that the phenomenon of the prodigy is at least more complicated and worthy of attention than it has been given in quite some time. I have even maintained that giving the prodigy its due means confronting the possibility that the historical role of the prodigy as a portent of change may not be as farfetched as it might seem.

Certainly the modern-day prodigy does not foretell changes in the social order as decreed by the gods. But I do think that by examining the prodigy phenomenon through a new lens we will change our understanding of the nature of human potential and how it can be harnessed and developed. For centuries, talent was considered to reside in the individual; while other factors were believed to make some difference in individual performance, the essential feature in conceptions of human ability was the individual's own native intelligence. Close examination of the process of developing prodigious talent has left little doubt that while individual talent is certainly a necessary factor, it is hardly sufficient: it is the delicate co-incidence, interplay, and balancing of a number of forces that allows talent to emerge and prosper. The prodigy phenomenon not only demands that we reconsider the individual-based unitary notion of ability, it provides a number of important clues about how one might work with co-incidence forces to try to optimize the development of potential in every individual.

I do not mean to draw a portrait here of a heaven on earth where every child is blissfully and self-absorbedly working away in some specialized field. Many factors critical to the development of ability cannot be controlled; much that goes into the co-incidence calculus is determined long before it becomes an immediate issue for any particular parent or child. Furthermore, there most certainly are individual differences in ability, and there are some children who would never display a particular talent, regardless of the delicacy and precision of alignment of other critical forces. Not all individuals will find and pursue a particular field with single-minded devotion for their entire lives. Those that do so are, and in all likelihood will remain, rare and unusual. Yet their very existence suggests that there are probably other individuals with the potential for great talent who, for one reason or another, are unable to develop or express it. As banal as it may sound, I would hope that one of the changes the twentieth-century prodigy can signal is a renewed dedication toward the realization of all human potential, with an attendant recognition of the value of diversity of interest, ability, and achievement.

Every child who has the persistence and potential to make a contribution should have the opportunity to do so. This means having a society that will put resources into the process of developing children's abilities and that will be committed to responding with care and dedication to children's efforts to utilize their talents. For most children the high-powered, focused, and organized regime of the prodigy is not at all optimal for nurturing their talents, and I would be the last to urge it. The trick is to recognize what is best for a given child at a given time and under a given set of circumstances. Responding optimally to a child's needs means having a wide range of instructional, personal, and psychological supports available at all times. Because prodigies are highly pretuned, they display a set of specific qualities for which very specific responses are necessary. A child with less specialized talents and a different set of temperamental qualities may require a more eclectic instructional approach. Again, the important idea is that diversity must be valued and embraced, both in terms of the possible paths a developing talent may take and in responses to the particulars of an individual developmental trajectory.

As I suggested earlier, sailing is a metaphor that seems to capture some of the spirit of harnessing co-incidence. Sailing requires that you understand a great deal about nature and about technology, and also about yourself in relation to them, but it does not mean having total control over any of these factors. The more one knows about sailing, the more respect one has for the power of wind and water, the uncertainty of events, and the impossibility of being completely in control of one's fate. Yet, with skill and experience and wisdom, it is possible to get from one place to another in reasonable safety and comfort. It is sometimes very hard work, requiring continuous vigilance and analysis, and may simply be overwhelming at times, but more importantly it is a journey that can also have moments of exhilaration and joy.

The joy of mastery is a theme that has become increasingly strong in the past fifty years. One of the primary changes in the concept of human development during this century has been to place greater and greater emphasis on free agency: the individual acts increasingly on the basis of self-generated and self-controlled goals. The prodigy dramatically reinforces this change in core beliefs about human development. In an almost uncanny fashion the prodigy seems to understand how great a gift is the opportunity to carry out a self-selected life plan. This is not to say that the plan does not depend heavily on the cooperation and good offices of quite a number of other forces—the co-incidence process in full harmony—but the point remains that a prodigy has the potential to be a modern person, a person of the twentieth century.

By modern I mean that there is a core, especially strong in the prodigy, that arbitrates, selects, and organizes the myriad possibilities and influences into a coherent plan of mastery. That core is aided and abetted by parents and mentors who participate in the process of developing an extreme talent. The prodigy reflects a fundamental increase in the integrity and existence of a sense of self and the notion that it is one's birthright to select one's own life course.

Psychological theories such as those of Erik Erikson and Jean Piaget invoke the idea of human uniqueness as a central organizing principle and place the autonomous individual in the center of the development process. Prodigies represent not only extreme talent but also unusual self-awareness and confidence. Where the ideal person in Eriksonian or Piagetian psychology seems somewhat removed or abstracted from the reality of actual people, the prodigy comes close to this in real life. Erikson even emphasized the crucial negotiation and balancing of forces that must take place among the child and those who care for and nurture him, share his space and resources, teach and guide him, establish bonds of friendship and intimacy, and who are in turn influenced by the child's own self-expression. And while Erikson's view of these forces is a psychodynamic one, he recognized that the child's development proceeds through a number of crucial interactions with the social world.

Of course, prodigies are not the cause of our changed view of where abilities come from and how they are developed. But the fact that they are being considered anew in their full complexity, without diluting the powerful feelings that they engender, may be a sign of change in current views of mind and self. By allowing some of the more ambiguous, ambivalent, complex qualities of the prodigy phenomenon to enter the discussion, it is possible to begin to acknowledge that there is much as yet not understood about the nature of intelligence. A change in perspective is called for.

Prodigies and Creativity

What we see when a prodigy appears is a concurrence of forces that gives us hints about how the development of potential works, but not necessarily how a new idea is fashioned, nor a domain transformed. We still know very little about how creativity, in the sense of making something new, operates. Still, by virtue of the close association of a child with a field, the uncanny match of individual and domain, the prodigy may offer some clues about the circumstances involved in matching individuals to their environments and vice versa. Were we able to better control the subtlety of such matches, we would, in all likelihood, not only produce more prodigies but also more individuals capable of contributing original and important new works.

One can think of the history of human development, of the emergence of cultures and societies, the development of technologies and crafts, the codification of knowledge and wisdom, as attempts to provide the resources necessary for people to make their unique contributions, to say what they have to say in a way that may stand the test of time. The more matches we can stimulate between individuals and domains, the better the chances of people finding their own voice and making a significant contribution.

Prodigies have taught us that human beings and their cultures play a crucial role in the evolution and expression of potential. When we see a prodigy we are seeing evidence that in certain respects humanity has made headway in the process of finding ways to use a particular talent, one that may have been "stored" genetically in the species for thousands of years. Whatever the expression of such talent might mean to the prodigy himself, it should indicate to the rest of us that we have, collectively, been able to lay before one of our own the distilled efforts of countless generations.

And in so doing, we have shown that we are capable of communicating even to a mere child the essence of a highly complex symbolic domain. The child prodigy is tangible evidence of progress in the collective human effort to cultivate and distill knowledge, to preserve it and pass it on.

The prodigy cannot answer all our questions about how development works or tell us what human history is about. Yet the phenomenon can draw our attention to aspects of human experience that, when understood more fully, may help illuminate both development and history. Development is a process that requires an understanding of the influence of several broad time frames as well as the coordination of individual qualities of mind and temperament with domains of knowledge that have their own histories, customs, pedagogies, and values. Understanding and learning to harness the factors influencing development should make it possible to better facilitate matches between individuals and domains. Such efforts at optimizing individual expression of ability will, in turn, enrich existing domains or lead to the construction of new ones, thus raising the probability that more people will find the path to express their unique potential. Clearly this view of development, inspired by the experience of observing prodigies, is one that encompasses much more than simple survival. It assumes that each person has something unique to say and desires to use his or her unique mix of talents and experiences to leave a lasting mark. Development means satisfaction and fulfillment, not just survival, and somehow in that desire for fulfillment humanity strives to give meaning to its own history. Through that process new possibilities for expression are created, and the long-term well-being of the species is enhanced.

12

Epilogue: Final Notes on Six Prodigies

I T IS NOW more than a decade since my study of prodigies began, and a great deal has happened in the lives of the children and their families. The oldest subject in the study is now approaching twenty, two others are nearly out of high school, and two others have just entered their teens. Only one is still below the age of ten, the upper age limit for my subjects when I began this research. I make no claim that what I have seen of these children captures what is most significant in each of their lives. As fascinating as each of the six cases is, my purpose was not to comprehend their lives as a whole, as was the aim of my teacher Robert White.[1] It was, rather, to see what could be learned about developmental processes from studying extraordinary talent.

Yet there is a natural curiosity about what has become of these children so far. What of the early promise that burst upon the scene? Have the guesses that I made about them been supported by their choices and decisions over the years?

Early Predictions

I had made my own informal predictions about what would happen with each of the cases during the first year that I knew them. The first three children in the study were Nils, Ricky and Franklin, a composer and two chess players. Having had little experience or direct knowledge of prodigies or training in their fields, I was at first dazzled, as many would be, by the sheer virtuosity of their performances. Since I was unable to observe their talents at onset (they had emerged at least two years earlier in each of the chess players' cases, and nearly six years before my study began in Nils's case), I was already seeing quite accomplished performances from the children. Perhaps if I had been a chess player myself or had been involved in music more than the five or six lackadaisical years I had logged taking accordion lessons, I would have had a somewhat different reaction to their abilities. Yet their teachers also believed that they were dealing with children of unusual promise. Nils's teacher, Daniel Aaron, conveyed to me a sense of unlimited potential in his prize student while, at the same time, maintaining a certain skeptical restraint intended to keep his young charge on the straight and narrow path that he and his fellow teachers had mapped out. The two chess coaches also expressed great confidence in their young players, and with good reason. Each was ranked in the top fifty players in the country under age thirteen; at age eight, they were the two highest ranked youngsters nationally in their age group at the time.

So it is no surprise that I believed during that first year that all three would go on to fame and fortune. Time and experience have shown me just how high the odds are against such a prediction. Still, one of the three, Nils Kirkendahl, has pursued his musical career without interruption, and although he is no longer a composer, he is a promising young concert performer. This is no guarantee, in and of itself, that Nils's path is well established. Remember the young pianist Erwin Nyiregyhazi, whose early career paralleled Nils's in many ways, and who took a decisive turn into obscurity in his early twenties. Nothing can be taken for granted. Yet it is not so foolhardy to look with some confidence at the record of Nils Kirkendahl and predict that his future as a musician will be rewarding and successful. Indeed, Nils is the oldest of my subjects and the only one who has had enough years behind him for any guesses to be taken very seriously.

By the time I gathered my second panel of children, in 1978, I was more sober about the realities of early prodigious achievement. I was then working explicitly on the idea of co-incidence and had begun to appreciate just how complex and delicate the whole process of expression of potential must be. By then I had also searched fruitlessly for children younger than ten in the fields of visual art and mathematics and knew that it was unlikely that such children could be found. Therefore, when I was told of a child of six who had been identified by Julian Stanley's study of precocious mathematics talent as a math prodigy, I was already guessing that mathematics was not all that likely to be his ultimate preoccupation. And from our first meeting there was evidence that his passion was for the natural sciences and not mathematics. For the purposes of the study, I hoped that he would embrace mathematics, but I did not really expect it.

The same could be said for my early impressions of Randy McDaniel. I knew that genuine literary output before the age of ten was extremely rare, and in those cases where it actually was present, rarely led to mature careers in literature.[2] That young Randy was behaving like a writer was clear, that he was producing reams of material was also well documented, and that some of it was exceptional was also evident. And yet, as so many have asked of young writers, what do children so young have to say? Still, Randy was impressive and we (by this time Lynn and I were working together) had never seen anything like him. He would be some kind of writer, we believed, but just what he would write about, and what form it would take (essays, novels, musicals, plays, comedy routines), would have to wait until Randy was older and showed a clear direction.

Finally, there was Adam. He was the youngest of the children when he came into the study. This in itself made his future activities more difficult to predict. In addition, his talent did not seem to take a strong specific direction or express itself in a single area, even a broadly defined one. He was said to show evidence of extreme precocity in languages, mathematics, natural science, music, and symbol systems. He did not really fit the definition of prodigy I had been working with, making prediction still more chancy. I decided to continue seeing Adam, not because I had any bright ideas about what would become of him, but because his was such a compelling case that I could not resist the opportunity to observe his development. In fact, I made up the term "omnibus prodigy" to justify including Adam in my study. Since any theory of development of prodigies was primitive anyway, why be restricted by that theory from studying what was by any account one of the most unusual children I had seen, read about, or imagined?

Update on the Subjects

Briefly, here is what has happened to our six young subjects. The two chess players, Ricky and Franklin, gave up competitive chess as they entered junior high school and have not gone back to it in any sustained way, although Ricky recently played for "fun" in high school competition. Nils is still going strong in preparing for a career as a concert violinist, the only one of the six prodigies who has gone more or less in a straight line from where he started to where he is now. As I suspected, Billy Devlin did not become a mathematician, but has moved at a rapid clip through high school to enter college at fourteen, studying natural science and engineering. Randy McDaniel has been seriously studying the guitar and is writing rock operas and other material for performance in a rock music format. And Adam has focused his energies on music for the past three years, not to the exclusion of other pursuits, but sufficiently seriously and productively to label him a music prodigy by even my earlier "strict" criterion. He has composed a number of orchestral pieces, most notably three symphonies, two of which have been performed professionally.

What is most striking at this point is that three of the six children are now seriously and deeply involved in music in one form or another. Nils, of course, has been on a music fast track since age three, with only the one major crisis when he had to decide to train as a performer and give up serious composition. But Randy has taken his penchant for writing and turned it toward libretti for rock operas. He also invented his own musical notation technique, which has served him well but which will soon need to be traded in for the one the rest of the world uses. And Adam, for all his many talents and interests, has put a major portion of his time and energy into playing the violin and composing. It is interesting that all three children could still legitimately be called prodigies, even though only one of them was strongly oriented toward music from the earliest age. I will say more later about what I think this drift toward music tells us about early prodigiousness and what it means for the encouragement of talent.

The two chess players have all but abandoned chess. This is in a way puzzling and in a way not. It probably says as much about the current status and viability of chess in this country as it does about my two subjects. Yet, other children, seemingly no more talented or more dedicated, have continued to perform as serious chess players. The most notable contemporary of Franklin and Ricky was probably Joel Benjamin (his real name), who was a couple of years older than my subjects when I was watching them in chess tournaments. Joel is currently a grandmaster, one of the top players in the United States. Why Joel Benjamin stayed with chess and my two subjects did not is difficult to say, although we can speculate on some of the reasons that my two subjects turned their attention to other pursuits. Here, then, are brief summaries of the current activities of the six prodigies.

NILS KIRKENDAHL

Nils has matured into a remarkably unaffected person. His precociousness as a nine-year-old has given way to a quiet confidence that is carried off without abrasiveness. Nils has followed the course set for him when he was three years old virtually without interruption. His track has been straight and it has been true. Not without certain pressure points and crises, yet Nils has never doubted for a minute that he would be a musician, and—although this specific outcome is not quite so assured—that he would stand one day on the concert stage as a recognized master of his instrument. The crisis during early adulthood of many musical prodigies, eloquently and compellingly detailed by researcher Jeanne Bamberger, seems not to have occurred with Nils.[3] It is possible that the decision to abandon serious pursuit of composition as a career was Nils's version of this "mid-life" crisis, but if so it took an unusual, early, and relatively mild form.

Even among prodigies Nils is unusual in his steadiness and steadfastness. He is tenacious without seeming in the least fanatic, dedicated without succumbing to the myopia of singlemindedness, ambitious without being cutthroat or vicious. When I asked Nils a year or so ago how he dealt with the fierce competition to secure exposure and opportunities to perform, he said that he tried not to compare himself to his fellow students, but only to think of his own performance and how to get better. This was not mere dogma. If he spent time comparing himself with those with whom he must compete, he said, he would be obsessed with competition for its own sake. He admitted that he was not immune from such comparisons, but said that he worked very hard not to get caught up in the competition mania. Perhaps his success to date has also allowed him to be a bit more relaxed about how he is doing relative to others; in fact he is doing very well.

Just how well is Nils doing? It is difficult for an outsider in the music world to judge the degree of his progress. He is one of Dorothy DeLay's more promising students, one who she apparently believes is now ready for management and contract commitments. He has been in some demand as a guest artist while still a student at Juilliard, and he has risen through the ranks at the Aspen Music Festival each summer. So far as I know, he is operating in the most demanding circles of the music world available to someone at his level of preparation and is faring well. He is clearly not getting the same attention as young Mi Dori, who, at age eleven, is already touted as one of the great violinists of the century.[4] Nils was relatively more modest in his accomplishments at the same age, in part, perhaps, because he had not begun to focus his energies on performance, perhaps because of his own developmental timetable, perhaps for both sets of reasons. In any case, he is certainly not the most dramatically successful musical prodigy we have seen in the past thirty years, but he is one among a small group of especially promising young performers.

Nils has come through a music regime at Juilliard that is skeptical of the whole idea of a prodigy. Perhaps having seen so many children flounder on the crises of adolescence and early career pressures, Nils's teachers and many others as well are chary of calling their charges prodigies. By avoiding the term they are not changing the reality of the child prodigy, for without doubt there are still children, Nils included, who are as talented as any of the most celebrated music prodigies of the past. The difference is that these young performers are now more protected from the publicity, attention, fawning adoration, and exploitation that have sometimes been their fate. Quite reasonably, teachers at Juilliard and elsewhere have become skeptical of the prodigy phenomenon as a public celebration and media event, and they have tried to hold their students in protected enclaves peopled mostly with other young musicians. Publicity is carefully screened and their performances managed with care. Given the especially voracious appetite of the media for stories about what prodigies are "really like," it is not surprising that those responsible for preparing young musicians for performing careers are wary of gratuitous public displays and media hoopla.

There was a point at which Nils welcomed the possibility of media coverage when it would help him get exposure for his performance career, but this has not been the case for several years. He is being groomed and prepared in a very quiet and careful manner, with little outside attention. The argument is that this gives him the time to develop a distinctive style and to perfect his technique without too much professional scrutiny and without the need to perform a repertoire night after night. These could prematurely crystallize his range of interpretation and constrain his development.

Perhaps in the current climate of instant celebrity and equally rapid obscurity, it is inevitable that commercial and media pressures would be put on promising young performers. For all of this, Nils Kirkendahl seems to have glided through his teen years without serious turmoil and is still right on track. Perhaps the "no prodigies any more" way of doing things really works, or perhaps with Nils it would have made little difference.

Now fully involved in his music, Nils nonetheless still maintains a set of other interests, including a lively fascination with the opposite sex. The last time we met he was carrying a photograph of a stunning fellow student and model who was his steady companion. Since then, his mother tells me that another, equally attractive young woman has entered the scene. This is not surprising. Nils is now six feet tall, handsome, and approachable, with the casual confidence that makes him exotic and attractive at the same time. He continues to be pragmatic in his outlook (taking courses at Columbia to better manage the business aspects of his career), bothers little with formal competitions because he has not seemed to need them to get exposure, and lives quite independently of his family in New York. He is soon to have the opportunity to play before the most important broker of young violinists, Isaac Stern. If it goes well, it could mean that we will be seeing and hearing much more of Nils Kirkendahl in the years to come. For my own part I am not concerned about these "crucial" episodes in his life. He seems to have reached a point where he has met life on its own terms, is reflective and thoughtful about what his own talent means and does not mean, and has the internal strength and confidence to deal with adversity.

Will he be one of the great violinists of the day? I do not know, nor am I in any position to judge. But he more than passes muster as an exceptional young man whose talent will shine one way or another, who has benefited from co-incidence and learned to use it.

ADAM KONANTOVICH

Adam is now ten years old. Were I starting this project again now, Adam would be the only subject still within the original age range set for the study. Surprisingly, he would also now qualify on the other criterion, namely that he is performing at the level of an adult professional in an intellectually demanding domain. That domain is music composition, one of the original four fields I selected for intensive study. The three-and-a-half-year-old child whom I had decided to include in my small sample, even though he did not qualify as a prodigy by my technical criterion of performance in a specific domain, has turned out after all to meet that criterion.

To be sure, Adam is an unusual music prodigy. Although he seemed musically inclined even as an infant, there was little evidence that he would focus his efforts on music before he reached the age of ten. Adam's talents were too diverse and unbounded to lead to predictions about what he was likely to be doing seven or eight years hence. In fact, were we to have predicted, we would have probably selected languages or possibly natural science as more likely pursuits. The only domain we would have probably eliminated during those early encounters was art, since Adam's work seemed to us advanced but not off the charts.

As for his general education, Adam continues to be taught mostly by Fiona and Nathaniel and by an ever-changing set of tutors in subjects ranging from Sanskrit to philosophy. Adam still tends to set his own curriculum and is dogged in his insistence that certain subjects be made available to him. He also tends to have difficulty maintaining long-term studies with some of his tutors, for reasons that Fiona and Nathaniel find somewhat puzzling. Adam is a teacher's dream: quick to learn, eager, dedicated, and curious almost beyond belief. Yet with the exception of some of his music teachers, few tutors have been able to stay for more than half a year or so, a fact that Fiona and Nathaniel now interpret as having to do with Adam's nonlinear learning style and omnivorous desire for knowledge, which leaves most instructors depleted and exhausted (see chapters 5 and 9).

Fiona reports that their insight about Adam's nonlinear approach to subject matter has led to a much more relaxed attitude toward his education. They have genuinely begun to accept that he will not learn in a "traditional" manner, and that school as organized in Western cultures is simply not an appropriate place for him to pursue his interests. As I reflect on our plan of a few years ago to have the family move to Boston, the concept of making the city's resources available to Adam was implicitly (though not explicitly) designed to engage his particular learning style. We hoped to provide Adam with access to the city's universities, museums, institutes, and instructors, from which he would then draw in his unique and idiosyncratic fashion. The structure of Adam's activities was to come from his own desires and interests without imposing a sequence of lessons or courses. I think this was probably an early example of Adam's "non-linearity," which we just did not interpret as such at the time.

Adam's gifts are of acknowledged value within our culture; in spite of his possibly non-Western approach to learning, he has never had his potential questioned seriously. In terms of actual performance in a field, as soon as Adam seems unengaged Fiona and Nathaniel are there to move him to more comfortable environs. And the most comfortable environment for Adam for the past three years has been a musical one. His musical education is substantially Western and classical, which raises some questions concerning Fiona's guess about Adam's style of learning and cast of mind. He does seem to grasp music theory issues with great speed, and to analyze the structure of music even as he is playing it for the first time. This is not usual. But for whatever reasons, and however achieved, music allowed Adam to soar and range freely with his talents; he has embraced it almost as a life preserver.

With all that music means to Adam, his parents still wonder whether it will ultimately be his main source of expression. Nathaniel thinks Adam may be a composer, and Fiona is not yet sure. Both parents believe that music serves a purpose for Adam now. Whether his musical compositions from this period will become cherished works of lasting value is uncertain. In any event, his parents are quite convinced that Adam will go on to other fields, and that music may be more of a way station than a final destination for him. In this respect, Adam is different from other music prodigies. He is not a pure case like Mozart, nor is he similar to Nils Kirkendahl. The music prodigy usually shows his or her talent very young and in strong and sturdy form, eliminating most other possible pursuits early and convincingly. This was clearly not the case with Adam. He did not begin serious musical studies until about six, and he did not catch fire instantly as did other music prodigies. For all of that, Adam is a serious musician and composer. He plays with a very good children's orchestra and studies hard. He composes works that meet the criteria of professional quality and complexity. Were we not to have had several years of earlier experience with Adam, we would have no reason to believe that he is anything other than a bona fide music prodigy. Only time will tell, of course, but for the moment he seems likely to continue with his music and to compose interesting works, at least for a while. On the other hand, the fact that he is less of a specialist than most music prodigies weighs against music for Adam in the long run.

RANDY McDANIEL

Randy, now fourteen, is the most gregarious and outgoing of the six children in the study. He can be counted upon to agree to interviews, radio and television appearances, and magazine articles: I can usually count on the McDaniels' interest and cooperation when a media project is in the air. This outgoing behavior is quite unusual for my subjects.

Darren and Jeanne have begun to wonder whether writing is going to be Randy's life now that his rock music phase, begun about six years ago, is in full swing. He continues to write for his summer camp newspaper, but this is no longer of vital importance to Randy. In fact, the experience of competing with writers as good as he is may have lessened his sense of accomplishment in that realm and discouraged Randy from continuing with his writing.

Uniqueness is still critical to Randy, as it is to Darren and Jeanne. Randy still believes that he is special and is hurt when his sense of uniqueness is not recognized and acknowledged. This need to feel special is central for Randy and his family. Some teachers and other children have had trouble accepting the fact that Randy is as special and as gifted as he and his parents know he is. And since in some ways that are important to schools Randy is not as traditionally talented as other classmates, there has been a continuous tension between the McDaniels and organized education. During much of Randy's life he has been taught at home, with Darren and Jeanne serving as faculty, staff, curriculum, and laboratory of the "McDaniel University." Thus, it is not at all surprising that Randy has channeled his energies into pursuits that express his particular sense of himself as a unique, dramatic, and specially talented child. He continues to have a sense of inner confidence even though the conventional world of the school sometimes had some doubts about the degree of his giftedness. In recent years, these doubts have begun to wane.

Two years ago Randy was accepted into an accelerated program in a public high school, and the "McDaniel University" closed its doors as a full-time institution. Randy's school performance there has been outstanding; he has maintained better than a 95 average in his coursework. Darren and Randy still spend a good deal of time together, much of which is focused on the examination of issues and topics of interest to Randy, but Randy is also very engaged in his schoolwork, especially his writing, which has matured considerably and become more journalistic.

The McDaniels maintain a rich and generous support system for Randy, including musical instruments and lessons, a stereo, frequent trips to movies, restaurants, and cultural events, library and record holdings that would impress any fourteen-year-old, as well as an unusually active and involved relationship with their son. Jeanne and Darren have maintained a secure and provident environment for Randy, and their family seems intact and secure.

Currently the McDaniels live in a university apartment a block or so away from Jeanne's office. Randy's music school is also only another block or so away and he spends a great deal of his time there after his regular high-school classes, even when he has no scheduled lessons. He plays in a jazz group at the New England Conservatory, which he likes largely for the camaraderie, even though by and large he prefers more contemporary music. He continues with his writing and composing of rock operas and other rock material, as well as music critiques of recent albums, and he plays and sings well. He has achieved a level of mastery of the guitar that is near professional quality. Randy has the same confidence about his capability that he had with his writing of stories and plays, and he loves to perform. He continues with his dramatics and his journalistic writing in the summer. Randy is, in short, fully engaged in his music, while maintaining some interest in writing and performing in plays.

Randy's new school program seems to be working out, and he and his parents seem pleased so far. He takes whatever courses he wants, is on a very flexible schedule, essentially coming and going as he pleases, and has made new friends. Randy's history with organized education has been spotty, but the fact that he has the chance to be among peers and friends during these critical adolescent years is certainly a promising development in Randy's life.

Randy is on the verge of adolescence. His feet, as is often the case, have announced the impending roar of hormones by stretching to canal boat proportions. The rest of his body is still wiry and childlike. It is possible that this period is one of tranquility before the inevitable storms of his impending teenage years. Given the extremely intense nuclear family relationships, this will almost of necessity be a critical period for Randy, Jeanne, and Darren, as with other families of prodigies. For all of that, the McDaniels have shown a remarkable resilience and deep belief in their own and Randy's uniqueness. One can only speculate that, whatever the next several years may hold, the McDaniels will figure out a way to make the most of them. Whatever their route through Randy's adolescence, it will likely reflect their unique, exuberant, caring, and positive way of looking at the world and at their only joint offspring. One thing seems quite certain: they will never go back to the farm, but they may find that it is not at all necessary to their mission.

BILLY DEVLIN

Billy has just finished his first year of college. He graduated from high school at fourteen and began studying engineering and physics at a nearby state university. His parents wanted Billy to be near enough that he could get home any weekend, and so they chose the best public university within commuting distance of their home. The choice seems to have been a good one for Billy. As was the case in high school, Billy went at his course work with tenacity and confidence. His confidence was on the whole well placed; he had a very solid first-year average in a demanding curriculum.

By the time Billy began high school at age nine it was pretty clear that his abilities were more those of an extremely academically talented child, the focus of the traditional "high IQ-gifted child" literature, and less those of the prodigy, whose specialized talents were the focus of my own interest. Billy had concentrated on science and mathematics from the time we met him and, according to his parents, even before that. But this is also true of many academically talented children, especially boys. Even though he took the most advanced courses in mathematics available at his excellent suburban high school while a ninth grader, it was clear even then that he was not necessarily going to do mathematics as a career. His teachers in mathematics knew that his "math intuition" was not so extraordinary as to clearly indicate that Billy was a budding young mathematician. On the other hand, he showed an ability to comprehend and master mathematics far in advance of his years.

I especially remember the reflections of one of Billy's science teachers, a woman of many years' experience who had seen several of her students go on to become scientists of the first rank. When asked about Billy, she did not hesitate to rank him among the very best she had seen come through her classroom over the years. Yet, she said that there was a quality that Billy had not shown, at least not up to that point. It was a quality she described as "curiosity" or "scientific intuition" that she had seen in the students who went on to take their place as leading scientists. In a few cases, we were told, these students were not necessarily the ones who did the best in their science studies, but they had a difficult to define sense of what was an interesting problem and always seemed to be able to get to the heart of it. She wondered whether this quality was simply not yet well developed in Billy because he was so much younger than her other students. This teacher, at least, wondered whether Billy had not been pushed too hard too fast to allow his natural talents to ripen, suppressing or obscuring his best intellectual qualities in a frenzy of high expectations for academic performance. It will be several years before we know to what extent this teacher's cautions and concerns were well placed, but it is important that they be noted. They are precisely the ones that have led some music teachers to try to ease the pressure on promising children who are performing at high levels.

There is, after all, a deeper message in the words of caution of well-meaning and sincere teachers. They worry in cases like Billy's and those of other bright students whether the emphasis on speed and early achievement is necessarily always in the best interest of the child. Now it is true that for some students the possibility of acceleration through a subject is not only welcome but a salvation from boredom, dullness, and tedium in school. Julian Stanley's work at Johns Hopkins has revealed several cases where students liberated from lock-step sequences of classes were able to make rapid and stunning progress.[5] The other side of the coin, though, is that acceleration itself tends to be taken as a measure of how gifted a person is. Inasmuch as the Devlins do not live far from where Stanley's project is located, and inasmuch as Billy was identified as one of the most promising young students ever to come through that project, it is not surprising that the emphasis in Billy's school career was on rapid acceleration through the standard curriculum. In a way it is also not surprising that Billy's teachers were skeptical of this emphasis. They saw that their own steady years of working with children, their own insights and wisdom gathered in the classroom were questioned and sometimes even devalued by the university-based Johns Hopkins team.

These tensions tended to focus on Billy who, as a product of the acceleration-oriented Johns Hopkins screening program but also a student in a regular (but proud) suburban high school, found himself being pulled in two directions at once. Clearly, moving rapidly through high school won out. More time must pass before we will know how valuable those early opportunities to study at advanced levels will turn out to be for Billy. What is my guess? Because Billy moved in the direction of science studies, and more and more into the conventional category of a highly academically "gifted" child, I have not followed his progress closely enough to feel any sense of confidence in my predictions. It is certainly reasonable to expect that he will continue to pursue some branch of scientific study, but which one, how, or where I would not try to predict. I do know that Billy's parents, as always, are careful, reflective, and unmoved by hype or bluster. Based on the thoughtful quality that has characterized all of their decisions, one can only have confidence in their advice and judgment about Billy's educational and career choices. Certainly Billy has lost none of his self-confident, almost brash, belief in his own capabilities. A good sign.

RICKY VELAZQUEZ

Ricky had given up chess by the time he was out of junior high school. In fact, he did not even want fellow students to know he had played the game. I remember a conversation with his sixth-grade teacher in which it was already clear that Ricky was putting his energies elsewhere. The elsewhere for Ricky was, and to a great extent still is, in sports. At age eight, he stood out as a gifted athlete when I watched him play baseball with much older teammates, and since then he has played soccer at the varsity level for all three years of high school. Chess seemed to make him different from his classmates in a way that was uncomfortable for Ricky. His father, too, felt that chess was not an activity likely to provide Ricky with either the future that sports could offer or the admiration of his peers. And he probably was right. His mother, though, always felt that Ricky (he wants to be called Rick these days) should keep up his chess, that it was a talent that was too rare and too rewarding in a personal if not social sense to let go completely.

And as fate would have it, Rick found himself playing chess again last year. The chess team at his high school needed a player to strengthen their chances of doing well in state competition. The coach and players appealed to Rick to help, and out of a feeling of school spirit, he reluctantly agreed. Without having picked up a chess piece in four years, Rick played very well. He tied for second place in the individual competition in the state, and he played a very strong board for his team. That he played as well as he did with virtually no practice suggests that, as John Collins, his instructor, had said several years earlier, his talent is as sharp as any he had seen, including that of Bobby Fischer. But as Mr. Collins also said, there is so much else that goes into being a great chess player that one would not hazard a guess about the future of any player younger than twelve or so. And he was right on target with Rick Velazquez, who, talented or not, gave up the game for more rewarding pursuits not too many years after those cautious words of the great teacher were spoken.

Now what does it mean that Rick Velazquez gave up chess? That he was not a prodigy? That his talent was not as extraordinary as it had seemed? I would suggest that neither of these is the most reasonable interpretation. More likely is that Rick was doubly and triply blessed, not only with chess talent but also with athletic ability and outstanding academic capability. With chess, especially in this country at this time, one would have to be extremely committed to the game to choose it over other options. There is little attention paid to chess in the media; it is not a major activity in most schools; there is little financial reward in tournament play except at the highest international levels; and the cultural and social benefits for playing chess well in this country are minimal. I remember being told of a lecture and demonstration by William Lombardy, then ranked number two in the country, to which only a handful of people showed up, not even enough to cover expenses. And this was in New York! Without the magnetism of a Bobby Fischer, most people don't even know or care who is ranked number one in the country in chess.

I am suggesting that staying with chess may be largely a matter of having no choice, of having unadulterated chess talent. If one can do anything else at all well, it is unlikely one will choose to continue playing serious chess. If chess is absolutely the most important thing in life, and one can do nothing else nearly as well, then it may be that chess will hold its place in the young person's life. This is not the only basis on which such decisions are made, but often it is. In Rick's case (as was true with Franklin Montana as well), chess was not part of his family's value system, recent tradition, or daily life. In contrast, Joel Benjamin, who is currently a college student at Yale, grew up in a family where chess was very important, where his father was a good player and coach, where he was encouraged to continue playing despite relatively little public reward. With Rick having too many other choices and a father who encouraged the non-chess options, Rick's commitment to chess was much less deep and he all but gave up playing the game.

It cannot be overemphasized that Rick Velazquez is a gifted student academically and a very social young man as well. He wanted and still wants very much to be accepted by his peers. Although Rick has his own version of inner confidence, it takes a different form from the other subjects in the study. He takes no pleasure in standing apart from his peers, has no desire to be different in order to sharpen and clarify his own identity. His has been a quintessentially social orientation. His specialness reflects the best qualities his peers aspire to. Rather than setting him apart, these qualities bring him closer to those with whom he associates. When his ninth-grade guidance counselor said "Ricky is special," I believe she meant it in this sense.

Now a high-school senior, Rick will be going to college with his age-mates this fall. He has decided he wants to go to Harvard, which in Rick's case is a perfectly reasonable choice. He is drawn to the great tradition, the social significance of the institution. He wants to go to the "best" place, which Harvard may be. He has broadly defined career goals, maybe to become a lawyer or a businessman. His qualifications are impeccable: excellent grades and recommendations from a reputable suburban high school; SAT scores combining to well over 1400; all-around athletic ability; and, of course, his "specialness," which is perceived and appreciated by virtually all who come into contact with him. Perhaps his chess achievements will help him a little as well.

The real question is what will Rick Velazquez do with his various talents? Chess has taken a back seat to other interests and probably always will. He has too much else going for him to play chess except as a hobby. The chances are that Rick Velazquez will reflect the American Dream in its best and most positive form, that he will personify those values of general intellectual and personal excellence that form the core of American culture. He could do a great deal worse.

FRANKLIN MONTANA

The Montana family has been experiencing a period of stress during the past few years, and our contact with them has been minimal. I did recently see Franklin when he made a trip to New England to interview at a university near Boston about transferring there next year. Franklin was an indifferent student in high school, having concentrated more on his various business enterprises than on his studies. He attributed his lacka-daisical performance to the fact that "I didn't believe in high school." Nonetheless, he graduated at age sixteen and took a year off before enroll-ing at the nearest branch of the state university. College has proven more of a challenge.

In some ways Franklin seems unchanged since I first met him in 1975. He is intense and tends to want to direct discussions and activities. In conversation, he jumps quickly from topic to topic, giving the impression that he somehow knows where he wants things to go, but is not sharing that information. He is at once very open and very guarded. He talked a great deal about his memories of his active years playing chess, asked about his counterpart in this study, Rick Velazquez, and inquired about many of the other people in the chess world. When he wondered aloud why he had not continued in chess, some of his fierce competitiveness seemed to return, if just for a moment. Not that he has lost his desire to win. He has simply turned it to different ends, primarily making money and playing sports. Franklin won the state title in wrestling for his weight class in eighth grade, played competitive tennis through high school, and at the same time built a successful and lucrative landscaping business. At one time he owned several trucks, a large inventory of equipment, part interest in a gasoline station, and had more than a dozen employees. During the year after high school Franklin put his business affairs into good order and sold out—for a very healthy profit. All the while he has been playing options and other sophisticated stock-market games, also with quite good results. When I asked whether he had perhaps given up serious chess play because there was no money in it, he agreed that was part of the reason.

Perhaps Franklin's most revealing observation about himself was that he has a tendency to get very good at something, and then to lose interest in it. He noted that he is unable to sustain a commitment to become the very best, to reach the real heights of accomplishment. Certainly this was the case with chess. The sum total of his chess playing over the past several years has been with a neighborhood doctor, with whom he plays a casual game from time to time. He said that he does not think that he has lost his underlying ability to play well, but that he has lost command of the various combinations and openings, and his competitive desire has not been kept at a keen edge. Franklin is aware of this pattern of intense early engagement with chess, sports, and business, which later gives way to disinterest; and he concludes that he still has no real idea of what he will do with his life, what he will become. I suggested that most people at age eighteen did not yet know their life plans, and probably should not expect to have a plan mapped out. Franklin replied that because of his earlier experiences as a prodigy it was hard for him not to be totally involved in some activity. What was a normal level of uncertainty for a typical young adult was for Franklin very jarring.

Franklin is now seeking admission to a more prestigious college. His mind is as active and purposeful as ever, but lacking a strong focus to give it direction. In one sense, he is the classic liberal arts student in search of a path to follow. Although he wonders if his passion for money is not leading to a dead end, he was the most animated when talking about his triumphs and defeats in the market. As I sat with Franklin in my office, I could see how he might drive his teachers to distraction. He goes his own way, he follows his own star, he does not do things in the usual way. This must be an especially difficult time for a young man gifted with such intensity, desire, ability, and drive, and who does not know quite what to do with it all. I can only speculate that when Franklin figures out what he will do next, the world had better be prepared.

Coda

Three of the six children in the study have become deeply involved in music. This is perhaps the most striking outcome of the project; while Nils Kirkendahl was immersed in music from toddlerhood, Adam and Randy have come to it as preadolescent children. I am impressed with this move toward music, although I am not sure what to make of it. The range of possibilities presented by music in this culture at this moment in history seems unprecedented. Indeed, each of the three prodigies has chosen a very different musical form to work within. Adam seems most inclined toward classical composition, although Nils was too at his age; Randy writes and performs more avant-garde music in the style of the seventies and eighties; and Nils has launched a concertizing career. In a way these three are involved in studies almost as different as if they were in different fields, particularly Randy versus the two classicists. I would not have predicted that Adam would go this route, nor for that matter Randy. Perhaps there is a special opportunity to be seized right now in studying musical development.

I am not the first one to have noticed that we have a wonderful natural laboratory for developmental psychology in the study of music. Some of our most distinguished developmentalists have been keenly aware of this. Some even have claimed that understanding musical development is one of the keys to understanding the development of thinking in general. Heinz Werner, Lev Vygotsky, and James Mark Baldwin, great contributors from the earlier decades of the century, were, each in his own way, tuned to the special opportunities presented by the arts, particularly music; and anthropologist Claude Levi-Strauss has written that all of the scientific disciplines must try to find an explanation for the mystery and magic of music. Jeanne Bamberger at MIT is now carrying on in that same tradition.[6]

The other three subjects, Franklin, Ricky, and Billy, have not continued their trajectory of prodigious achievement, at least in the sense that their early promise has not sustained itself through adolescent commitment to the same field. These three prodigies have moved closer to the concept of giftedness found in the traditional "gifted child" literature, having more than their share of general academic talent. All three have done well in school—although Franklin has been a marginal student at times—and have shown themselves to be fine college prospects. Their career goals fit more closely with those of the larger group of academically gifted children, with the broader specialties like law and medicine and engineering capturing their energies. For these three subjects, the signs of early specialization were apparently more like those episodes in most children's lives where they go from passion to passion without a long-term commitment, although in the case of my subjects the mastery was more profound, as was perhaps the potential for continued extraordinary achievement.

It must be said that at least in the case of the chess players, their level of commitment during their three or four active years was exceptional, their level of performance remarkable, and their ability to direct and sustain concentrated energy in their field genuinely unusual. Still, it is now apparent that for them, at least, chess was a passing fancy, although a serious one. Billy Devlin's course has turned from one aspect of natural science to another over the years, while his early achievement in mathematics was the more temporary area of intense concentration. Yet all in all, his path, too, has been relatively straight and true.

Reflecting on the six prodigies and their families, I am struck both by how much I have learned about them and by how little I know. I suppose this is what most researchers experience when they reach the end of a long and complex project, at least in those fortunate instances where the material is rich and challenging. It seems trite to say so, but it feels as though the prodigy as a topic of study is one that is still barely touched. My predecessor Geza Revesz, who in 1925 published the only full-length research study of a child prodigy, wrote:

> In this work I have endeavoured to put before the public the result of my researches on the mentality of an unusually gifted child. If I have been successful in selecting, from among a number of observations, those which are most characteristic and which serve to complete the picture of little Erwin, I may perhaps have succeeded in throwing some light on the great mystery of evolution.[7]

With fifty years of hindsight, we now know that Revesz indeed provided us with a marvelously detailed account of a prodigy, Erwin Nyiregyhazi, who then proved in life that the prodigy phenomenon is in some respects as mystifying as ever. I, too, have endeavored to glean from my observations of prodigies insights that might shed light on "the great mystery of evolution," although I cannot be sure that Revesz and I mean the same thing when we use the term. Revesz could not have imagined how incomplete his work actually was in revealing the essential qualities of little Erwin. It is a humbling lesson to be kept in mind when dealing with the unknown. Even though the life span of the individual is the shortest of the four time frames we have considered in this book, we will have to observe many more prodigies over their lifetimes to approach an adequate explanation for this ancient and revealing phenomenon. In this manner we may hope to increase the likelihood that nature's gambit will prevail.

NOTES

Chapter 1. Out of the Usual Course of Nature

1. This definition is from Webster's *Third International Dictionary*.

2. Robert Graves, *Claudius the God* (New York: Vintage Books, 1962, pp. 558–59).

3. Eberstark reflects on his own prodigious abilities in his Introduction to Steven B. Smith's book, *The Great Mental Calculators: The Psychology, Methods, and Lives of Calculating Prodigies, Past and Present* (New York: Columbia University Press, 1983). Eberstark's quote can be found on page xi.

4. Fred Barlow, *Mental Prodigies* (New York: Greenwood Press, 1952, p. 47). Barlow's book is a collection of short biographies documenting the lives and abilities of children with prodigious mental abilities. As an example of exploitation of prodigies, consider Barlow's description of the childhood of George Parker Bidder (1805–78). An English calculating prodigy, Bidder and his father toured the country giving performances. According to Barlow, "This was so profitable for the father that the boy's education was entirely neglected. Even at the age of ten he was only just learning to write; figures he could not make" (pp. 29–30). Bidder was luckier than many other children of his era who displayed curious talent: he did eventually receive an education, becoming an engineer with a distinguished career. His son, George Parker Bidder, Jr., was also a calculating prodigy.

5. Olaf Stapledon's novella, "Odd John," about an individual with a superior intellect who nonetheless lives on the fringe of society, offers a fictionalized view of how unusual ability may threaten the status quo. Odd John is disdainful of the rest of humanity, calling them "cows," at the same time that he is unable to function within the society established by those of more modest abilities. He eventually connects with others of similar, extraordinary abilities. This group of superior, yet outcast, individuals go off and begin a new colony which, presumably, will reflect their higher level of ability and sensitivity, and which will provide the basis for further human evolution. See Olaf Stapledon, *Odd John and Sirius: Two Science Fiction Novels* (New York: Dover Press, 1972).

6. See especially Herbert Simon and William Chase's article, "Skill in Chess," in the *American Scientist*, 63, no. 4 (1973):346–403, and A. D. de Groot's book, *Thought and Choice in Chess* (The Hague: Mouton & Co., 1965). These treatments of chess and chess ability are not strictly psychometric in approach, for they are not interested in linking chess skill to general levels of intellectual functioning. They are motivated instead by a branch of psychological theorizing known as information processing. Their understanding of unusual ability is nonetheless similar to the psychometricians in the identification of underlying thinking capacities that can account for all levels of performance.

7. For a discussion of these issues, see David Henry Feldman, *Beyond Universals in Cognitive Development* (Norwood, N.J.: Ablex, 1980).

8. I have been reminded that Jung also used the term co-incidence, although for a somewhat different purpose. Jean Shinoda Bolen, a Jungian writer, puts it as follows: "Synchronicity is a *co*-incidence of events that is meaningful to the participant; thus each synchronistic experience is unique." See her book *The Tao of Psychology: Synchronicity and the Self* (San Francisco: Harper & Row, 1979).

9. *Time Magazine*, August 5, 1985, p. 55. Ruth Lawrence is a young English prodigy who recently completed her undergraduate studies at St. Hugh's College, Oxford University, at the age of thirteen with honors in mathematics. She is described in the media as a child with an omnivorous intellect and the ability to grasp complex concepts rapidly and with ease. While her accomplishments are truly prodigious, she has not yet—as her tutor has noted—found her own voice in the field.

Chapter 2.   A Study of Six Prodigies

1. Howard Gruber presents a virtuoso piece of cognitive detective work and one of the finest essays on creativity in *Darwin on Man: A Psychological Study of Scientific Creativity*, 2d ed. (Chicago: University of Chicago Press, 1981). Using Darwin's notebooks as evidence, Gruber reconstructs the development of Darwin's formulation of random variation and natural selection as the process underlying biological evolution. This study of a single case occupied Gruber for more than ten years.

2. Julian C. Stanley, Professor of Psychology at the Johns Hopkins University, began his Study of Mathematically Precocious Youth (SMPY) in 1971. The project is designed to identify mathematically gifted elementary school-aged children, as assessed by their scores on the quantitative section of the Scholastic Aptitude Tests (SATs)—a college entrance examination routinely taken by high-school juniors and seniors. The project also offers enrichment classes in an effort to promote the mathematical education of the children they have identified through their testing efforts. For descriptions and discussions of Stanley's program, see the following: Julian C. Stanley, "Rationale for the Study of Mathematically Precocious Youth (SMPY) During Its First Five Years of Promoting Educational Accelera-tion," in *The Gifted and Creative: A Fifty Year Perspective*, ed. Julian C. Stanley, William C. George, and Cecelia H. Solano (Baltimore, Md.: The Johns Hopkins Press, 1977); Julian C. Stanley, Daniel P. Keating, and Lynn H. Fox, eds., *Mathematical Talent: Discovery, Description, and Develop-ment* (Baltimore, Md.: The Johns Hopkins University Press, 1974); and Daniel P. Keating, *Intellectual Talent: Research and Development* (Baltimore, Md.: The Johns Hopkins University Press, 1975).

3. Halbert B. Robinson developed and headed a longitudinal study of children with ad-vanced intellectual abilities at the University of Washington in Seattle. Like the Stanley project, the assessment of abilities in this project relies heavily on standardized IQ tests, although parental reports and individualized assessments are also used. In addition to the research, the Seattle project sponsored several practical programs aimed at facilitating the education of high-IQ children, including both a Child Development Preschool and a High School on the University of Washington campus.

For an overview of the Seattle project, see: Wendy C. Roedell, Nancy E. Jackson, and Halbert B. Robinson, *Gifted Young Children* (New York: Teachers College Press, 1980).

4. For a description of Nadia's abilities and disabilities and for examples of her work, see Lorna Selfe, *Nadia: A Case of Extraordinary Drawing Ability in an Autistic Child* (London: Academic Press, 1977).

5. Although Yani has not yet become a phenomenon in the West, she is well known (and carefully observed and instructed) in her own country. For a commentary on her early development and reproductions of some of her extraordinary watercolors, see Li Shufen and Jiang Cheng'an, *Yani's Monkeys* (Beijing, China: The Foreign Language Press, 1984).

6. Although it appears that mathematicians are most productive between the ages of twenty-five and thirty-five, there are a number of famous men who continued to make significant contributions late in their lives—for example, Euler, Legendre, and Mobius. (See E. T. Bell, *Men of Mathematics* [New York: Dover Publications, 1937] and Harvey C. Lehman, *Age and Achievement* [Princeton, N.J.: Princeton University Press, 1953].) For an account of a contemporary world-famous mathematician who remains extraordinarily prolific in his eighth decade, see J. Tierney, "Paul Erdos is in Town. His Brain is Open." *Science '84*, October 1984, pp. 40–47, and Gina Bari Kolata, "Mathematician Paul Erdos: Total Devotion to the Subject." *Science*, April 8, 1977, pp. 144–45.

Chapter 3.   Talent and Transition in a Writing Prodigy

1. At the turn of the century there were two young girls who received considerable publicity for their writing. Winifred Stoner authored a number of published stories and

poems before she was twelve years old. Her publications ceased at that age and there is no further public record of her activities. Her mother, Winifred S. Stoner, detailed young Winifred's childrearing and education in her book *Natural Education* (Indianapolis: Bobbs-Merrill, 1914). See also Lois Taniuchi, *The Creation of Prodigies Through Special Early Education: Three Case Studies* (Report for the Van Leer Project on Human Potential, Harvard University, 1980). Daisy Ashford was an English girl who published *The Young Visiters* [*sic*] in 1890 at the age of nine. Her book depicted a child's-eye view of Victorian life; it sold thousands of copies during its long publication history. Like Winifred Stoner, Daisy stopped publishing as she entered her teens, although she lived until the age of ninety. For more on Ashford and other prodigies, see Roderick MacLeish's article "Gifted by Nature, Prodigies Are Still Mysteries to Man" in *Smithsonian Magazine*, March 1984, pp. 71–79.

2. Howard Gruber has made this point about the psychological distancing of the creative individual from everyday society in his Afterword to my book *Beyond Universals in Cognitive Development* (Norwood, N.J.: Ablex, 1980), pp. 175–80.

3. Norman Geschwind and his co-workers at Beth Israel Hospital in Boston have even documented a syndrome that they labeled interictal personality disorder, or "Geschwind's syndrome," for cases of brain-damaged patients who display, among other characteristics, hypergraphia, the tendency to write compulsively but make little coherent sense. Geschwind's observations on hypergraphia are briefly described in R. J. Trotter's article, "Geschwind's Syndrome: Van Gogh's Malady," *Psychology Today*, November 1985, p. 46.

4. This information came from Howard Gardner in a personal communication.

Chapter 4. Domains That Produce Prodigies

1. See David Henry Feldman, *Beyond Universals in Cognitive Development* (Norwood, N.J.: Ablex, 1980).

2. Howard Gruber's chronicle of Darwin's changing conceptions of the processes underlying biological evolution is an exception to this generalization. Yet his work, while oriented toward the psychological, is a single case study and not an effort to trace changes within an entire discipline. See Howard E. Gruber, *Darwin on Man: A Psychological Study of Scientific Creativity*, 2d ed. (Chicago: University of Chicago Press, 1981).

3. Howard Gardner has recently proposed a view of intelligence that takes these kinds of different proclivities into consideration. Conceived as an alternative to the standard psychometric views of intelligence, Gardner's view is that there are at least seven distinct kinds of thinking that function relatively independently of each other: verbal, musical, visual/spatial, logical/mathematical, kinesthetic, interpersonal, and intrapersonal. An individual may display high levels of one of these kinds of intelligence and show average or even below average abilities on another. The kinds of domains and activities that a child finds interesting and engaging are assumed to reflect his or her underlying abilities. For a detailed account of his theory, see his *Frames of Mind* (New York: Basic Books, 1983).

4. Benjamin Bloom and his colleagues have recently reported the results of a study of 120 individuals who have achieved world-class status in one of six fields—piano performance, sculpture, swimming, mathematics, tennis, and neurosurgery. He found that the subjects' progress in their fields could generally be divided into three learning phases: an early, romantic engagement with the field; a middle period of disciplined and intensive study; and a later phase when their crafts were tempered and shaped with the help of a master teacher/practitioner. It was often the case that as subjects moved from phase to phase they also moved from teacher to teacher. It was unusual for a single teacher to carry the student from the most elementary levels of the field to the most subtle and complex ones. This pattern held particularly for fields where private tutoring plays a major role, such as piano, tennis, swimming, and sculpture. See Benjamin Bloom, *Developing Talent in Young People* (New York: Ballantine Books, 1985).

5. See, for example, Ann Roe, *The Making of a Scientist* (New York: Dodd, Mead & Co., 1952). Roe interviewed and tested sixty-four eminent scientists (biologists, physicists, and social scientists). Many of these men reported being undistinguished students until they met a teacher who helped spark their curiosity and interest in the field.

6. In recognition of the increasingly rare skills possessed by master artisans and craftsmen,

in the 1950s Japan took the unprecedented move of institutionalizing as "Living National Treasures" those who practice the traditional crafts at the highest level. This program is, in part, directed at trying to interest young people in learning these crafts and thereby preserving knowledge and practice that is in danger of dying out: some of the individuals who have been designated as treasures are the only ones still practicing their crafts in the time-honored ways. See Dorothy Field's article, "Holders of Most Important Intangible Cultural Properties" in *Smithsonian Magazine,* January 1980, pp. 50–58.

7. For a discussion of the difference between the development of drawing ability and artistic ability, see David Henry Feldman, "The Concept of Nonuniversal Developmental Domains: Implications for Artistic Development" in the 1985 issue of *Visual Arts Research* edited by G. W. Hardiman and T. Zernick (pp. 82–89).

8. See Mihalyi Csikszentmihalyi and Rick Robinson, "Culture, Time, and the Development of Talent," in *Conceptions of Giftedness,* ed. Robert J. Sternberg and Janet E. Davidson (Cambridge, England: Cambridge University Press, 1985).

9. Franziska Baumgarten observed, interviewed, and tested a number of European prodigies in the 1920s, one of whom was a budding cartographer. The child seemingly had an unerring sense of direction and a highly developed ability to represent his spatial knowledge in maps. For her descriptions and discussions of this child and eight others, see her (untranslated) book, *Wunderkinder Psychologische Untersuchungen* (Leipzig: Johann Ambrosius Barth, 1930).

10. The promising young chess prodigy K. K. Karanjan reports that he was drawn to a chess set in a toy store, although neither he nor his parents knew anything about playing the game. (See public television's "Nova" program entitled "Child's Play: Prodigies and Possibilities" first aired in March 1985.) See also Vladimir Nabokov's novel *The Defense* (New York: G. P. Putnam's Sons, 1964).

Chapter 5.   Families: Catalysts and Organizers of Co-incidence

1. Marie Winn, "The Pleasures and Perils of Being a Child Prodigy," *The New York Times Magazine,* December 23, 1979, p. 39.

2. This quote was taken from an unpublished manuscript, "Prodigy II," written by "Fiona Konantovich" for a presentation in October 1983.

3. See Evelyn Goodenough Pitcher and Lynne Hickey Shultz, *Boys and Girls at Play* (South Hadley, Mass.: Bergin & Garvey, 1983).

4. See *Mindstorms* (New York: Basic Books, 1980), written by LOGO's developer, Seymour Papert.

5. Leslie Lemke's story is presented in "The Miracle of May Lemke's Love" by Joseph P. Blank in the *Reader's Digest,* October 1982, pp. 81–86 and in the film *May's Miracle: An Idiot Savant,* produced by the Canadian Broadcasting Company.

6. Joseph P. Blank, "The Miracle of May Lemke's Love," *Reader's Digest,* October 1982, p. 84. Excerpt from "The Miracle of May Lemke's Love" reprinted with permission.

Chapter 6.   Choosing Teachers and Changing Directions

1. See Benjamin Bloom, *Developing Talent in Young People* (New York: Ballantine Books, 1985).

2. See George Kane, *Chess and Children* (New York: Scribner, 1974).

3. John Collins discusses his principles for winning chess play in *Maxims of Chess* (New York: David McKay Company, 1978). He recounts personal and professional stories of the chess prodigies he has tutored in *My Seven Chess Prodigies* (New York: Simon & Schuster, 1974).

4. Lionel Menuhin Rolfe, *The Menuhins: A Family Odyssey* (San Francisco: Panjandrum/Aris Books, 1978), p. 125. See also Robert Magidoff, *Yehudi Menuhin: The Story of the Man and the Musician* (New York: Doubleday, 1955), p. 25.

5. Vladimir Nabokov, *The Defense* (New York: G. P. Putnam's Sons, 1964).

6. K. K. Karanjan recounted this story on the public television program in the "Nova" series called "Child's Play: Prodigies and Possibilities," first aired in March 1985.

Chapter 7. Social and Emotional Issues in the Lives of Prodigies

1. See Franziska Baumgarten, *Wunderkinder Psychologische Untersuchungen* (Leipzig: Johann Ambrosius Barth, 1930).

2. Dr. Laibow has recounted this story on film: see the public television program in the "Nova" series, "Child's Play: Prodigies and Possibilities," first aired in March 1985.

3. Norbert Wiener, *Ex-Prodigy: My Childhood and Youth* (Cambridge, Mass.: MIT Press, 1953, pp. 118–19).

4. For biographies of these famous prodigies, see Norbert Wiener, *Ex-Prodigy: My Childhood and Youth* (Cambridge, Mass.: MIT Press, 1953); Geza Revesz, *The Psychology of a Musical Prodigy* (1925; reprint, Freeport, N.Y.: Books for Libraries Press, 1970); Wolfgang Hildesheimer, *Mozart* (New York: Vintage Books, 1983); Marcia Davenport, *Mozart* (New York: Scribner, 1960); Yehudi Menuhin, *Unfinished Journey* (New York: Knopf, 1977); Robert Magidoff, *Yehudi Menuhin: The Story of the Man and the Musician* (New York: Doubleday, 1955).

5. Norbert Wiener, *Ex-Prodigy: My Childhood and Youth* (Cambridge, Mass.: MIT Press, 1953, pp. 161–62).

6. Michael Deakin, *The Children on the Hill* (Indianapolis: Bobbs-Merrill, 1972).

7. This quotation is from Jack McClintock, "The Edith Project," *Harper's*, March 1977, p. 23. For Aaron Stern's own description of his Total Educational Submersion Method, see his book, *The Joy of Learning* (North Miami Beach, Fla.: Renaissance Publishers, 1977).

8. Jeanne Bamberger has described this unraveling of confidence and even abilities themselves as prodigies' "mid-life crisis." She attributes its occurrence to the underlying shifts in thinking that all children undergo in their early adolescent years. For prodigies this often requires reformulating their strategies for performance, and understanding anew the structure of their special domain. See her article "Growing Up Prodigies: The Mid-Life Crisis," in *Developmental Approaches to Giftedness and Creativity*, ed. David Henry Feldman (San Francisco: Jossey-Bass, 1982).

Chapter 8. The Cultural Context

1. See Carol Gilligan, *In a Different Voice* (Cambridge, Mass.: Harvard University Press, 1982).

2. Stephen Jay Gould offers an alternative to Darwin's account of evolution as a process of continual, slow change in his article "Darwinism and the Expansion of Evolutionary Theory," *Science* 216 (1982):380–87.

3. For a summary of the meteor hypothesis of dinosaur extinction, see Michael Allaby and James Lovelock, *The Great Extinction—the Solution to One of the Great Mysteries of Science: The Disappearance of the Dinosaurs* (Garden City, N.Y.: Doubleday, 1983).

4. For a fascinating discussion of this period of Austrian history, see Allan Jarvik and Stephen Toulmin, *Wittgenstein's Vienna* (New York: Simon & Schuster, 1973). The authors discuss how the sociocultural milieu of turn-of-the-century Vienna shaped the preoccupations of its artists, writers, and philosophers.

5. John Gardner, *Excellence* (New York: Harper & Row, 1961, pp. 130–31).

6. This quote is also taken from John Gardner, *Excellence* (New York: Harper & Row, 1961, p. 47).

7. For discussions of the Suzuki teaching method from a psychological standpoint, see Lois Taniuchi, *The Creation of Prodigies Through Special Early Education: Three Case Studies* (Report for the Van Leer Project on Human Potential, Harvard University, 1980) and Howard Gardner, *Frames of Mind* (New York: Basic Books, 1983).

8. See Francis Galton, *Hereditary Genius: An Inquiry Into Its Laws and Consequences* (New York: D. Appleton & Co., 1891: originally published 1869).

9. Simonton adopts an analytic technique used primarily by historians in order to ask psychological questions about the factors that influence creativity and leadership. This method is based on statistical analysis of data drawn from large numbers of historical cases. For further description of this technique and the results of its application, see Dean Keith Simonton, *Genius, Creativity, and Leadership: Historiometric Inquiries* (Cambridge, Mass.: Harvard University Press, 1984).

10. Dean Keith Simonton, *Genius, Creativity, and Leadership: Historiometric Inquiries* (Cambridge, Mass.: Harvard University Press, 1984, p. 165).

11. Seymour Sarason has also written about the importance of understanding the societal, cultural, and historical contexts that influence individual psychological development and functioning. He laments the shortsightedness of the mainstream American psychological community, which has tended to consider the individual as autonomous, divorced from these broader contextual forces. See Seymour Sarason, *Psychology Misdirected* (New York: The Free Press, 1981) and "An Asocial Psychology and a Misdirected Clinical Psychology," *American Psychologist*, 36 (1981):827–36.

Chapter 9.   Beyond Co-incidence

1. Roberta Elliott, "Small Wonder: Israel's Piano Prodigy," *Hadassah Magazine*, November 1983, p. 13.

2. See Lionel Menuhin Rolfe, *The Menuhins: A Family Odyssey* (San Francisco: Panjandrum/ Aris Books, 1978), and Norbert Wiener, *Ex-Prodigy: My Childhood and Youth* (Cambridge, Mass.: MIT Press, 1953).

3. Francis Galton, *Hereditary Genius: An Inquiry Into Its Laws and Consequences* (New York: D. Appleton & Co., 1891: originally published 1869).

4. For more on the hypothesis that there are family patterns of handedness, immunological and hormonal disorders, and extreme behavior (either intellectual difficulties or talents), see Norman Geschwind and Peter Behan, "Left-handedness: Association with Immune Disease, Migraine, and Developmental Learning Disorder," *Proceedings of the National Academy of Sciences,* August 1982; Norman Geschwind and Albert Galaburda, "Cerebral Lateralization," *Archives of Neurology,* 42 (1985): 428–59; and Linda Garmon, "Of Hemispheres, Handedness, and More," *Psychology Today,* November 1985, pp. 40–48.

5. Wade Davis's book *The Serpent and the Rainbow* (New York: Simon & Schuster, 1985) offers a fascinating look into Haitian voodoo culture through the eyes of an American scientist who was allowed privileged access to its practices and secrets.

6. See Lionel Menuhin Rolfe, *The Menuhins: A Family Odyssey* (San Francisco: Panjandrum/ Aris Books, 1978).

Chapter 10.   The Game: To Create Conditions That Express Potential

1. See Fritjof Capra, *The Tao of Physics* (New York: Bantam Books, 1977); also Jean Shinoda Bolen, *The Tao of Psychology: Synchronicity and the Self* (San Francisco: Harper & Row, 1979).

2. Stephen Jay Gould, *The Mismeasure of Man* (New York: Norton, 1981).

3. Linda Matchan, "A Mania for Thimbles," from the "Calendar" section of *The Boston Globe,* August 14, 1980.

4. Paleontologist Stephen Jay Gould provides a readable account of the evidence in *The Mismeasure of Man* (New York: Norton, 1981). A more traditional scholarly piece is S. Washburn and F. Howell, "Human Evolution and Culture," in *The Evolution of Man,* vol. 2, ed. S. Tax (Chicago: University of Chicago Press, 1960).

5. For a report of research on the development of different symbol systems, see Howard Gardner and Dennis P. Wolf, "Waves and Streams of Symbolization," in *The Acquisition of Symbolic Skills,* ed. D. R. Rogers and J. A. Sloboda (London: Plenum Press, 1983).

6. An important article on the issue of "cultural prosthetics" as facilitators of thinking and learning is by Jerome S. Bruner and David R. Olson, "Learning Through Experience and

Learning Through Media," in *Media and Symbols,* ed. D. R. Olson (Chicago: University of Chicago Press, 1974).

7. For a novelized version of B. F. Skinner's utopian vision based on control of environmental variables, see his *Walden Two* (New York: Macmillan, 1948).

8. See Roger Brown, *A First Language* (Cambridge, Mass.: Harvard University Press, 1973).

9. Biographers seem to agree that Mozart was not a man of letters, nor one of introspection or particular interpersonal skill; his genius seems to have begun and ended in the musical domain. It has been suggested that his failure to secure a regular court appointment was due to his lack of interpersonal skills and his inability to maneuver politically within the musical scene. He is often described as something of a boor. His nonmusical interests ran more toward carousing with friends than to introspection or study; his letters were often peppered with scatological references. See Wolfgang Hildesheimer, *Mozart* (New York: Vintage Books, 1983) and Marcia Davenport, *Mozart* (New York: Scribner, 1966).

10. See, for example, Jerome Bruner's discussion of generalists and specialists in his paper, "The Nature and Uses of Immaturity," *American Psychologist,* 27 (1972): 1–22.

11. Lionel Menuhin Rolfe's search for the origins of his family's sometimes incomprehensible behavior led to the realization that the Menuhins have been a prodigy-producing group for centuries. See his book *The Menuhins: A Family Odyssey* (San Francisco: Panjandrum/Aris Books, 1978).

Chapter 11.   Harnessing the Forces of Co-incidence

1. This anecdote was found in a review in *The New York Times Book Review* (June 30, 1985) by Michael A. Guillen of *Mathematical People: Profiles and Interviews,* ed. D. J. Albers and G. L. Alexanderson (Boston: Birkhauser, 1985).

2. Hollander remembered this story of his childhood on the public television "Nova" program "Child's Play: Prodigies and Possibilities," first aired in March 1985.

3. Theresa M. Amabile argues in her book *The Social Psychology of Creativity* (New York: Springer-Verlag, 1983) that internal motivation is, in fact, the key to understanding the creative process.

Chapter 12.   Epilogue: Final Notes on Six Prodigies

1. Robert White's classic text is *Lives in Progress,* 2d ed. (New York: Holt, Rinehart & Winston, 1966). See also his more recent work, *The Enterprise of Living: Growth and Organization in Personality* (New York: Holt, Rinehart & Winston, 1972).

2. Two good examples of early prodigiousness in literary efforts are those of Daisy Ashford and Winifred Stoner. In 1890, at age nine, Ashford published the novel *The Young Visiters* [*sic*], which was a commercial smash. Winifred Stoner's early poetic accomplishments are documented in a book written by her mother, Winifred S. Stoner, entitled *Natural Education* (Indianapolis: Bobbs-Merrill, 1914). Neither child's talent survived the teenage years. For more about the teenage crisis facing most prodigies, see note 8 from chapter 7.

3. For a good discussion of the "mid-life crisis" as it manifests itself in musicians, see Jeanne Bamberger, "Growing up Prodigies: The Mid-Life Crisis," in *Developmental Approaches to Giftedness and Creativity,* ed. David Henry Feldman (San Francisco: Jossey-Bass, 1982).

4. See *Geo Magazine,* January 1984. In addition, the "Nova" program on public television, "Child's Play: Prodigies and Possibilities" (first aired March 1985) showed Mi Dori and her teacher, Dorothy DeLay, at work.

5. *Time Magazine,* June 6, 1977, covered the Johns Hopkins program. See also Julian C. Stanley, "The Student Gifted in Mathematics and Science," *National Association of School Psychologists Bulletin,* March 1976, pp. 28–37.

6. See James Mark Baldwin, *Thought and Things,* vol. 3 (London: Swan Sonnenschein, 1911); Lev S. Vygotsky, *The Psychology of Art* (Cambridge, Mass.: MIT Press, 1971); Heinz Werner, *Comparative Psychology of Mental Development* (New York: International Universities Press, 1957);

and Claude Levi-Strauss, *The Raw and the Cooked* (New York: Harper & Row, 1969). Jeanne Bamberger is currently writing a book summarizing her research on musical development. Its working title is *Musical Development*.

7. Geza Revesz published *The Psychology of a Musical Prodigy* in German in 1925. It is now available in translation through Books for Libraries Press (Freeport, New York, 1970). The quote is from the Preface, p. viii.

INDEX

Laibow, Rima, 149–50, 153, 255*n*2
Landseer, Sir Edwin, 21
Lawrence, Ruth, 15, 251*n*9
Learning Place, The (pseudonym), 39, 49, 51, 104–10, 159
Legendre, Adrien Marie, 252*n*6
Lehman, Harvey C., 252*n*6
Leibnitz, Gottfried von, 181
Lemke, Joe, 115–18
Lemke, Leslie, 93–94, 114–19, 122, 254*n*5
Lemke, May, 115–18
Lennon, John, 60
Lévi-Strauss, Claude, 249, 248*n*6
Li Shufen, 252*n*5
Literary prodigies, *see* Writing prodigies
LOGO, 107–8, 254*n*4
Lombardy, William, 125
Lovelock, James, 255*n*3
Lyman, Shelby, 176

Ma, Yo-Yo, 66
McClintock, Jack, 255*n*7
McDaniel, Darren (pseudonym), 37, 40, 45–49, 51, 60–63, 65, 66, 104, 127–28, 177, 194, 240–42
McDaniel, Jeanne (pseudonym), 36, 37, 40, 45, 48, 49, 51, 62, 63, 65, 66, 104, 127, 193–94, 240–42
McDaniel, Randy (pseudonym), 21, 36–40, 43–76, 87, 88, 104, 106, 149, 175, 234, 248–49; adolescence of, 63, 235, 240–42; domain of writing, 59–60; early childhood of, 45–47; effect of success on, 162; examples of writing by, 37–39, 50–56, 67–75; family tradition and, 177; friends and, 159; mystical behavior of, 187–88, 190, 192–94, 200, 204; relationship with parents, 62–63, 152, 154; in rock group, 60–63; at school, 48–49, 63–64; teachers of, 127–28; technology and, 176
Mach, Ernst, 173
Machiavelli, Niccolo, 180
MacLeish, Roderick, 225, 253*n*1
Mann, Ruth, 210

Marx, Karl, 180
Mary Poppins (movie), 87
Massachusetts Institute of Technology (MIT), 249; Computer Center, 105, 107–8
Massachusetts State Department of Education, 36
Mastery: desire for, 167, 170; ease of, 222; joy of, 229; levels of, 80–83; motivation for, 226
Matchan, Linda, 256*n*3
Mathematical prodigies, 3, 5, 7, 15, 16, 19, 22, 234; age of, 91; families of, 94; formal organization and, 88; general intellectual abilities and, 214; levels of mastery of, 82; methodologies and, 84; teachers of, 128–29; *see also* Calculating prodigies; Devlin, Billy
May's Miracle: An Idiot Savant (movie), 254*n*5
Mendelssohn, Fanny, 16
Mendelssohn, Felix, 13, 113
Mental calculators, 5, 251*n*4
Mentors, 17, 129; apprenticeship with, 81; methodologies and, 84; overdependence on, 215; parents' selection of, 95; for writers, 65–66
Menuhin, Hephzibah, 157
Menuhin, Yalta, 157
Menuhin, Yehudi, 81, 87, 131, 152, 157, 158, 216
Menuhin family, 189, 191, 216
Messianic Age, 4
Methodologies of domains, 83–84
Michelangelo, 21
Microchip technology, 173
Mill, John Stuart, 16, 59
Millais, Sir John, 21
Mismeasure of Man, The (Gould), 209
Mobius, August, 252*n*6
Monroe, James, 174
Montana, Frank (pseudonym), 27–30
Montana, Franklin (pseudonym), 21, 27–31, 176, 233, 246, 249; adolescence of, 235, 247–48; effect of success on, 162; family tradition and, 177; general intellectual ability of, 214; motivation of, 166; relationship with par-

Montana *(continued)*
ents, 154; sibling and, 156–57; teachers of, 124–27, 130
Montana, Jane (pseudonym), 27–29
Montana, Keith (pseudonym), 28–29
Montana, Tricia (pseudonym), 28–29
Moral prodigies, 90, 92
Motivation, 163–67, 208; and development of ability, 226; Freudian theory of, 165–67; internal, 44
Mozart, Nannerl, 16, 157
Mozart, Wolfgang Amadeus, 9, 13, 16, 113, 120, 152, 156–58, 174, 208, 215–16, 240, 257n9
Musical prodigies, 3–5, 8, 16, 19; accessibility and, 87, 248; age of, 91; developmental psychology and, 249; education of, 85; effects of success on, 161; families of, 92, 94–96; formal organization and, 88; genetics and, 211–12; levels of mastery of, 81, 82; methodologies and, 84; motivation of, 165; myths about, 131; performance standards for, 80; teachers of, 129–48; *see also* Kirkendahl, Nils
My Favorite Year (movie), 168–69
Mystical aspects of prodigiousness, 187–204
Mythology, 46

Nabokov, Vladimir, 131, 254n5, n10
Nadia, 21–22, 252n4
Nazis, 196–98
NBC Symphony, 94
Neumann, John von, 16
New England Conservatory, 241
New York Horticultural Society, 199
Newton, Isaac, 13, 120, 181
Nobel Prize, 83
"Nova" (television series), 46, 205, 254n10, 255n2, n6, 257n2, n4
Novices, 80–81
Nuclear holocaust, 173
Nyiregyhazi, Erwin, 16, 152, 215, 233, 250

O'Brien, Tom (pseudonym), 49, 104, 109
Olson, David R., 256n6
Omnibus prodigy, 109, 234; *see also* Konantovich, Adam
Organization of domains, 87–88
"Out of body" experiences, 202
Oxford University, 251n9
Ozawa, Seiji, 103

Pandolfini, Bruce, 28, 125
Papert, Seymour, 254n4
Parents: directing prodigies' development of abilities, 94–95, 98, 122, 155–56, 224, 226; general child-rearing characteristics, 155, 159; motivation and, 120, 164, 166; peer relationships encouraged by, 160; prodigies' relationships with, 151–56, 159–60; *see also* Families
Patronage system, 172
Peer Gynt (Ibsen), 46
Perceptual capacity, 83–84
Performance standards, 79–80
Perinatal memories, 199–200
Philosophical orientations, 180
Physical demands of domains, 88–89
Physics, 205–7
Piaget, Jean, 79, 88, 102, 108, 229
Picasso, Pablo, 21
Pitcher, Evelyn Goodenough, 254n3
Pizarro, Francisco, 174
Plato, 173
Political milieu, impact on creativity of, 180
Prenatal memories, 199–200
Probabilistic prediction, 182
Prophecy tradition, 4, 6–9, 18, 187, 204, 227–30

Ramanujan, 13
Rathbone, Basil, 39